the blues

From Robert Johnson to Robert Cray

THIS IS A CARLTON BOOK

Text and Design copyright © 1997 Carlton Books Limited

ISBN 0 02 864862 5 (hardcover)
ISBN 0 02 864886 2 (paperback)

Schirmer Books
An Imprint of Simon & Schuster Macmillan
1633 Broadway
New York, NY 10019

Prentice Hall International
London Mexico City New Delhi Singapore Sydney Toronto

1 2 3 4 5 6 7 8 9 10

Printed and bound in Dubai

This paper meets the requirements of ANSI/NISO 239 48-
1992 (permanence of paper)

Library of Congress Cataloging-in-Publication Data
Author: Tony Russell
    The Blues –
    From Robert Johnson to Robert Cray
    Includes index
    Russell/THE BLUES 97-67479   CIP

Title page picture: Jimmy Rushing and jiving dancers.
Contents picture: Billy Branch.

Schirmer
Books

the blues

From Robert Johnson to Robert Cray

TONY RUSSELL

contents

INTRODUCTION
THE TWENTIETH-CENTURY BLUES

SOME TIME IN THE EARLY SIXTIES THE BLUES SANK ITS TEETH FIRMLY INTO THE BACKSIDE OF POPULAR MUSIC. IT WAS MORE OF A SHOCK THAN A MAD DOG'S BITE – POP DIDN'T TURN OVERNIGHT INTO A BLUES-BELLOWING MONSTER. BUT IT DID GET THE POINT. EVER SINCE THEN, POPULAR MUSIC HAS ALWAYS HAD THE BLUES IN MIND.

t here have been times when pop and blues have been bedfellows. The deeply American rock of the early Rolling Stones, the Yardbirds or the Animals was chiselled out of a stratum of pure blues. At their gigs the Stones not only played wall-to-wall cover versions of obscure American blues but told the audience what labels the originals could be found on. Heavy metal began as a kind of simplified but vastly overblown blues – bomp and circumstance. Punk, in scorning pop's pretensions and returning to three-chord fundamentals, unconsciously re-enacted the musical rebellion of skiffle 20 years earlier, and skiffle had a long taproot in the blues.

Waterside taverns, docks and levees, railroad tracks and factory chimneys – every detail in this landscape has a blues resonance.

In fact, that old bulldog blues has been yapping at the heels of popular music for most of the century. The basic musical architecture of the blues, the three-line twelve-bar verse, became recognizable through early jazz, which used it to build enduring monuments like Louis Armstrong's 'West End Blues'. In the mid-Twenties a dance craze called The Blues washed over Britain and the United States. On the eve of World War II there was an international craze for boogie-woogie, which was nothing but the blues set to an eight-to-the-bar pulse. Meanwhile Joe Loss, king of the English

dancehall circuit, delighted foxtrotters from Southend to South Shields with his signature tune 'In The Mood': that was a blues too.

Fast forward to the Fifties, the decade of Bill Haley's 'Rock Around The Clock' and Elvis Presley's (or, if you prefer, Carl Perkins's) 'Blue Suede Shoes', of Little Richard's 'Tutti Frutti', Buddy Holly's 'Oh Boy!' and Ray Charles's 'What'd I Say'. All blues.

But the blues' ambush of pop in the Sixties marked something more significant than pop songwriters' fondness for borrowing 12 bars rather than thinking up a new tune. A generation of musicians emerged then who had learned their trade on guitars rather than pianos or saxophones, from records rather than sheet music or orchestra scores. They looked around and saw a musical landscape of dull suburban competence, a music industry stuck in the age of the danceband and the "vocal refrain". Imagine what it was like to discover, beneath those well-kept, well-swept streets, an underworld of secret music, stuff you never heard anywhere else, made by men and women with strange names: Muddy Waters, Howlin' Wolf, Fats Domino, Lightnin' Hopkins (not to mention Bo Diddley or Sugar Pie Desanto). Above ground, singers were Walking Back To Happiness, or taking Three Steps To Heaven, or trying on Itsy-Bitsy Teeny-Weeny Yellow Polka-Dot Bikinis. Down in Bluestown they were taking a Key To The Highway or Dusting their Brooms, or slipping on High-Heel Sneakers to match that Soulful Dress. All to music that was hardly fancier than a heartbeat – instrumentation stripped to its essentials. Lean. All muscle.

Ritual caning of the bad boys and girls of the Sixties is a popular sport nowadays. The tone gives it away, the vengeful sneer of those who were afraid to be cool. "We told you the party wouldn't go on for ever, and we were right. Nyeh, nyeh, nyeh." Admittedly, it's hard to put much heart into defending violet and lime green revolutionary rants printed in the alternative press, or empty-headed doodling on flute, tambourine and sitar. It's still possible to agree with the songwriter John Hartford that a lot of good things went down, back in the good old days.

One medal the Sixties can wear with pride is a lifesaver's award for keeping the blues afloat. The music might not have drowned, but it was surely drifting out of sight. B.B. King declares unequivocally that without the intervention of musicians like Eric Clapton or Mick Jagger he might never have been known outside black America. It took mediators from the other side of the culture, or the Atlantic, to awaken middle America to the blues within.

By now the reader will have a fair idea of the author's allegiances, but this historical background is not sketched as a credential, still less as a fond reminiscence. The intersection of the blues and the Sixties was a crucial crossroads in the history of the music, not only for the musicians who were that history, or hoped to add to it, but for the process of becoming a traceable history at all.

In 1962 a blues bookshelf might have held half a dozen titles: Paul Oliver's *Blues Fell This Morning* and Sam Charters' *The Country Blues* (tablets from the mountain in those days, set texts on the subject); a few volumes on jazz with chapters about blues; maybe an expensive reprint of an early collection of "Negro songs". There were no blues magazines: jazz periodicals gave some space to blues articles and record reviews, but not much, because there was not much to write about. The most energetic, inquisitive and thick-walleted enthusiast would

Though never well-known, Arthur "Montana" Taylor was an exquisite boogie-woogie pianist.

have had trouble amassing as many as 200 blues albums.

Today you can stroll into a branch of Tower Records, pick out 200 CDs and scarcely dent the stock. One label – typically, it is a European one, Document Records in Vienna – has issued over 600 discs of blues all recorded more than half a century ago. A comprehensive blues collection would run beyond 3,000 albums.

Similarly, a working library of blues books has swollen to at least 100 titles, without even touching adjacent subject areas like soul, gospel or jazz. A dozen magazines dedicated to the blues circulate in the United States and Europe alone (see page 221), and many mainstream music periodicals have blues columns. Add extensive coverage on radio (hundreds of US stations engage in blues programming), TV, video and several blues sites on the Internet.

Meanwhile the practitioners, the real people behind the paper or Web page or the anonymous sheen of a CD, can expect, if they are very lucky, to find sporadic work. Some may get to play in Europe, Australia or Japan. A few may make a decent living from the blues.

Structures are beginning to form

that encourage and even subsidize the blues artist. Colleges and community groups fund posts or regular performing opportunities. Blues, like rock, is being absorbed into the heritage business.

But at the same time blues is inextricably involved in the world of entertainment. As it should be: after all, it started there. Ma Rainey in 1920 was a top-of-the-bill concert attraction, not the grateful recipient of a National Heritage Fellowship or a Blues In The Schools outreach programme. Three generations on, there cannot be a major city in the United States that does not boast a blues bar and a resident band. Many will have several. There are thriving blues scenes not only where you might expect them, in Chicago and Los Angeles and Oakland, but in Boston and Detroit, Austin and Indianapolis, Portland, Oregon, and Providence, Rhode Island. Also in Clarksdale, Mississippi – one sign that after all the years of movement in the opposite direction, south to north, the blues is

finally coming home. Yet despite this vast change in the blues' fortunes, unimaginable in 1962, it is still far from clear what people expect of the music, what point it is meant to be making, what purpose it serves, what its options are at the marking of the millennium and, give or take a few years, its own centenary.

The reader's perception of the blues may be derived from images that no longer accurately represent it. The woman slumped on an unmade bed in a cheap hotel, the man rocking on the porch of a one-room country shack – familiar images of album covers and book jackets – are figures in a disappearing landscape. The strutting guitar warrior with a headband and a thousand watts of power is just as misleading. Perhaps more so, because he or she reinforces the notion that the blues is just about music, and mainly guitar music at that. And this is a gigantic misconception. Blues, as numberless practitioners have patiently explained, is a story, a personal testimony. More, it's a history – an oral archive of experiences and memories, legends and aphorisms, jokes and secrets: things that need to be remembered, and so are passed on.

The blues community of musicians and listeners and commentators grows every day larger and more heterogeneous, spreading not merely from Memphis, Tennessee, to Madison, Wisconsin, but to Manchester and Maastricht and Milan. It is multilingual, multicultural, multicoloured. The blues singers of the future will write their own history, and it will be different. Already in the songs the computer is replacing the cotton-picker and the singles bar the juke-joint.

Thanks to paper and vinyl, and whatever it is that CDs are made of, the old songs will

An early collaboration that bridged the colour line: T-Bone Walker and pianist Freddie Slack, Los Angeles, about 1942.

stand – but for what? When a young blues-man like Corey Harris sings a Charlie Patton song from the Twenties, we may wonder if he is doing anything significantly different from, say, a young folkclub singer in Newcastle retelling a nineteenth-century coal-miner's ballad. We may feel like calling the pair of them archivists. But when each of their songs hauls behind it a freight of meaning, about race or class or exploitation, perhaps we should hesitate before consigning them to the museum. It could just be that these subjects are not exhausted, that raising them in song still has a role, that the stories, though old, are not yet stale. Maybe we should stick around the blues: we might learn something.

But the blues is more than history. Turn it into a degree course, however benevolent-ly meant, and you risk pulling its teeth – hid-ing its improprieties, deadening its vigour, neutralizing its magic, diluting its language, reducing it to a literal world of description. Blues is more subtle than that, more layered with meaning and implication. "The sun's gonna shine in my back door some day" is not a weather forecast. The blues comes from a culture in which men and women chose their words carefully, always bearing in mind whom they were talking to and who might be listening. We should expect blues language, rooted as it is in everyday patterns and rituals of speech, to be equally guarded.

Perhaps the most persistent misunder-standing of the blues is that it is made by people who feel low in spirit, and addressed to others in the same condition. (That unmade bed again.) "Got the blues, can't be satisfied", sang Mississippi John Hurt. "I believe to my soul", replied Skip James, "I'm my mama's bad luck child." You could string together quotations like that all night, until the case for the blueness of the blues seemed unassailable, but only because you had ignored the other side of the case – the drinking, screwing, partying blues: songs,

in Jelly Roll Morton's phrase, of hokum and hilarity. When the black writer W.E.B. DuBois spoke of "the sorrow songs" he meant not blues but spirituals. He knew that while the spirituals are grounded in sub-mission to divine will, the blues is an affir-mation of life and the will to survive. "I done seen better days," sang "Rabbit" Brown, "but I'm puttin' up with these."

There is yet more to the blues, though, than this dialectic of suffering and joy, depression and resolve. Blues are not just complaints or celebrations. Sleepy John Estes' 'Floating Bridge' is an autobiographi-cal memoir about nearly drowning, while his

Lucille Bogan: "Got a sign on my door – 'barbecue for sale'."

'Lawyer Clark Blues', dedicated to a white patron in his home town, hovers between a praise-song in the manner of a West African *griot* and an advertisement. Lonnie Johnson's 'Sleepy Water Blues' is an ode to the Old South, where mammy stands forever waiting at the cabin door. Andy Boy's 'House Raid Blues' is a gleeful account of a brawl, Bo Carter's 'Cigarette Blues' a nudge-nudge joke, Memphis Minnie's 'Ma Rainey' an obitu-ary, Sonny Boy Williamson I's 'Win The War Blues' a recruiting poster.

Guitarist and songwriter Skip McDonald heads the 1990s blues band Little Axe.

There are blues that amuse and ones that inform, soliloquies and broadsheets, lovesongs and lullabies, letters home and letters to whom it may concern, boasts and confessions, texts and subtexts. When the singer Georgia White tried to define the blues she couldn't settle on any one answer, and the song title duly appeared on the record label as 'The Blues Ain't Nothin' But . . . ???' Seldom have six punctuation marks been more accurately employed.

This rich complexity of meaning and reference does not reveal itself at first sight. The documents in the case are the accumulated subject matter of eight decades, not the night's set list of a Seattle or Sydney bar band. Some of the costumes the blues has worn in the past are currently in storage, waiting for a change of fashion, or maybe the moth. There

are blues by men that speak of women with bitterness and brutality, and blues by women that reply just as intemperately: neither sort, perhaps, will be heard for much longer.

Other songs are glued firmly into the scrapbook of the past by their allusions to passing fashions – defunct dance crazes, for instance, like the Georgia Grind, the Truck or the Suzi-Q. The Memphis Jug Band's 'Cave Man Blues' and 'Lindberg Hop' refer to news stories that held the front pages of American papers for weeks in the Twenties, but only social historians now remember the trapped potholer Floyd Collins or the transatlantic aviator Charles Lindbergh. Any music serving a fickle audience and disseminated by a commercial system based on quick returns will always produce ephemeral songs, and the blues has just as much stale-dated material as pop or country music. Yet like them it also gave birth to songs and performers that stand outside time, telling stories that

are still worth hearing, in language too sharp and bright to rust.

The reader coming new to the blues will soon meet, in books and magazines and album-titles, terms like "country blues", "city blues" and "classic blues". A word of advice here: they are almost meaningless. They are survivals from a time when blues fans, like their jazz counterparts in the great war of Traditional versus Modern, were engaged in territorial disputes about the superiority of one kind of music over another. Inventing categories was a way of identifying the enemy. "Country blues" meant men with acoustic guitars, "city blues" men with electric guitars. "Classic blues", incomprehensibly, meant women not with guitars but with pianos or jazz bands.

As a three-way division of the blues, assuming one wanted such a thing, this is not quite useless, but the terms beg far too many questions. Why is an unamplified guitar "country" but not an acoustic piano? Many of the artists who wear the "country blues" tag were based in cities like Memphis, Atlanta and Dallas. Conversely, the singer-guitarist R.L. Burnside, who plays electric guitar and has recorded with a rock band, has spent his entire life in rural Mississippi. What do we call him? Lucille Bogan, a singer active in the city of Birmingham, Alabama, was often accompanied by Walter Roland, usually on piano but sometimes on acoustic guitar. Was her music "classic", "city" or "country"?

Labels like these are short cuts to nowhere. They make it no easier for us to find our way round the blues map. In fact they deceive us into thinking that there *are* easy ways. We would do better to judge blues musicians not in terms of their instruments or their birthplaces but by discovering the role their music plays in their lives and their communities. We might usefully distinguish between the career musician and the one who plays as a sideline, or between the dance musician and the street-singer. Some artists have divided lives, playing blues when asked to do so by a blues-dedicated record label but taking a quite different repertoire into the neighbourhood club where they earn their regular money.

While that thought hangs before the reader's eyes, this seems a good moment to explain what this book attempts to do, and what it leaves to be investigated elsewhere. It is not, except incidentally, a social history of the blues' world: there are excellent books about that already. Primarily, it is a users' guide. The way in to the blues is by listening to it, and unless the reader lives down the street from a great blues club, his or her primary resource will be recorded music. There is an enormous amount of this, and the aim has been to point out rewarding directions.

In addition to about 50 essential albums described in Milestone Recordings, and hundreds more cited in the sections titled Blues Legends and A–Z Blues Artists, artists' biographies are often sketched around their recording careers. This is not to say that records are the most important events in a musician's life, or always the best representations of his or her abilities, merely that they are the most accessible. And, of course, for the artists who are no longer around, they are almost our only point of contact.

The selection of the musicians covered in Blues Legends and A–Z Blues Artists inevitably reflects a subjective judgement of who is important or interesting or promising. But it is not a flag-waving exercise on behalf of favourite artists. The aim has been to convey the sweep of blues history from Los Angeles to London and from Papa Charlie Jackson to Stevie Ray Vaughan, duly noting the great and good but not tilting the balance too much in favour of the dead. There are

some gambles on the future, a handful of mavericks, a few spells of tub-thumping for figures who seem undeservedly neglected, and one or two pointed omissions.

No one writing a book about a living art form in 1997 can avoid a peep around the millennial corner. So – how are things with the blues? How are they likely to change?

Young lovers sell their Levi's to buy gas. An old man's hands wander over a piano keyboard painted in the colours of Budweiser. Female office workers gaze longingly at a hunky construction worker, his throat muscles taut as he tips back a Diet Coke – 30-second clips from that epic fantasy *Selling America To The World*, each one soundtracked by the blues. Odd, isn't it, that music born out of a hard-up, hand-to-mouth existence should serve the interests of million-dollar TV advertising campaigns? When Skid Row gets cheques from Madison Avenue, there must be, as the blues singers say, strange things happening in the land.

Perhaps the blues seems like a rock of normality in a crazy world. Direct, down-to-earth, genuine, it embodies qualities any ad agency would want you to reflect on when buying Coke or Bud or, especially, jeans, which are both the most democratic and the most American of garments, a blue denim metaphor for the pioneer spirit. Buy Levi's or drink Coke and you are consuming America. And what could be more grittily, plain-speakingly American than Etta James growling 'I Just Want To Make Love To You'?

What keeps the blues alive, and may preserve it far into the twenty-first century, is its ability to remain both-feet-on-the-ground natural in a world that daily grows more and more artificial. You don't have to be an old hippy or a New Age prospector to feel that the blues can sometimes rattle the rusty cage of received ideas, penetrate the senses a little deeper and more meaningfully than the mechanistic boogie of the Whole Earth Ballroom.

ALBUM NOTES

The album citations listed at the end of the A–Z Blues Artists entries consist of album title and record label. (The abbreviation MR indicates an album discussed in Milestone Recordings.) A record label is not repeated when it applies to two or more consecutive albums. For example, the recommendations in the Johnny Copeland entry are given as *Texas Twister*, *When The Rain Starts Fallin'* Rounder; *Catch Up With The Blues*, *Jungle Swing* Verve – meaning that the first two albums are on Rounder, the third and fourth on Verve. If two labels are attached to an album, they indicate licensees for different territories, which are specified. Thus Smokey Hogg's *Angels In Harlem* Specialty [US]/Ace [UK] has been issued in the United States on Specialty and in the United Kingdom on Ace. Citations are confined to American, British and some European labels. All recommended albums, here and elsewhere, are CDs, and all were reportedly in print at the time of going to press, but availability is a changeable concept in the record industry and unfortunately cannot be guaranteed.

Oddly enough, the older the recording, the more likely it is to remain in print. The reader interested in blues of the Twenties and Thirties should have few problems of supply with specialist labels like Document, Yazoo and Indigo. In contrast, much interesting material from the Fifties and Sixties is (at time of writing) out of print. The catalogue of the premier Chicago blues label, Chess, is gradually being reinstated by its owners, MCA, but important recordings, for instance by Jimmy Rogers, still await reissue. For reasons like this, a few of the lists of recommended albums are skimpier or less representative than they might have been, and in a very small number of cases it has been impossible to give any recommendation at all. At the other end of the scale, the handful of suggestions for the John Lee Hooker, Lightnin' Hopkins or Sonny Terry & Brownie McGhee admirer should not be taken as implying that there is nothing else as good in their enormous output.

BLUES TIME

▲ FIRST RECORDINGS OF
★ HIT RECORDS

1912 Publication of first blues compositions: 'Memphis Blues' by W.C. Handy, 'Dallas Blues' by Hart Wand.

1917 First jazz recording by Original Dixieland Jazz Band from New Orleans.

1920 Prohibition begins. American women win right to vote. Mamie Smith records 'Crazy Blues', first recording with a blues title by a black artist.

1921 ▲ Alberta Hunter, Ethel Waters, Edith Wilson.

1922 Paramount Records initiates first catalogue devoted to African-American jazz, blues and gospel music.
▲ Trixie Smith, Sara Martin.

1923 Lucille Bogan's 'The Pawn Shop Blues' cut in Atlanta in June, first Southern location recording by a blues artist. Sylvester Weaver records first blues guitar instrumentals, 'Guitar Blues'/'Guitar Rag'.
▲ Bessie Smith, Ma Rainey, Ida Cox, Sippie Wallace, Clara Smith.

1924 Singer-guitarist Ed Andrews is first male blues artist recorded in the South. Whistler & His Jug Band make first jugband recordings. Daddy Stovepipe and Stovepipe No. 1 (Sam Jones) first blues one-man bands on disc.
▲ Papa Charlie Jackson. Gershwin's 'Rhapsody In Blue' premiered, New York. Crossword craze begins.

1925 Electrical recording replaces acoustic system.

▲ Lonnie Johnson.
★ Bessie Smith's 'The St Louis Blues', Trixie Smith's 'Railroad Blues'.

1926 ▲ Blind Lemon Jefferson, Blind Blake, Peg Leg Howell. Savoy Ballroom opens, New York. African-American poet Langston Hughes publishes first collection, *The Weary Blues*.
★ Lonnie Johnson's 'Falling Rain Blues', Victoria Spivey's 'Black Snake Blues'.

1927 Mississippi River floods leave 675,000 homeless. *The Jazz Singer*, with Al Jolson in blackface, first sound film. De Ford Bailey records first blues harmonica solo, 'Pan-American Blues'. Hillbilly singer Jimmie Rodgers records 'Blue Yodel' ('T For Texas').
▲ Blind Willie McTell, Memphis Jug Band, Barbecue Bob, Big Bill Broonzy, Frank Stokes, Furry Lewis, Texas Alexander.
★ Jim Jackson's 'Kansas City Blues', Blind Lemon Jefferson's 'Match Box Blues', Barbecue Bob's 'Mississippi Heavy Water Blues', Bessie Smith's 'Back-Water Blues'.

1928 *Blackbirds Of 1928*, all-black revue, opens in New York. Archive of Folk Song opens at Library of Congress.
▲ Mississippi John Hurt, Cannon's Jug Stompers, Bo Carter.
★ Leroy Carr and Scrapper Blackwell's 'How Long – How Long Blues', Tampa Red and Georgia Tom's 'It's Tight Like That'.

1929 Herbert Hoover becomes US President. St Valentine's Day Massacre, Chicago. Wall Street Crash (29 October) precipitates Depression.

Death of Blind Lemon Jefferson. Bessie Smith stars in short film *St Louis Blues*. *Hallelujah!* first Hollywood movie with all-black cast.
▲ Charlie Patton, Memphis Minnie, Roosevelt Sykes, Henry Townsend, Sleepy John Estes.

1930 First supermarket opens, Queens, New York.
▲ Walter Davis, Mississippi Sheiks, Son House, Booker White, Little Brother Montgomery, Peetie Wheatstraw.
★ Mississippi Sheiks' 'Sitting On Top Of The World'/'Stop And Listen Blues', Memphis Minnie and Kansas Joe's 'Bumble Bee'.

1931 ▲ Skip James.
★ Tampa Red & Georgia Tom's 'New Strangers Blues'.

1932 US Highway 66 ("Route 66") opens. Paramount Records ceases trading. Location recording in South virtually abandoned.

1933 Franklin D. Roosevelt inaugurated as US President, launches New Deal programme of economic and social recovery. Prohibition repealed. Walter Roland records 'Red Cross Blues'. John A. Lomax begins recording African-American material for Library of Congress's Archive of Folk Song, encounters Leadbelly.
▲ Buddy Moss.

1934 Blues recording revives after Depression: Bluebird, Brunswick/Vocalion and Decca dominate industry. Apollo Theatre in Harlem reopens.
★ Joe Pullum's 'Black Gal What Makes Your Head So Hard?',

Kokomo Arnold's 'Milk Cow Blues', Leroy Carr's 'Blues Before Sunrise'/ 'Mean Mistreater Mama'.

1935 Works Progress Administration (WPA) set up to create employment. First recordings of electric guitar. Death of Leroy Carr.
▲ Blind Boy Fuller, Big Joe Williams, Washboard Sam.
★ Peetie Wheatstraw's 'Good Whiskey Blues', Georgia White's 'You Done Lost Your Good Thing Now'.

1936 ▲ Robert Johnson, Harlem Hamfats.
★ Washboard Sam's 'Don't Tear My Clothes', Blind Boy Fuller's 'Truckin' My Blues Away', Casey Bill (Weldon)'s 'W.P.A. Blues'/'Somebody Done Changed The Lock On That Door'.

1937 US Supreme Court upholds 1935 National Labor Relations Act, supporting workers' right to unionize. Black boxer Joe Louis becomes world heavyweight champion. Death of Bessie Smith.
▲ Sonny Boy Williamson I.
★ Johnny Temple's 'Louise Louise Blues', Washboard Sam's 'Back Door', Curtis Jones's 'Lonesome Bedroom Blues'.

1938 Stock-market crisis raises spectre of second Depression. First *Spirituals To Swing* concert, Carnegie Hall, New York, with Joe Turner, Sonny Terry, Big Bill Broonzy. Boogie-woogie craze begins. Death of Robert Johnson.

1939 *Gone With The Wind* released: former blues singer Hattie McDaniels wins Oscar for role of Scarlett O'Hara's maid.

▲ Louis Jordan's Tympany Five, Jimmy Yancey, Tommy McClennan.

1940 American Negro Exposition, Chicago. Black novelist Richard Wright's *Native Son* published. Blind Willie McTell records for Library of Congress.
▲ Brownie McGhee.
★ Jazz Gillum's 'Key To The Highway', Walter Davis's 'Come Back Baby', Blind Boy Fuller's 'Step It Up And Go', Tampa Red's 'Don't You Lie To Me', Memphis Slim's 'Beer Drinking Woman', Lil Green's 'Romance In The Dark'.

1941 Japanese attack on Pearl Harbor brings US into World War II. Muddy Waters, Son House record for Library of Congress (and in 1942). Sonny Boy Williamson II begins broadcasting on *King Biscuit Time*, KFFA, Helena, Arkansas.
★ Lil Green's 'Why Don't You Do Right?', Big Maceo's 'Worried Life Blues', Memphis Minnie's 'Me And My Chauffeur Blues', Big Joe Williams' '(Baby) Please Don't Go', Big Bill Broonzy's 'All By Myself'.

1942 Savoy Records founded in Newark, New Jersey. James C. Petrillo, president of American Federation of Musicians, imposes union ban on recording which lasts almost two years.
★ Little Son Joe's 'Black Rat Swing', Lonnie Johnson's 'He's A Jelly-Roll Baker'.

1944 King Records founded in Cincinnati.
▲ Eddie "Cleanhead" Vinson, Ralph Willis. Brownie McGhee & Sonny Terry begin recording as a duet.
★ Cecil Gant's 'I Wonder'.

1945 Death of Franklin D. Roosevelt, US President since 1933. Modern and Imperial labels founded in L.A.
▲ Jimmy McCracklin, Johnny Otis.
★ Charles Brown's 'Drifting Blues', Joe Liggins' 'The Honeydripper', Arthur "Big Boy" Crudup's 'Rock Me Mama', Dinah Washington's 'Evil Gal Blues'.

1946 Specialty and Aladdin labels founded in L.A.
▲ Lowell Fulson, Muddy Waters, Johnny Shines.
★ Roy Milton's 'R.M. Blues', Roosevelt Sykes's 'The Honeydripper', Jack McVea's 'Open The Door Richard'.

1947 Jackie Robinson is first African-American to play major league baseball. Chess brothers found Aristocrat label in Chicago. Atlantic Records founded in New York. Alan Lomax records worksongs on Parchman, Mississippi, prison farm, later issued on album *Murderers' Home*; also records Big Bill Broonzy, Memphis Slim, Sonny Boy Williamson I playing and talking pseudonymously for album *Blues In The Mississippi Night*.
▲ Lightnin' Hopkins, "Gatemouth" Brown, Sunnyland Slim, Johnny Young, Jimmy Witherspoon.
★ Charles Brown's 'Merry Christmas Baby', T-Bone Walker's 'Bobby Sox Blues'.

1948 Second AFM recording ban: chiefly affects major labels. Long-playing record (LP) first marketed.
▲ Howlin' Wolf, John Lee Hooker, Jimmy Rogers, Snooky Pryor.
★ T-Bone Walker's 'Call It Stormy Monday', Amos Milburn's 'Chicken Shack Boogie', Pee Wee Crayton's

'Blues After Hours', Wynonie Harris's 'Good Rockin' Tonight', Lonnie Johnson's 'Tomorrow Night'.

1949 Peacock Records founded in Houston, Texas, and Regal in Newark, New Jersey. First appearance of 45 rpm single. Death of Leadbelly.
▲ Mercy Dee Walton, Ray Charles.
★ Jimmy Witherspoon's 'Ain't Nobody's Business', Little Willie Littlefield's 'It's Midnight', Dinah Washington's 'Baby, Get Lost'.

1950 US enters Korean War. Muddy Waters' 'Rollin' Stone' first blues release on Chess.
★ Fats Domino's 'The Fat Man', Roy Brown's 'Hard Luck Blues', Lowell Fulson's 'Every Day I Have The Blues', Ivory Joe Hunter's 'I Almost Lost My Mind', Piano Red's 'Rockin' With Red', Percy Mayfield's 'Please Send Me Someone To Love'.

1951 Korean War prompts J.B. Lenoir's 'I'm In Korea', Arthur "Big Boy" Crudup's 'I'm Gonna Dig Myself A Hole' and other blues. First blues issues on Sun label. Big Bill Broonzy plays throughout Europe.
▲ Sonny Boy Williamson II, J.B. Lenoir.
★ Jackie Brenston's 'Rocket 88', Wynonie Harris's 'Bloodshot Eyes', John Lee Hooker's 'I'm In The Mood', B.B. King's 'Three O'Clock Blues', Joe Turner's 'Chains Of Love', Charles Brown's 'Black Night'.

1952 First year in which no African-American citizen is lynched since 1881. Willie Dixon joins Chess Records as producer. Lonnie Johnson tours Britain.

▲ Earl Hooker.
★ Elmore James's 'Dust My Broom', Little Walter's 'Juke', Eddie Boyd's 'Five Long Years', Big Mama Thornton's 'Hound Dog', Rosco Gordon's 'Booted', Willie Mabon's 'I Don't Know'.

1953 Korean War ends. Vee Jay label founded in Chicago, Excello label in Nashville.
▲ Jimmy Reed, Albert King, Junior Wells, Little Milton.
★ Guitar Slim's 'The Things That I Used To Do', Willie Mabon's 'I'm Mad', Big Maybelle's 'Gabbin' Blues', Jimmy Wilson's 'Tin Pan Alley'.

1954 US Supreme Court decides against segregation in public schools.
★ Muddy Waters' 'I'm Your Hoochie Coochie Man', 'Just Make Love To Me' and 'I'm Ready', Joe Turner's 'Shake, Rattle And Roll'.

1955 Bill Haley's 'Rock Around The Clock' starts rock 'n' roll craze.
★ Lowell Fulson's 'Reconsider Baby', Sonny Boy Williamson II's 'Don't Start Me Talkin'', Little Walter's 'My Babe', Jimmy Reed's 'You Don't Have To Go', Jack Dupree's 'Walking The Blues'.

1956 US Supreme Court declares segregation on buses unconstitutional. Elvis Presley is a national star. Piano Red makes first live blues recording, Magnolia Ballroom, Atlanta. His brother Speckled Red makes first blues album on Delmark label.
★ Howlin' Wolf's 'Smokestack Lightnin'', Otis Rush's 'I Can't Quit You Baby', John Lee Hooker's 'Dimples', Bill Doggett's 'Honky Tonk', Joe

Turner's 'Corrina, Corrina', Ivory Joe Hunter's 'Since I Met You Baby'.

1957 Dr Martin Luther King heads Southern Christian Leadership Conference. Controversial integration of Central High School, Little Rock, Arkansas. Introduction of stereo recording.
★ Fats Domino's 'I'm Walkin'', Slim Harpo's 'I'm A King Bee', Bobby Bland's 'Farther Up The Road', Jimmy Rogers's 'Walking By Myself'.

1958 Muddy Waters makes first visit to Britain. Death of Big Bill Broonzy.
★ Jimmy McCracklin's 'The Walk', Albert Collins's 'Freeze'.

1959 Alan Lomax makes field recordings in South for LP series *Southern Folk Heritage* (Atlantic) and *Southern Journey* (Prestige). Harry Oster records Robert Pete Williams and other artists in Louisiana. Death of Blind Willie McTell. Publication of Sam Charters' *The Country Blues* and companion album.
★ Ray Charles's 'What'd I Say'.

1960 Muddy Waters plays Newport Jazz Festival. Mance Lipscomb's *Texas Sharecropper And Songster* first album on Arhoolie label. Bluesville is first all-blues LP label. Publication of Paul Oliver's *Blues Fell This Morning* and companion album.
★ Freddie King's 'Hideaway'.

1961 Origin Jazz Library releases first reissue LP of Charlie Patton, also *Really! The Country Blues* with recordings by Skip James, Tommy Johnson, etc.
★ John Lee Hooker's 'Boom Boom'.

1962 James Meredith first African-American student at University of Mississippi. Release of *King Of The Delta Blues Singers*, first reissue album of Robert Johnson. First American Folk Blues Festival tours Europe. Memphis Slim emigrates to Paris.

1963 Dr Martin Luther King gives "I Have A Dream" speech, Washington, D.C. US President John F. Kennedy assassinated, Dallas. Death of Elmore James. Bob Koester of Delmark Records opens Jazz Record Mart, Chicago. British magazine *Blues Unlimited* launched. John Mayall forms Bluesbreakers. Eric Clapton joins Yardbirds.

1964 Newport Folk Festival presents Son House, Skip James, Sleepy John Estes, Robert Wilkins, Fred McDowell. B.B. King records *Live At The Regal*, Chicago. Vee Jay Records bankrupt. Marquee Club opens in Wardour Street, London. Rolling Stones top British pop chart with Willie Dixon's 'Little Red Rooster'.

1965 Selma-Montgomery Freedom March. Riots in Watts, Los Angeles. Death of Sonny Boy Williamson II.
★ Little Milton's 'We're Gonna Make It'.

1966 Release of John Mayall's *Blues Breakers* with Eric Clapton.
★ Albert King's 'Laundromat Blues', Koko Taylor's 'Wang Dang Doodle'.

1967 Worst race riots in US history, Detroit. Son House, Skip James, Booker White tour Europe with American Folk Blues Festival. Eric

Clapton forms Cream. Death of J.B. Lenoir.
★ Albert King's 'Born Under A Bad Sign'.

1968 Dr Martin Luther King assassinated, Memphis. Muddy Waters records *Electric Mud*. Death of Little Walter. London hosts first National Blues Convention.

1969 Fleetwood Mac and various Chicago artists record *Blues Jam At Chess*. The Rolling Stones record Robert Johnson's 'Love In Vain' on *Let It Bleed*. Luther Allison and Jimmy Dawkins make first albums. First Ann Arbor Blues Festival. Death of Magic Sam.
★ B.B. King's 'The Thrill Is Gone'.

1970 Johnny Otis Show makes historic appearance at Monterey Jazz Festival. Howlin' Wolf records in London with British blues musicians. Death of Otis Spann, Earl Hooker. First issue of *Living Blues* magazine, Chicago.

1971 Alligator Records founded in Chicago. Muddy Waters records in London with British blues musicians.

1972 Death of Fred McDowell.

1975 Antone's club opens in Austin, Texas. Death of T-Bone Walker, Louis Jordan.

1976 Death of Howlin' Wolf, Jimmy Reed.

1977 US TV series *Roots* attracts 80 million viewers nightly. Alberta Hunter makes comeback at The Cookery, Greenwich Village.

1980 Movie *The Blues Brothers* released.

1982 Robert Cray's *Bad Influence* issued. Willie Dixon sets up Blues Heaven Foundation to aid young musicians. Brownie McGhee & Sonny Terry break up. Death of Lightnin' Hopkins, Big Joe Williams.

1983 Stevie Ray Vaughan's *Texas Flood* issued. Death of Muddy Waters, Roosevelt Sykes.

1985 *Live Aid* concerts held simultaneously in London and Philadelphia; Albert Collins appears. *Showdown!* by Collins, Robert Cray and Johnny Copeland wins Grammy award.

1988 B.B. King records 'When Love Comes To Town' with U2.

1989 John Lee Hooker's *The Healer* internationally successful. Willie Dixon's *Hidden Charms* wins Grammy Award.

1990 Robert Johnson's *The Complete Recordings* best-selling album ever by a pre-war blues artist.

1991 Buddy Guy's *Damn Right, I've Got The Blues* issued.

1992 Death of Willie Dixon, Albert King. First House Of Blues opens on Sunset Boulevard, Los Angeles.

Nine Ages of Blues

Amateur night contest in Memphis, Tennessee. Disc-jockey Nat Williams holds the microphone for a young hopeful as she belts out her song.

THE BIRTH OF THE BLUES

LIKE THE MOVIE AND THE MUSICAL, THE BLUES IS A PRODUCT OF THE TWENTIETH CENTURY. BUT ITS ROOTS TWINE BACK BEFORE 1900 – YEARS, EVEN DECADES BACK, TILL WE LOSE THEM IN THE SUBSOIL OF AFRICAN-AMERICAN FOLK MUSIC. THE BLUES GREW OUT OF A COMPOST OF RAGS AND REELS, SONGS OF THE STREET AND THE STAGE, THE CHURCH AND THE MINSTREL SHOW, AND THE PLANTATION DANCE MUSIC OF FIDDLE AND BANJO.

the first blues ever sung came long before records and tapes. We shall never hear it. But can we put a date on it? In his autobiography, the composer and bandleader W.C. Handy tells a story. Handy's 'The Memphis Blues', published in 1912, would be one of three tunes on the market that year with "Blues" in the title – the first time the word was used for a musical composition. He would go on to write 'The St Louis Blues' and 'Beale Street Blues'. In the arena of music publishing and dance orchestras he held the title of Father

Blues grew up not only in Mississippi cotton country but in the tobacco fields of Virginia.

of the Blues, but reading his book we find a more complicated lineage.

In 1903 Handy took a job as the director of a black band in Clarksdale, Mississippi. It called for a lot of railroad travel. "One night at Tutwiler as I nodded in the railroad station while waiting for a train, life suddenly took me by the shoulder and wakened me with a start. A lean, loose-jointed Negro had commenced plunking a guitar beside me while I slept. . . . As he played, he pressed a knife on the strings of the guitar in a manner popularized by Hawaiian guitarists who used steel bars. The effect was unforgettable. His song, too, struck me instantly.

    'Goin' where the Southern cross' the
       Dog.'

"The singer repeated the line three times, accompanying himself on the guitar with the weirdest music I had ever heard."

This is a priceless glimpse: a first-hand account, by an African-American musician rather than a white folklorist, of the blues taking shape in the first decade of the century. (Handy had left Mississippi by 1908.) It is also the earliest description of slide guitar playing.

Handy went on to quote other songs he had heard in Mississippi and his home town of Florence, Alabama. They are obviously blues, with the familiar three-line verse. But he had another memory to share. He was playing for a dance in Cleveland, Mississippi, when a listener suggested that a local group take over for a while. "Their band consisted of just three pieces, a battered guitar, a mandolin and a worn-out bass. . . . They struck up one of those over-and-over strains that seem to have no very clear beginning and certainly no ending at all."

Only pages after his discovery of an early blues, Handy has stumbled upon another archetype of African-American music, the reels and rags of the string band. Was he lucky? Anything but. The landscape of Southern music in the last two decades of the nineteenth century and the first two of

the twentieth was dotted everywhere with bands like this, white as well as black. We can just catch their music, before it fades away, on a few Twenties recordings by black groups like the Dallas String Band or Peg Leg Howell's Gang in Georgia, and rather more loudly on discs by white hillbilly fiddle bands, who often learned tunes from their black neighbours.

Or shared them. Black and white music in those days were not two separate portfolios. There was a huge common stock of songs and tunes that everybody sang and played: dance tunes like 'Turkey In The Straw', the story-songs of 'John Henry' and 'Casey Jones', minstrel-show favourites like 'I Got Mine'. Thanks to those Hawaiian guitarists Handy mentioned, whose music was a craze of the early century, every musician knew about the sound effects of knife or bottleneck on a guitar string. The banjo

Informal plantation gatherings were one of the social contexts of the blues.

songs and breakdowns of the blackface minstrel shows filtered down into the backwoods and bayous to be remembered decades later by black and white alike.

The blues singer, the man or woman who sang nothing but blues, was a creation of the Twenties, probably a by-product of the record business. In earlier days musicians put their personal songbooks together from all the musics that floated in the air about them. The recording microphone arrived almost too late to document that diversity, and in its obsession with blues it was deaf to much of the other music that was around. Fortunately it was switched on for Leadbelly, Mississippi John Hurt, Henry Thomas, the Memphis jugbands and other musicians with memories longer than the blues.

THE EARLY TWENTIES

Showgirls, 1929 style: the chorus line at Small's Paradise. This Harlem club's stage was one of the great training-grounds of African-American dance.

AT FIRST EVERYONE THOUGHT IT WAS A PASSING CRAZE. BUT THE BLUES CAPTURED THE HEARTS AND IMAGINATIONS OF ITS AUDIENCE INSTANTLY AND PERMANENTLY – BECAUSE IT WAS ABOUT THEM. INSTEAD OF AN IMAGE FROM SOME ROMANTIC DAYDREAM, THE BLUES SHOWED PICTURES FROM EVERYDAY LIFE.

the blues hits of the early Twenties – songs like Lucille Hegamin's 'Everybody's Blues', Alberta Hunter's 'Down Hearted Blues', Ethel Waters' 'Down Home Blues', Sippie Wallace's 'Up The Country Blues', Trixie Smith's 'Freight Train Blues', Ida Cox's 'Chicago Bound Blues' – spoke directly to black listeners everywhere. A population on the move, as so many African-Americans were or wanted to be, knew what Sippie Wallace meant when she sang about "going up the country", and why Ida Cox was "Chicago bound". When Trixie Smith evoked the sound of a freight train's whistle, she not only grounded her song in common experience but hinted at movement, change, opportunity.

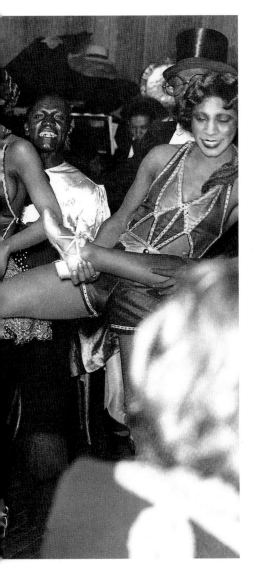

All those songs were by women, because singing the blues on records was seen as women's business. The first black singer to declaim a blues into a recording horn was Mamie Smith, in August 1920. 'Crazy Blues' sold in hundreds of thousands and created a sensation. It gave African-Americans a modern medium of their own – "Race Records for the Race".

Smith was a polished vaudeville singer, and many of the artists who followed her on to record, such as Ethel Waters and Alberta Hunter, came from a similar show-business world of revue and musical comedy. Others emerged from less polite backgrounds – taverns and dancehalls. Some sang blues only as long as it was fashionable, but artists like Ma Rainey, Bessie Smith, Sippie Wallace

and Victoria Spivey devoted themselves almost exclusively to blues, accompanied by musicians who created on trumpet or clarinet voice-like timbres that echoed and replied to the singers' growls and moans.

For the first half of the Twenties women ruled the blues market. The period rapidly created its stars. Ma Rainey was so popular that she had her picture on a record label. Lucille Hegamin's 'Everybody's Blues' and 'Arkansas Blues' were issued on ten or a dozen different labels simultaneously. The latter started a fad for state-songs: before you could turn round there was a 'Mississippi Blues' and a 'Georgia Blues', custom-written to appeal to the nostalgia of new Northerners.

Some of the singers wrote their own blues, others took anything they were handed, which might mean novelty blues with titles like 'You Can Have Him, I Don't Want Him, Didn't Love Him Anyhow Blues' or 'Crossword Papa (You Sure Do Puzzle Me)'. Blues was a new game, and old hands in the music business did not always grasp the rules. Often they just tacked "Blues" on to an ordinary pop song, as if that would magically transform it.

Women's monopoly of the blues was breached here and there, but no male singer of any importance appeared until Charlie Jackson from New Orleans popped up in 1924. He went down well on record, but his vaudeville singing and banjo-playing did not distance him very far from the female singers. The momentous change came in 1926, with the arrival of Blind Lemon Jefferson, the first Southern bluesman to make an impact on disc as both singer and guitarist.

It's extraordinary that Jackson and Jefferson should have co-existed in time. Their approaches to music could not have been farther apart. Jackson's natural home was the minstrel-show stage, his music urbane, sophisticated and jolly. His blues brought no tear to the eye, no lump to the throat, no clench of the fist. Jefferson was a

man of the open street and the town square. 'Got The Blues', his first recording, could hardly have had a duller title, but his piercing holler over a writhing, squabbling guitar scorched the ears like a Texas twister. Not even the most imposing of the blues women could match this.

The immediate effect of Jefferson's runaway success was to uncover a new and unsuspected anthill of blues activity. Bluesmen and women – but this time mostly men – declared themselves all across the South, from Texas to Florida. They might be grateful to Jefferson for opening a door, but few were minded to copy him. Some of them had been singing and playing the blues for ten or fifteen years already, and they had developed highly personal styles. Now they would be heard outside the plantation, beyond the unpaved, unlit streets of their town's "coloured section". The five years after the Jefferson starburst would be the first golden age of the blues.

Bessie Smith, 1924. "I'm a young woman, ain't done runnin' round."

THE LATE TWENTIES

THERE WAS NO BIG BANG IN THE HISTORY OF THE BLUES. EVEN BEFORE RECORDS, EARLY SONG-COLLECTORS WERE COPYING DOWN BLUES VERSES FROM BLACK FIELDHANDS, CONVICTS AND HOUSE SERVANTS EVERYWHERE AT ONCE: GEORGIA AND THE CAROLINAS IN THE EAST, THE DEEP SOUTH STATES OF ALABAMA AND MISSISSIPPI, THE SOUTH-WESTERN PRAIRIES OF TEXAS. BLUES EVERY WHICH WAY.

Charlie Patton grew up on this Mississippi plantation.

the curtain that lifted on this boiling diversity in the late Twenties revealed groupings of musicians who shared musical ideas so intimately that they had a kind of family resemblance. Linking these outposts of local style was a network of routes travelled by footloose musicians. "I rode freight trains practically all over the country", recalled the Texas pianist Buster Pickens. "Just wherever it was booming, I'd hear about it." City or small town, at any time some wandering blues singer might suddenly show up on the main street or courthouse square, playing for small change on market days, impressing the locals in the taverns, here today, somewhere else tomorrow.

So while blues artists like Charlie Patton, Frank Stokes or Sleepy John Estes were anchored to their communities, singing about home boys and home-town affairs, even dropping street addresses, others, like Blind Lemon Jefferson or Little Brother Montgomery, inhabited a wider world of travel and curiosity.

One way to move around in the South was with a medicine show. "It was just a show where the man sold all kinds of medicine and soap and stuff", remembered the pianist Speckled Red. "'One medicine good for a thousand things' – and it wasn't good for *nothin'*." The troupe would roll into town, set up a stage and pull in an audience with its singers, dancers and comedians. When a crowd gathered, the self-styled "doctor" would talk up his product – pills or panaceas, liniments, elixirs or draughts to restore "vitality", a polite code for flagging male potency. For many musicians the shows were a short, sharp course in the entertainment business. Besides singing and playing they learned to dance, tell jokes and go round the audience extracting quarters and dimes. But it wasn't only pills and bottles they dispensed – it was the new and invigorating tonic of the blues.

Twice a year during the late Twenties, small convoys of cars would head south out of New York City. They were not carrying

holiday-makers to the Florida sunshine or asthmatics to the pure air of the Blue Ridge Mountains. The cars were packed with machinery, and the men driving them had the absorbed look of technicians.

They were recording crews on the way to Atlanta, Memphis, New Orleans and Dallas, where they would set up temporary studios in hotel rooms, radio stations or warehouses. In Memphis they used the YMCA meeting-hall. Musicians would flock into town, some prebooked, some on the off-chance. Often there was a local contact, usually a music store owner who knew the musicians and could identify the ones with good material. One such, H.C. Speir in Jackson, Mississippi, fixed up recording opportunities for Charlie Patton, Tommy Johnson and Son House.

One of the hothouses of Southern music that the Northern scouts stumbled into was Memphis, the river city at the junction of Tennessee, Mississippi and Arkansas. Thanks to cotton, highways and railroads it was one of the busiest commercial centres in the South. There was money in Memphis, and many ways to spend it, especially on Beale Street – shows at the Palace Theater, gambling at the Monarch, the Panama or Pee Wee's, prizefighting at the Vintage and whores everywhere. "Sportin' class of women runnin' up and down the street all night long", remembered Will Shade, leader

of the Memphis Jug Band. "There was so much excitement down there on Beale Street it'd take me a year and a day to tell you about it all."

When the recording men came to town they might not spend more than a week and a day, but they would hear a lifetime's music. Ditties from the bars like Speckled Red's 'Dirty Dozen', and stomping guitar duets by Frank Stokes and Dan Sane, the Beale Street Sheiks. Furry Lewis sliding a steel bar over his strings, Memphis Minnie and her husband Kansas Joe McCoy jiving each other over their interlocking guitars.

Other cities, other styles. Atlanta rang with the 12-string guitars of Barbecue Bob and Willie Baker. Dallas had saloon pianists like Whistling Alex Moore. Jugbands in Louisville, harmonica players in Nashville, string bands in New Orleans. And up in Indianapolis, the calm piano and guitar music of Leroy Carr and Scrapper Blackwell, whose 'How Long – How Long Blues' was not only the biggest blues hit of the closing decade but a forecast of how the blues would sound in the next.

Railroad lines like the Louisville & Nashville or the Baltimore & Ohio have left their tracks in countless blues stories.

THE THIRTIES

THE TWENTIES HAD BEEN THE AGE OF THE SOLOIST: THE THIRTIES WERE AN ERA OF COLLABORATIVE BLUES, SINGER WITH BAND. TAKE-IT-OR-LEAVE-IT INDIVIDUALISTS LIKE BLIND LEMON JEFFERSON OR CHARLIE PATTON MOVED OVER FOR RELIABLE, ADAPTABLE STUDIO MUSICIANS LIKE TAMPA RED AND BIG BILL BROONZY.

t he Thirties were a time of stability. It seems an odd way to describe a decade one-third sunk in the shadow of the Great Depression, but "the Thirties" in blues-speak actually span the eight years from 1934, when the record industry, like other sectors of the US economy, began to stir with life again, to 1942, when the nation's attention turned to war.

The early Thirties are a dark age in blues history. Record sales diminished to a tiny fraction of their Twenties levels, and most of the companies went bankrupt. Some first-generation blues artists had died, like Jefferson and Barbecue Bob, or got religion,

like Georgia Tom Dorsey. Yet there were optimistic bursts of activity. Big Bill and Memphis Minnie might have disappeared for a time, but you could hear the introspective guitar blues of Buddy Moss, or the lively collaborations of his fellow Georgians Blind Willie McTell and Curley Weaver. In Birmingham, Alabama, Lucille Bogan retailed hard-luck stories about women of the street, while her piano player Walter Roland took a dubious view of welfare handouts in his 'Red Cross Store Blues'.

But such artists were going out of style. Instead of the rural accents of Texas Alexander or Booker White, records offered the civil, conversational tones of Jazz Gillum or Bumble Bee Slim, framed by the unobtrusive discourse of the small group. Style was subordinated to content. Record-buyers wanted, or were presumed to want, a snappy song with enough distinction to last three months on the jukeboxes sprouting in every tavern. There was a flood of blues about talking-points of the times like "hobo jungles" – cardboard cities of the homeless – or federal work programmes for the unemployed, or urban redevelopment that reshaped and sometimes eradicated black neighbourhoods.

The nerve centre of Thirties blues was Chicago. Blues production was confined to the output of three companies, Victor, Brunswick/Vocalion and Decca, all with Chicago offices. The first two subcontracted much of their blues recording to a local producer, Lester Melrose. Almost all the most popular artists lived in Chicago or other Midwestern cities with large black populations like St Louis and Indianapolis. So did the session musicians who composed the record companies' house bands: Big Bill and Tampa Red, the versatile McCoy brothers, pianists Blind John Davis and Black Bob and Joshua Altheimer, bassmen Ransom Knowling and Alfred Elkins. Chicago had a studio elite years before Nashville. Henry Ford would have smiled upon the blues record business: it faithfully followed the principles of his automobile factory production line. Any colour of song you want, so long as it's blue.

Yet it would be unjust to pass over such beloved and idiosyncratic performers as Peetie Wheatstraw, with his gruff cry of "ooh, well, well" in every verse, or Sonny Boy Williamson I, who put the blues harmonica into overdrive, or the vast-voiced Roosevelt Sykes, nicknamed The Honeydripper, because, he said, he played so sweet: believe it if you like. Characters like these outweighed production line journeymen such as Washboard Sam and Johnny Temple.

Meanwhile, the success of Blind Boy Fuller in North Carolina or Joe Pullum in Texas indicated that not all the first-rate blues artists had left the South. Northward migration had slowed during the Depression: why go to jobless Chicago when you could stay in Dixie where, as blues singers like to say, "the weather suits my clothes"?

Talent scouts realized that they could not sustain a lively catalogue by sitting in their offices in Chicago or New York and phoning the usual suspects every three months. As in the late Twenties, they looked southwards, renewing their old contacts in the field. Once again, cars loaded with recording equipment were on the road, bound for tried locations like Dallas, Memphis and Atlanta, as well as once-only visits to Augusta, Georgia, or Hot Springs, Arkansas. Mostly this highway-hopping led them to intriguing but obscure

figures like the south-western pianists Big Boy Knox and Black Ivory King, the Texan slide guitarist Black Ace or the Memphis street-singer and songwriter Little Buddy Doyle. But twice the travelling recordists rendezvoused in Texas with that hurried, haunted young man Robert Johnson.

Right at the end of the Thirties the Chicago A-team had an unexpected challenge. Tommy McClennan hit town, a countryman in overalls from Yazoo City, Mississippi. Whamming enthusiastically on his guitar and hoarsely chanting "you got to bottle up and go!", he sounded like a bumpkin beside Big Bill or Tampa Red, but he was a bumpkin everyone wanted to hear. No one in Chicago knew it, but within a few years the city would be full of Southern country boys toting guitars, harmonicas and high hopes.

Rosetta Howard with the Big Three Trio: Willie Dixon, Bernardo Dennis, Leonard Caston.

POST-WAR CHICAGO

1945. THE WAR WAS OVER AND A NEW WORLD WAS DAWNING. THE OLD-GUARD BLUESMEN LIKE BIG BILL, TAMPA RED AND SONNY BOY WILLIAMSON I WERE STILL NAMES TO RESPECT, BUT THERE WERE FRESH FACES IN TOWN. CHICAGO HAD CHANGED. THE RURAL SOUTH WAS EMPTYING INTO IT AGAIN, AND WHERE THERE ARE NEW PEOPLE, YOU FIND NEW BLUES.

Much of Chicago's South Side was within the sound range of the "L", the city's elevated railroad.

round about 1945 fellows used to meet over here on a Sunday", reminisced the bluesman Johnny Williams. "Be musicians lined all up and down the street. Muddy Waters, Moody Jones, One Leg Sam, old Daddy Stovepipe, Porkchop – well, you know, we had a couple of Porkchops – and Washboard Sam. So this was where the music world began, right there on Maxwell Street."

Playing for shoppers in an open-air street market may not sound like much of a gig, but it was how many of the new Chicagoans just arrived from Mississippi or Arkansas broke into the music scene. Some of the first records of the new music,

including the debut disc of the teenaged Little Walter, appeared on the label of a Maxwell Street store. Musicians like Moody and Floyd Jones, Johnny Young, Snooky Pryor and Sunnyland Slim played rough-and-ready blues that expressed the shock of life in the Windy City, like Floyd and Slim's 'Tough Times':

Now the company and the union men
    begin to meet:
"Slow production –
    we'll give you four days a week."
Hard times, hard times here with me now,
If they don't get no better,
    I believe I'll leave this town.

The workshops of Chicago blues in the Forties and Fifties were the clubs of the South and West Side ghettos: Theresa's, Sylvio's, Pepper's Lounge, the 708, Smitty's Corner, Gatewood's Tavern, the Du Drop Inn. At the Zanzibar, female patrons sat entranced as the snake-eyed Muddy Waters sang "I wanna show all you good-looking women just how to treat your man". The classic Chicago line-up of guitars, harmonica, piano, bass and drums was developed over years of tireless clubbing, and the perfected model of the rollercoasting blues band was demonstrated on the records of Muddy Waters, Howlin' Wolf and their peers, mostly for the powerful Chess label.

The glory years were the early Fifties, the era of Muddy's 'Hoochie Coochie Man', Wolf's 'Smokestack Lightnin'', Little Walter's 'Juke', Elmore James's 'Dust My Broom', Eddie Boyd's 'Five Long Years' and Jimmy Reed's 'Ain't That Lovin' You Baby'. They were not only great songs but nationwide hits. Yet musical change was accelerating all the time, and by mid-decade the tight ensemble of the Muddy Waters band was being nudged aside by a radical new format, the subtler rhythms and more open textures of the bands led by young singer-guitarists like Buddy Guy, Freddie King, Otis Rush and Magic Sam – the West

Side sound. Harmonicas gave way to saxophones, acoustic bass to electric, and democratic free-for-all polyphony yielded to a music with guitar as the autocratic leading voice.

There was more to the West Side sound than musical innovation. Its intensity came from frustration and anger. "Hey, hey – they say you can make it if you try", Rush sang in his brilliant song 'Double Trouble', but added bitterly, "Some of this generation is millionaires – it's hard for me to keep decent clothes to wear."

It's no coincidence that the West Siders were all guitarists. Amplified to the point of distortion, pushed to the limits of its potential, the guitar expressed more keenly than any other instrument the anguish and isolation of the black blues singer in white America. It was the music of people who had gained little or nothing from the United States' post-war prosperity.

But at the same time it had a wealth of its own, a wealth of ideas from new

Music on Maxwell Street in the early 1940s: guitarist Moody Jones (centre), Ed Newman (bass), John Henry Barbee (guitar, left) and James Kindle (tenor banjo).

directions. Its pulse and the freedom it gave the soloist were inspired partly by contemporary jazz. Rush listened to the jazz guitarists Wes Montgomery and Kenny Burrell and organist Jimmy Smith. But the outstanding model for the West Siders, as for their Sixties successors Luther Allison and Jimmy Dawkins, was B.B. King. The intense, dramatic, highly strung vocal, interspersed with the guitar's shafts and slivers of glancing light, was a logical progression from King's Fifties work such as 'Three O'Clock Blues' or 'Please Love Me'.

In the years to come it would be King, far more than Muddy or Wolf or anyone in the Chicago blues establishment, who would influence the style of the city's young musicians.

WEST AND SOUTH

WHILE THE CHICAGO BLUES FACTORY REBUILT THE SOUTHERN DOWNHOME BLUES OF GUITARS AND HARMONICAS AS A SUPERCHARGED URBAN MODEL, MUSICIANS IN CALIFORNIA TOOK THE BIG-BAND LINE-UP APART, STRIPPED IT DOWN TO A FEW HORNS AND A RHYTHM SECTION AND CREATED MUSIC THAT JUMPED WITH LIFE. BUT THERE WERE STILL PLACES WHERE A CROWD WOULD HUSH FOR ONE MAN AND A GUITAR.

Café scene in the early 1950s on Beale Street, where, Memphians like to say, "the blues began".

i n the recharged atmosphere of the blues scene after World War II, a new style bloomed on the West Coast: jump blues. Basically that was what it was: blues for leaping up and dancing to, lively jazzy music made by small bands trying to sound like big ones.

The defining jump blues records were a pair of massive hits of the mid-Forties, Joe Liggins's 'The Honeydripper' and Roy Milton's 'R.M. Blues', both medium-tempo blues based on repetitive, seductive riffs. Milton modelled his six-piece band, the Solid Senders, on Louis Jordan's Tympany Five, the hippest black combo of the Forties, known on every jukebox for their peppy party songs like 'Saturday Night Fish Fry', 'Let The Good Times Roll' and 'Five Guys Named Moe'.

While Jordan and Milton wooed the jitterbugs in the dancehalls, the West Coast's

more intimate nightspots offered the quiet, almost genteel music of trios like the Three Blazers, featuring the crooning pianist Charles Brown and his wispy, smoky 'Driftin' Blues'. This understated style had been introduced at the beginning of the decade by Nat King Cole. Years before he had hits with 'Mona Lisa' and 'Unforgettable', Cole fronted a piano-guitar-bass trio, deftly improvising on standards. The lucid lines of his guitarist Oscar Moore were echoed by his brother Johnny, leader of the Three Blazers.

Brown and contemporary singer-pianists like Ivory Joe Hunter and Cecil Gant had some background in jazz and mainstream popular music themselves, but lacking Cole's speed and imagination they chose a mixture of flashy boogie-woogie, pop songs of the day like 'How High The Moon' and dreamy nocturnal blues, in which the melancholic interlacing of voice, piano and discreetly amplified guitar created a mood of lost hopes and broken dreams.

Meanwhile the more optimistic Floyd Dixon and Amos Milburn pounded the keys in a frenzy of boogie-woogie hedonism, as they lip-smackingly hymned African-American nightlife in 'Hey Bartender' and 'Chicken Shack Boogie'. There was a boogie riot on the other side of the tracks, too, as hillbilly guitar-pickers like the Delmore Brothers or Merle Travis, or even bluegrass bandleader Bill Monroe, exploited the energy of the eight-to-the-bar beat.

Dixon, Milburn and Brown were all Texans who had gone west as young men. "California was beautiful", Charles Brown rhapsodizes. "Streets full of people, street cars loaded with shipyard workers. Hollywood Boulevard – all up and down that street, entertainment, nightclubs such as the Swing Club, Susie-Q, Florentine Gardens and many others. Everything at its best." Guitar-playing contemporaries like Lowell Fulson and T-Bone Walker made the same journey. Walker's supremely relaxed singing and playing were a whole blues style by themselves,

one that eventually percolated down to Texas again to inspire Clarence "Gatemouth" Brown, Johnny Copeland and Joe Hughes.

But in the late Forties and early Fifties the most distinctive sound to come out of the South-West was the cry of Lightnin' Hopkins, a John Wayne with a guitar, reasserting the worth of the individual blues singer. "Lightnin'" seems an unkind nickname for a man as slow-talking as Sam Hopkins, but he got it duetting with pianist "Thunder" Smith.

The hard-handed piano players of the Thirties barrelhouse circuit had almost all disappeared, but descendants like Smith and Leroy Ervin still played their lonesome, windswept blues. "It's a long freight train, with a red and green light behind", sang Ervin in 'Rock Island Blues'. "The red means danger, and the green means a ramblin' mind."

Lightnin' Hopkins proved that the solo storyteller could still be a force in blues, and in Detroit John Lee Hooker backed him up, but in most places the mood of the public favoured band music. Memphis, as always a crossroads, witnessed a collision of Chicago and Californian styles, a kind of downhome jump blues. Downriver in Helena, Arkansas, station KFFA's daily show *King Biscuit Time* became an informal college of the blues, presided over by Sonny Boy Williamson II and turning out graduates like Robert Jr Lockwood, Earl Hooker, Jimmy Rogers and Little Walter. Many of Chicago's stars were alumni of King Biscuit Academy.

Clarence "Gatemouth" Brown lit up the Houston blues scene of the 1950s.

THE SIXTIES

Little white roosters: the Rolling Stones got down and dirty with the blues.

AT THE BEGINNING OF THE SIXTIES THE BLUES SEEMED A SPENT FORCE. BY THE END OF THE DECADE, THOUSANDS OF MUSICIANS IN A DOZEN COUNTRIES WERE ABSORBED IN REPRODUCING BLUE-COLLAR BLACK MUSIC AS IT WAS PLAYED IN SOUTHERN JUKE-JOINTS AND CHICAGO CLUBS.

the blues went completely dry at one point around the end of the 1950s", Willie Smith remembers. He had started out as a harmonica player, but when harp gigs vanished he took up drums, eventually playing in Muddy Waters' band. "Muddy couldn't get work. Even B.B. King wasn't getting the work. He used to have almost an orchestra, you know, and he had to cut down to three or four pieces. It got so bad, I finally quit in '64 and took a job driving a cab."

He was not the only one to give the blues up as a bad job. Carey Bell worked in a car-wash, Jimmy Dawkins in a factory, Buster Benton as a car mechanic. Labels that once supported the blues turned to soul, as Motown and Stax set a new agenda for black music. Muddy and Wolf were yesterday's men beside Otis Redding, James Brown or Marvin Gaye.

Yet by the end of the Sixties Muddy, Wolf and many of their peers were internationally famous. They had made overseas tours, appeared at pop festivals and in vast rock auditoriums, got back into recording again. Their audiences were no longer black and tending towards middle age but white and young. What earned them this born-again career, apart from talent and persistence, was the discovery of the blues by white musicians half their age, many of them not even American. Paul Butterfield, Mike Bloomfield, Canned Heat

and their British counterparts John Mayall, Eric Clapton and the Rolling Stones, by introducing the blues to new listeners, also revalidated it for the old players. "Before the Rolling Stones", said Muddy Waters, "people didn't know anything about me and didn't want to know anything. I was making records that were called 'race records'. I'll tell you

The 1965 American Folk Blues Festival was Europe's introduction to Fred McDowell and J.B. Lenoir.

Lippmann+Rau present

FOLK

BLUES

AMERICAN

FESTIVAL '65

A documentation of the authentic blues with the best blues artists of america in concert

MICHEL + WEBER

CHICAGO BLUES

John Lee Hooker
Roosevelt
Sykes
J.B. Lenoir
Buddy Guy
Big Walter
Shakey Horton
Lonesome
Jimmy Lee
Doctor Ross
Freddie Below

Big Mama
Thornton
Eddie Boyd
Mississippi
Fred
McDowell

what the old folks would have said to kids who'd bought my records. They'd have said, 'What's that? Take off that nigger music!' Then the Rolling Stones and all those other English bands came along, playing this music, and now the kids are buying my records and listening to them."

What was the attraction? "The romance of it", says Rod Stewart in a *Mojo* article. "Just the name, Muddy Waters' Chicago Blues Band, sounds so romantic. It's funny, you think you're the only one who's listening to it and then ten years later you realise that everyone was listening to it at the same time – the Stones, the Yardbirds. Everybody in their own little corner. . . . Long John Baldry had this one album [*The Best Of Muddy Waters*] and I borrowed it, and he said, 'You must bring it back in two days because Mick [Jagger] wants to borrow it.'"

"The Rolling Stones", according to Keith Richards, "were a white London imitation of South Side Chicago blues. It all starts there." Before the Sixties were out, imitators and masters would be playing side by side on Muddy's and Wolf's *London Sessions* albums. Even the Beatles claimed "the sort of numbers we like doing best are the rhythm-and-bluesy things." During the "beat group" boom you could throw a stone at random in London or Liverpool clubland and bet on hitting a band doing 'Hoochie Coochie Man".

But though Chicago needed an infusion of respect, blues activity elsewhere could support itself, at least for a while, like the big-band blues of Junior Parker and Bobby Bland, or South Louisiana's "swamp blues" clique of Lightnin' Slim and Slim Harpo, who dismantled the styles of Muddy Waters and Jimmy Reed and rebuilt them to sound more rural and archaic. Then there was New Orleans, where music lives in the street, the home turf of parade bands and Mardi Gras dancers, echoing to horns and drums. New Orleans had a wonderful time in the early Sixties, turning out witty, weightless R&B classics like Lee Dorsey's 'Ya Ya' and Chris Kenner's infectious 'I Like It Like That'.

The blues' main territorial gain in the decade was its friendly invasion of foreign parts. Under the banner of the American Folk Blues Festival (AFBF), a concert party annually visited Europe. It was something to witness Otis Rush or Junior Wells, but the older artists could be even more mesmerizing. In 1967 fans had the opportunity, never repeated, to see and hear Son House, Skip James and Booker White – on the same bill.

THE SEVENTIES AND EIGHTIES

IN THE SEVENTIES AMERICA REPOSSESSED THE BLUES FROM ITS EUROPEAN PATRONS AND CREATED A WEB OF WORK OPPORTUNITIES, RECORDING OUTLETS AND MEDIA CONNECTIONS. A FRESH GENERATION OF ARTISTS FOUND WORK IN A NEW CLUBLAND. BUT BY THE EIGHTIES THE BLUES WAS INTERNATIONAL ON A LARGER SCALE THAN EVER BEFORE.

The Checkerboard Lounge, owned by Buddy Guy, was one of Chicago's leading blues nightspots in the 1970s.

the spirit of Woodstock was still in the air at the beginning of the Seventies. Annual blues festivals were staged in Washington, D.C., San Francisco, Memphis and the university town of Ann Arbor, Michigan. Blues artists appeared in profusion at mixed events like the University of Chicago Folk Festival and the New Orleans Jazz & Heritage Festival.

The event most typical of its time was Ann Arbor, founded in 1969 with a jaw-dropping opening line-up of John Lee Hooker, Lightnin' Hopkins, Son House, Howlin' Wolf, B.B. King, Freddie King, Fred McDowell, Magic Sam, Muddy Waters, T-Bone Walker and more. After some problems it was refloated in 1972 as the Ann Arbor Blues & Jazz Festival, the organizers expressing the hope that this might "raise the consciousness a little higher" and promising "on-site 'policing' by the Psychedelic Rangers of the Tribal Council."

By 1973 *Living Blues*, the first American blues magazine (another creation of the Seventies), could refer to Ann Arbor as "the biggest, best-known and most broad-based festival in America", but ambition and right-on politics did not go hand in hand with efficiency. The 1974 event was moved to the Detroit suburb of Windsor, Ontario, scaring off many potential visitors who didn't care to risk a drug search when crossing into Canada. It was the last Ann Arbor for almost 20 years.

The seeds of the blues festival idea nevertheless scattered far and wide, to bloom in other places and other varieties. The large college-town festivals were supplemented by regional events with local artists and sponsors, like the Mississippi Delta Blues Festival or Atlanta's Georgia Grassroots Music Festival. Some were underwritten in part by taxpayers' money, which helped to legitimize blues and put it on the same fundable level as folk art and old-time fiddlers' conventions.

MEMPHIS SLIM

EXCLUSIVITÉ DISQUES

fontana

In the 1960s and 1970s Memphis Slim was Europe's most visible blues artist.

Australia and Japan opened up as blues markets. In March 1979 B.B. King played in the USSR, the first time a blues band had ventured beyond the Iron Curtain. The *Living Blues* booking guide listed contacts in a dozen European countries. Britain was now a minor player: the blues' best friend in Europe was France, thanks partly to distinguished emigrés like Memphis Slim who were attracted by the relaxed and unthreatening atmosphere of Paris, a home away from home for black American musicians since the Twenties. France also boasted Europe's best jazz festivals, which were hospitable to blues musicians.

Even more importantly for artists trying to get exposure, French companies like Black & Blue afforded recording opportunities few American labels were offering. This rapidly growing catalogue became a kind of reproof to the American blues business, especially when, in the mid-Seventies, the French producer Michelle Morgantini began flying to Chicago to record promising artists like Willie Kent or Jimmy Johnson under the noses of the locals.

Perhaps goaded into action, Alligator Records conceived a six-album series called *Living Chicago Blues*, to proclaim to the world that the city's blues was alive, well and continually renewing itself. The cast-list was mainly composed of youngish men and women with reputations to make: Jimmy Johnson, Lacy Gibson, Queen Sylvia Embry, Andrew Brown, Lonnie Brooks, The Sons Of Blues.

The streets these young guns strode down still had some of the old club names like Theresa's, Pepper's Lounge, the Checkerboard, Florence's and Ma Bea's, but during the Seventies a new clubland had grown up among the boutiques and pizza parlours of the North Side. Venues like the Wise Fools Pub, Kingston Mines, B.L.U.E.S. and Biddy Mulligan's drew a mainly white clientèle of students and young professionals, but booked many of the same artists as the black neighbourhood clubs – acts like Son Seals, Lonnie Brooks and Mighty Joe Young. Still, Chicago could not possibly support the dozens of bands based in the city, and another source of income opened up, club gigs in Midwestern college towns like Madison, Wisconsin, and Lincoln, Nebraska.

Having previewed the Eighties with *Living Chicago Blues*, Alligator did the same for the next decade with their 1987 compilation *The New Bluebloods*, introducing "The Next Generation of Chicago Blues". There were few survivors from the earlier team. The blues was on the move again, and at high speed.

THE BLUES TODAY

Beale Street today is unrecognizable to its old habitués, but the blues is still heard there.

robert Cray is one of the most important figures in the blues of the last dozen years. Not just in himself, as a blues personality, but because he steered the music into new territory, pointing out a direction that others could follow by their own paths. Meanwhile, by galvanizing the more familiar forms of electric guitar blues, Stevie Ray Vaughan refreshed the whole genre with his virtuosity. In the short term his influence seems even more extensive than Cray's, his work inspiring a generation of guitarists much as B.B. King's and Jimi Hendrix's did, two or three decades ago.

If you define "blues" by the rigid categories of structure rather than the flexible language of feeling and allusion, Cray and contemporaries like Larry Garner, Joe Louis Walker and James Armstrong are a new and uncategorizable breed, their music blues-like rather than blues, each of them blending ideas and devices from a variety of sources – soul, rock, jazz, gospel – with a sophistication beyond the reach of their forerunners.

Best, then, not to cling to the old rules. "The blues is everywhere," maintains Skip McDonald of Little Axe. "But blues with different stylistic parameters, not confined to the geography of the Mississippi Delta and 12-bar structure."

There is a profound difference in the position of the blues today from that of earlier times. Successive waves of soul, funk, hip-hop and rap have swept black artists from the outskirts of musical culture

AFTER 20 YEARS, THE BLUES TRAIN THAT HAD TAKEN ON A FRESH LOAD OF COAL IN THE SIXTIES WAS BEGINNING TO RUN OUT OF STEAM. ONCE AGAIN AN EAGER BUNCH OF FIREMEN WAS WAITING TO JUMP ON BOARD AND GET THE WHEELS ROLLING AGAIN. AT THE HEAD OF THE RESCUE CREW WERE ROBERT CRAY AND STEVIE RAY VAUGHAN.

to its centre. Never the dominant music even in black America, blues today exists far out on the margin. Many African-Americans look on it as an unwanted legacy of an unlamented past, tainted by memories of deference and discrimination.

Yet some young African-Americans are beginning to dispute that interpretation. They find messages and attitudes in the blues that they can be proud of, musicians they can respect, ideas they can build on to create a music that belongs alike to the past, the present and themselves.

This rediscovery has been expressed in widely different ways. By the "new country blues" of Keb' Mo', Alvin Youngblood Hart, Corey Harris, Eric Bibb and Guy Davis. In the old-fashioned bar-band blues of Magic Slim or Little Mack Simmons, who deliberately turn back the clock to Fifties Chicago. Or through the fiercely contemporary fusions of blues, rap, reggae and world music explored by Little Axe, Ben Harper, Michael Hill or Lurrie Bell.

But this is only half the picture. By now it is perfectly clear that the future of the blues lies in white as well as black hands. Not all of those white inheritors are American. Some do not speak English as a first language, or at all. Among the new members of the blues community are the Czech-German slide guitarist Rainer Ptáček, the Japanese Freddie King admirer Fusanosuke Kondou, groups ranging from Barrelhouse in the Netherlands to the Blues Mobile Band in Russia.

Blues, like jazz before it, has become an international musical language, a rootsy Esperanto. Characters in TV dramas and sitcoms drop blues references without sponsors or audiences turning a hair. Someone in the *E.R.* TV series plans a night at a Chicago blues club.

B.B. King appears on *Blossom*. Through TV ads and film soundtracks, in national newspapers and on the Internet, sounds and images of the blues criss-cross the world.

What comes next?

There have been moments when it has looked as if the blues would settle into a dull middle age, follow the weary footsteps of traditional jazz or Fifties rock 'n' roll, become a perpetually

recycled repertory for stolid bands in pubs and bars and Holiday Inn lounges, until all blues bands sounded like the Blues Brothers Band. Right now, near the turn of the century, this doesn't seem such a serious risk.

There have been glum predictions of the death of the blues ever since Big Bill Broonzy died, 40 years ago. Yet new singers and players show up year after year to turn the funeral ceremony into a celebration of life and continuity.

Eric Bibb, one of the young musicians who are refurbishing the blues.

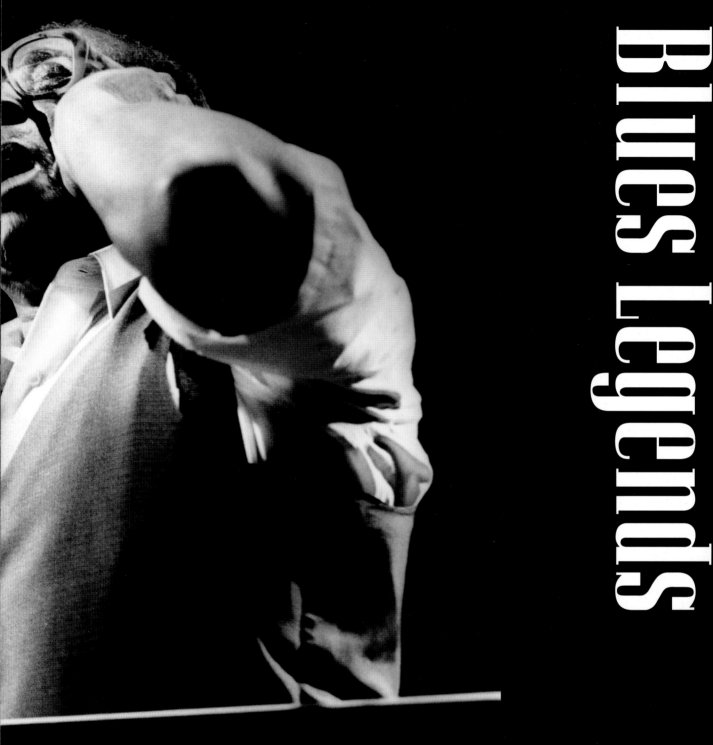

Blues Legends

Albert King. "If it wasn't for bad luck, baby, I wouldn't have no luck at all."

Leadbelly

LEADBELLY THE PERFORMER AND THE LEADBELLY SONGBOOK ARE TWIN PEAKS ON THE MAP OF AMERICAN MUSIC. HIS ENORMOUS REPERTOIRE HAS NO PARALLEL IN BLACK FOLKSONG.

he sang everything, ballads and blues-ballads, dance-songs and children's rhymes, hymns and gospel songs, memories of minstrelsy and freshly made songs about his own rapidly changing circumstances. To his amazed white audiences he seemed a mythic figure, a lone carrier of all-but-lost messages from black worlds of field and prison farm.

Today we can link some of his repertoire to other artists' and view him within a tradition, but without subtracting an inch of his colossal stature. He was a supreme narrative artist. Many of his songs are spoken as much as sung, with an earnestness that separates them from the sardonic talking blues of his contemporary and acquaintance Woody Guthrie. When he rears back and sings, there

are flickers of the sharp light of Blind Lemon Jefferson, rising and falling cadences that speak of the early blues. Yet Leadbelly is curiously constrained by the blues format, and little of his very best work is found there, though pieces like 'The Bourgeois Blues' and 'Good Morning Blues' are priceless.

He was born in Mooringsport, Louisiana, and learned accordion, piano and harmonica before he picked up a guitar. At 15, having fathered two children and been arrested and fined for a shooting incident, he was singing in the red-light district of Shreveport, Louisiana. A few years later he was living in Dallas, where he met and learned a few songs from Blind Lemon Jefferson and acquired his first 12-string guitar.

Much of Leadbelly's middle life was spent either in prison or on the run. Twice he sang his way to a pardon with an obsequious lyric aimed at the state governor. But in 1933, while in prison in Angola, Louisiana, he was given the chance of a new life when he met the folklorist John A. Lomax, who was travelling through the South making recordings for the Archive of American Folk Song at the Library of Congress. Lomax found in Leadbelly not only a deep source of material but a key to unlock the songs of other informants, and when the

singer was released in 1934 he became Lomax's collecting assistant.

Leadbelly made dozens of recordings for the Archive, and began to perform for folk-song societies. His exposure to New York's liberal and progressive circles failed

Leadbelly – a good title for a hard man, but it came from his given name, Huddie Ledbetter.

to discipline his temper, and he again served time on an assault charge. This did no harm to his reputation as a dangerous man, which for some listeners added a frisson to his music. "Without that violent past", Lomax's son Alan would remark later, "the white audiences never would have noticed him."

During the Forties Leadbelly was part of a circle of musicians and left-wing folksong enthusiasts (some of them also musicians) including Alan Lomax, Josh White, Brownie McGhee, Sonny Terry, Guthrie and other members of the Almanac Singers. He recorded lavishly for at least half a dozen labels, toured with the musical-political group People's Songs Inc. and even spent some time in Hollywood, hoping to get into films. But by 1947 he was back with his wife Martha in New York, where he spent his remaining years before dying of motor neurone disease. He made just one trip outside the United States, to the 1949 Paris Jazz Fair.

Already his songs had begun to acquire a celebrity larger than even he could confer on them, as they were taken up by artists closer to mainstream popular music. 'Goodnight Irene', his reconstruction of a nineteenth-century minstrel song, was a hit for the Weavers in 1948, and in 1956 the jazz banjoist and singer Lonnie Donegan signalled go to the British skiffle train with 'Rock Island Line'. 'Midnight Special', 'Cotton Fields' and 'Boll Weevil' were also skiffle favourites, but have outlived that craze to settle in the repertory of Anglo-American folkclub music.

KEY recordings

King of the Twelve-String Guitar,
Columbia. Leadbelly's only recordings for the blues market, made in 1935. Includes long versions of 'Roberta' and 'Death Letter Blues'.

Midnight Special, The Titanic,
Rounder. Volumes 1 and 4 of six CDs devoted to the Library of Congress recordings. The former concentrates on blues-ballads, the latter on (often topical) blues. Some of his strongest work.

The Very Best Of Leadbelly,
Music Club. Inexpensive and well-chosen sampler of the Library of Congress and later Folkways recordings. 'Midnight Special', 'The Bourgeois Blues', 'Rock Island Line', 'Goodnight Irene'.

Goodnight Irene,
Tradition. Fine 1939 sides with drop-in appearances by Sonny Terry and Josh White. 'New Orleans' is Leadbelly's 'House of the Rising Sun', and 'Where Did You Sleep Last Night' was recorded by Nirvana.

In The Shadow Of The Gallows Pole,
Tradition. Blues, reels and worksongs, and rare examples of Leadbelly playing piano and accordion.

Leadbelly's Last Sessions,
Smithsonian/Folkways. Several hours' continuous flow of songs and stories in a handsome four-CD set.

JOHNSON WAS THE MOST RECORDED BLUESMAN OF THE TWENTIES. HE WAS ALSO ONE OF THE MOST INFLUENTIAL, AND NOT JUST IN THAT DECADE – ECHOES OF HIS DOLEFUL PURPLE VOICE AND SUMPTUOUS GUITAR-PLAYING RING THROUGH THE YEARS FROM ROBERT JOHNSON TO B.B. KING.

Johnson's 12-string Gibson was a finer instrument than many blues guitarists ever saw, let alone played.

beyond the blues, he held his own as a guitarist in the most challenging jazz company, while he could deliver a pop ballad or a golden oldie with technique and feeling that Nat King Cole would have appreciated. Almost incidentally, he was a notable blues violinist as well.

Even at the start of his recording career in 1925, when disc-making was primitive and it took a strong singer to make much impression on the acoustic microphone, Lonnie Johnson's voice and guitar-playing had body and clarity. "I'm not a country blues singer," he once said, and he was right. His stately delivery and excellent diction ally him with Bessie Smith rather than with Blind Lemon Jefferson. At times he wasn't even primarily a blues singer. The trio he led in the Forties was a lounge act playing standards, while his last clutch of albums was sprinkled with songs like 'Summertime' and 'My Mother's Eyes'.

Johnson disliked looking back and left few clues to his past. He may have been born in New Orleans, or may only have spent some of his youth there. By the mid-Twenties he was in St Louis playing guitar, violin or banjo with his equally versatile elder brother James "Steady Roll" Johnson. He won a talent contest and with it a recording contract. On his debut disc for OKeh he picked lithe guitar in 'Mr Johnson's Blues' and bowed a mournful violin for 'Falling Rain Blues'. The songs' perfunctory lyrics seem designed to show off his playing, which was ahead of the competition on both instruments.

The record was a hit and over the next seven years, as well as dozens of vocal blues, he cut astounding guitar solos and duets with the jazz guitarist Eddie Lang like 'Blue Guitars' and 'Two Tone Stomp', made guest appearances with Louis Armstrong

Lonnie Johnson

'Tomorrow Night'. He spent five years with King, cutting R&B ballads with small jazzy units, but disappeared for most of the Fifties. In 1959 a jazz-DJ admirer found him working as a Philadelphia hotel janitor. The meeting led to some new work opportunities – Johnson's first booking was at the Chicago Playboy Club – and a stack of LPs, several for the new Bluesville label. While these records delighted his jazz friends, they held little interest for the new blues audience, which fidgeted with embarrassment while Johnson sang 'I Left My Heart In San Francisco'.

In 1965 Johnson accepted an engagement in Toronto and liked the city so much that he stayed there and opened a club. He was injured in a traffic accident in 1969 and died a year later.

Johnson and Blind John Davis – American virtuosi who sometimes played the blues.

('Savoy Blues') and Duke Ellington ('Hot And Bothered'), joined Lang, King Oliver and songwriter-pianist Hoagy Carmichael in a novelty studio group called Blind Willie Dunn's Gin Bottle Four, and accompanied a score of other singers from Texas Alexander to Victoria Spivey and his wife Mary Johnson. No blues musician of his time could draw up a CV half so varied.

The years 1932–37 are almost blank. Johnson was living in Cleveland, Ohio, separated from his wife and playing only sporadi-

cally. Then he moved to Chicago, got a gig at the Three Deuces jazz club and began recording again. It was production line stuff by now – he once said he'd copyrighted the same melody over a hundred times, and for subject matter he returned over and over again to the theme that women can't be trusted and men are pretty much rats as well. Nobody ever mistook Lonnie Johnson for a romantic.

Frequently finding himself on sessions with the pianist Blind John Davis, he teamed up with him for a while in the Forties before signing with King Records in 1947 and surprising both the company and himself with a gigantic hit first time out, the pop ballad

AMONG MISSISSIPPI SINGERS OF THE FIRST BLUES GENERATION, CHARLIE PATTON WAS FAR AND AWAY THE MOST CELEBRATED IN HIS OWN COMMUNITY. PERHAPS IN A REACTION TO THE IDOLATRY SURROUNDING ROBERT JOHNSON, HE HAS INSPIRED A UNIQUELY FIERCE DEVOTION IN MANY BLUES-LOVERS. HIS SINGING – GRUFF, BARKING, EXTRAORDINARILY

Charlie Patton's songs like 'Pony Blues' or 'High Water Everywhere' seem to burst from the very bedrock of the blues, yet like any musician of his day he responded to, and worked with, the other music around him: blues-ballads like 'Frankie And Albert', popular songs like 'Some Of These Days', sacred songs such as 'I Shall Not Be Moved'. Nevertheless, the sheer weight of his performing style pressed everything he sang and played into an utterly distinctive shape – so much so that when he unloads his gritty voice on to the slender melody of 'Sitting On Top Of The World' (in his 'Some Summer Day'), the effect is almost comically overpowering.

So Patton is best remembered for his blues, which is all the more extraordinary when you decipher them (if you can – he is one of the hardest blues singers to under-

stand), for they are as specifically local as a telephone directory. To someone living in the megalopolitan West of the late twentieth century the world Patton describes seems microscopic: a handful of cotton-country towns, a railroad line or two, a clutch of girl-friends. He doesn't simply sing about being in jail, but names the small-town police officers who put him there. Hearing his songs is like spending an afternoon travelling the back roads with a local historian . . . Look, that's where the flood reached in '27 –

Backwater at Blytheville,
    done struck Joiner town,
It was 50 families and their children,
    some of them sank and drowned
. . . and that's the juke-joint with the prettiest girls –

There's a house over yonder
    painted all over green,
Some of the finest young women,
    Lord, a man most ever seen

Charlie Patton

RESONANT– AND HIS RICHLY ACCENTED, PERCUSSIVE GUITAR-PLAYING PUT HIM AMONG THE MOST INFLUENTIAL BLUES ARTISTS OF HIS TIME AND REGION.

northern and central Mississippi and built a name that won him, in 1929, a recording session with Paramount. The couplings 'Pony Blues'/'Banty Rooster Blues' and 'Mississippi Boweavil Blues'/'Screamin' And Hollerin' The Blues' were good sellers for the time, but even so Patton was fortunate to make more than 50 recordings, some with Willie Brown playing second guitar, others with the fiddler Henry Sims.

In the early Thirties he settled down in Holly Ridge, Mississippi, playing for local functions. In 1934 he went to New York for a last session, joined on some sides by his singing wife Bertha Lee. Many of the recordings were rejected and lost. He died of a heart condition a few months later.

Apart from 'Pony Blues', the songs of Patton's time and place that have become standards belong rather to Tommy Johnson or to Big Joe Williams. His music survived less as a repertoire than as a grandiose sound effect, echoing through the years not only in the South but in the new Chicago blues of the post-war Mississippi migrants. His stylistic legatees include not only Robert Johnson but Muddy Waters and Howlin' Wolf.

. . . and here comes the Pea Vine train: listen to that whistle!

A highly particularized landscape, yet its general contours would have been recognizable to contemporaries in many parts of the South. Besides, what immediately seizes the listener is not so much the detail as the shock effect, the striding guitar rhythms, the voice as thick as molasses. Men like Booker White and Howlin' Wolf heard it once and

were changed for ever. In a world where plantation workers might be less valuable than the mules they drove, it was something to imprint yourself so boldly upon a landscape, to assert your individual worth.

Patton spent much of his life on the Dockery plantation near Ruleville, Mississippi, where he encountered fellow blues singers and guitarists Tommy Johnson and Willie Brown, but he played throughout

Bessie Smith

START A DEBATE ABOUT THE GREATEST MALE BLUES SINGER, AND IN NO TIME THE ROOM WILL BE IN UPROAR. BUT ASK WHO HEADS THE LIST OF BLUES-SINGING WOMEN AND, NINE TIMES OUT OF TEN, THE RESPONSE WILL BE "BESSIE SMITH, OF COURSE. NEXT QUESTION."

She had rivals like Ma Rainey, Ida Cox, Sippie Wallace and Clara Smith, but none matched her combination of gifts and skills. In particular, no one ever sang with the sheer intensity of lived or imagined experience in which she steeped her blues.

Whenever we hear a woman singing the blues, whether on some dim recording or with a cheerful jazz band on a cruising riverboat, we almost always hear something of Bessie. With its broad brush-strokes and its fine shading, from the indigo melancholy of 'Nobody Knows You When You're Down And Out' to the swaggering jollity of 'Gimme A Pigfoot', her singing teaches almost every lesson a blues vocalist needs to know.

Bessie was born in Chattanooga, Tennessee, and learned her trade as a singer in travelling shows, for a period with the older blues singer Ma Rainey. By the early Twenties she was based in New York, where she began recording for Columbia in 1923. Although her first release, 'Down Hearted Blues'/'Gulf Coast Blues', recycled songs that had been successful for other singers, it was an enormous hit, selling in hundreds of thousands, and assured her of a busy recording schedule for the rest of the decade. During that period she starred in revues such as *Harlem Frolics*, *Yellow Girl Revue*, *Steamboat Days* and *Happy Times*, which played at every significant black theatre in the country.

When touring she took her own band, but on her earliest records she tended to sing with just a pianist – Clarence Williams if she was lucky, otherwise Fletcher Henderson.

By 1924 she had discovered the men who would be her favourite studio partners, the cornetist Joe Smith and trombonist Charlie Green. She was also memorably accompanied by Louis Armstrong ('The St Louis Blues', 'Careless Love Blues'), cornetist Tommy Ladnier ('Dyin' By The Hour'), guitarist Eddie Lang ('I'm Wild About That Thing') and with particular grace by the pianist James P. Johnson on 'Back Water Blues' and 'Lock And Key'. But as the dedicated listener will find out, between these rewarding encounters she sometimes had to endure a session's worth of ineptitude from someone like the altoist Ernest Elliott. She also recorded a few winsome duets with the blues singer Clara Smith – no relation but a sister Columbia artist.

No one would call Bessie Smith a versatile singer like, say, Ella Fitzgerald, yet she tackled a wide range of material with aplomb. While marmoreal blues like 'Dyin'

By The Hour' bring out the noblest qualities of her voice, she is charmingly jaunty in the pop songs 'Alexander's Ragtime Band' and 'Cake Walkin' Babies (From Home)' and a thoroughly believable sex-kitten – though not averse to showing her claws – in 'I'm Wild About That Thing'.

The slump in record-making that came with the Depression seemed to have ended Bessie's career in 1931, but two years later the producer John Hammond, who had hunted her down to the seedy Harlem theatres which were now the best gigs she could get, set up a session for her and hired a splendid band including the trombonist Jack Teagarden, Frankie Newton on trumpet and Chu Berry on tenor. The four songs she recorded are among her admirers' favourites, especially the party anthem 'Gimme A Pigfoot' ("and a bottle of beer"), but they were out of tune with the favoured singing styles of the swing era and proved to be her swansong.

Four years later, while on tour in the South, Bessie was seriously injured in a road accident in northern Mississippi and died before she reached hospital. Hammond reported to the press that her treatment had been delayed by discrimination and that she had been turned away from a whites-only hospital, but this proved to be mistaken.

Bessie Smith's musical legacy has been shared by singers as different as Dinah Washington and the gospel diva Mahalia Jackson, while her life story has inspired writers like James Baldwin, Edward Albee and Amiri Baraka.

Her most poignant memorial, however, apart from her recordings, is the short film drama *St Louis Blues*, in which she sings a magnificent extended version of that most famous song.

Bessie Smith in 1923, as she stepped into the spotlight of recording stardom.

RECORDED COUNTRY BLUES DIDN'T START WITH BLIND LEMON JEFFERSON, BUT IF IT HADN'T BEEN FOR HIS IMMEDIATE AND WIDESPREAD SUCCESS, THERE MIGHT NEVER HAVE BEEN THE RUSH TO RECORD MEN WITH GUITARS THAT HAS LEFT US SO MUCH REMARKABLE MUSIC. HE WAS THE FIRST MALE SINGER AND GUITARIST TO FIRE THE

IMAGINATION OF RECORD-BUYERS AND RIVAL MUSICIANS ALIKE. ALMOST 70 YEARS AFTER HIS DEATH, HE STILL STALKS THE BATTLEMENTS OF CASTLE BLUES.

Blind Lemon

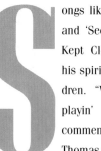

Songs like 'Match Box Blues' and 'See That My Grave Is Kept Clean' live on among his spiritual great-grandchildren. "Wasn't nobody else playin' when he played," commented blues guitarist Thomas Shaw. "Everybody else was standin' around him, hopin' they could do what he could do. . . . Wherever he pull his guitar out, he was the king there." We can catch the atmosphere of those admiring, envious gatherings by listening to 'Match Box Blues', one of Jefferson's earliest and most copied recordings. It's a stunning display of shifting rhythms, boogie-woogie bass runs, pulls and rippling tremolos. Over three minutes the tempo builds from sedate to breathless. 'Match Box' is exceptional, but there are passages of hectic invention ("crazy-quilt riffing", as Stephen Calt calls it) in many of his performances.

But this was only half of Jefferson's music. The range, penetration and tonal subtlety of his singing are hardly less extraordinary, while his lyrics are packed with vivid images: "If your heart ain't rock, it must be marble stone . . . I feel like jumpin' through a keyhole in your door . . . The blues come to Texas, lopin' like a mule." When John Lee Hooker builds a blues on the phrase "bad like Jesse James" he is recycling a half-line from Jefferson's 'One Dime Blues'. As for 'Match Box Blues', some of its wry jokes would still be resonating in rock 'n' roll lyrics 30 years later:

I'm sittin' here wonderin'
  will a matchbox hold my clothes,
I ain't got so many matches
  but I got so far to go.

Jefferson was born in Wortham, Texas, about 60 miles south of Dallas, in 1897 according to blues reference works, but possibly a decade or even more earlier. We know hardly anything of his youth, how he became blind, where he picked up his ideas about music. His history virtually begins in 1926 when

'Got The Blues'/'Long Lonesome Blues', his second blues release, was the first best-selling blues record by a black male singer. Soon he had a new car, a bank account and a billing as one of the stars of the Paramount label, the leading producer of "race" records, for whom he made almost a hundred sides in less than four years. His death is as mysterious as most of his life: he is supposed to have died in Chicago in the winter of 1929, frozen on the streets in a blizzard, but his producer Mayo Williams' account, that he collapsed in his car and was abandoned by his chauffeur, seems more plausible.

He was well known for his independence. The stories told by Leadbelly and others about acting as Jefferson's guide are probably fictional, but even so he seems to have covered a vast amount of ground in his travels. Sightings have been reported by musicians all over the South. Maybe pretenders learned his songs and assumed his identity, as would happen years later with B.B. King.

Jefferson impressed white musicians no less than black and was remembered with respect by Roscoe Holcomb in Kentucky and Hobart Smith in Virginia. 'Match Box Blues' has been repeatedly recorded by white artists over more than half a century, from Western Swing bandleader Bob Wills to Carl Perkins to The Beatles. Meanwhile in blues circles his songs have been recycled by Mance Lipscomb, Lightnin' Hopkins, Leadbelly and many other musicians. His instrumental technique is beyond most guitarists, and even today, when every second blues guitar enthusiast can bring off a passable impression of Robert Johnson, hardly anyone takes on the challenge of replicating Jefferson's darting unpredictability.

Cordially Yours Blind Lemon Jefferson

Jefferson

SHE WAS THE ONLY FEMALE BLUES ARTIST WHO MATCHED HER MALE CONTEMPORARIES AS BOTH A SINGER AND AN INSTRUMENTALIST. ACCORDING TO BIG BILL BROONZY, WHOM MEMPHIS MINNIE ONCE BEAT IN A BLUES BATTLE, SHE COULD "PICK A GUITAR AS GOOD AS ANY MAN ... MAKE A GUITAR CRY, MOAN, TALK AND WHISTLE THE BLUES."

more adaptable than some of her rivals, too, she confronted the stylistic changes in Thirties blues by swapping the two-guitar country blues format of her early recordings for a contemporary Chicago band sound that kept her music fresh into the late Forties.

Lizzie Douglas (as she was born) spent the first seven years of her life in Algiers, Louisiana, not far from New Orleans. Algiers was a centre of the Afro-American magic industry – home of the companies that manufactured mojo hands, dream books and John The Conqueror root, charms for success in love and gambling. Her own charms and her magic as a guitarist would attract several musician boyfriends, including Charlie Patton's friend Willie Brown and Will

Weldon of the Memphis Jug Band. She grew up in Walls, Mississippi, in the countryside south of Memphis and by the early Twenties was playing music on the city's streets. In 1929 she made her recording debut with her partner Joe McCoy. Following the lead of the hit recording duo Tampa Red & Georgia Tom, they called themselves Kansas Joe & Memphis Minnie.

Their rippling guitar duets and saucy backchat on numbers like 'Can I Do It For You?' were a novel blues format, and the coupling 'Bumble Bee'/'I'm Talking About You' (1930) was a big enough hit to keep them recording follow-ups practically every month for the next two years. They also made guest appearances on disc with the Memphis Jug Band – Minnie sang 'Bumble Bee' again – and with harmonica player Jed Davenport's Beale Street Jug Band. Early in the Thirties they moved to Chicago, but by 1935 their partnership, musical and marital, was over.

Memphis Minnie

stage, they stayed together until his death in 1961.

Minnie retained her popularity into the war years. In his newspaper column for the *Chicago Defender*, the African-American poet Langston Hughes wrote admiringly after seeing her at a Chicago club, "she beats out a good old steady down home rhythm on the strings – a rhythm so contagious that often it makes the crowd holler out loud. Then, through the smoke and racket of the noisy Chicago bar float Louisiana bayous, muddy old swamps, Mississippi dust and sun, cotton fields, lonesome roads, train whistles in the night, mosquitoes at dawn and the Rural Free Delivery that never brings the right letter. All these things cry through the strings on Memphis Minnie's electric guitar."

Later in the Forties Minnie lived in Indianapolis and Detroit, returning in the early Fifties to Chicago, where she found herself overtaken by the new Chicago blues generation of Muddy Waters and Howlin' Wolf. After a few more recordings, some disappointing and none commercially successful, she retired and spent her remaining years in Memphis.

Minnie spent the second half of the decade as a blues star in the same constellation as Big Bill and Tampa Red, performing in Chicago clubs like Gatewood's Tavern, where she held roistering 'Blue Monday' parties. Her records were now in the prevailing Chicago combo format, thickly textured with piano, bass and sometimes trumpet.

In 1939 she acquired another blues-guitarist husband, Ernest Lawlars, known as Little Son Joe. Some of her most potent and enduring work was made with him in the early Forties, such as the partly autobiographical 'Nothing In Rambling' and 'In My Girlish Days', 'Looking The World Over' and the lilting 'Me And My Chauffeur Blues', now a blues standard. Though Minnie had a short fuse when she saw Son Joe's eyes straying, and thought nothing of throwing his drink in his face or knocking him about on

KEY recordings

Bumble Bee,
Indigo. An excellent introduction, covering most of Minnie's career with many of her best-known songs.
Memphis Minnie & Kansas Joe Volumes 1–4,
Document. Everything they recorded, 1929–34 – the two-guitar years. Further Document CDs complete the story.
Hoodoo Lady (1933–1937),
Columbia. 'Ice Man', 'My Butcher Man', 'Good Biscuits' and other homely recipes.

IF YOU WERE BORN BLACK AND POOR IN RURAL MISSISSIPPI AROUND THE TURN OF THE CENTURY, YOU DIDN'T SET YOUR SIGHTS TOO HIGH. EVEN A MUSICIAN MIGHT NOT EXPECT TO MAKE A LIFELONG LIVELIHOOD SIMPLY OUT OF MUSIC. SO BIG BILL BROONZY WAS TRULY EXCEPTIONAL, BECAUSE HE HAD NOT ONE LIFE IN THE BLUES, BUT TWO.

f irst he was a leader of the Chicago blues gang in the Thirties and Forties, then in the Fifties he was the father figure of "folk blues". Imagine that Big Bill's career didn't span 25 years, hundreds of songs, thousands of miles travelled, but ended abruptly in the slump of the early Depression. Strangely, he would be venerated by record-collectors today chiefly as an extraordinarily fast and inventive guitarist, picking his way through exhilarating dance-tunes like 'Pig Meat Strut'.

It wasn't until the mid-Thirties that he fully revealed himself as one of the most accomplished of blues singers. His timbre was warm and rich, every word was understandable, and he seldom indulged in the whoops, cries and half-yodels favoured by many of his contemporaries. If he did, it was a deliberate joke, like the time he artfully

Big Bill in the 1940s, a jukebox star of the blues with records like 'All By Myself', 'When I Been Drinking' and 'I Feel So Good'.

Big Bill Broonzy

prefaced his bustling 'W.P.A. Rag' (1938) with a rustic field holler.

More than anything else, it was that fine, strong voice that made him so accessible to the white audiences of the Fifties who learned about blues and black folksong from him and from Josh White, Brownie McGhee and Sonny Terry. He also had great presence on stage and a capacious memory for songs, and was able and willing to adapt to his listeners' expectations. The small-band music of his Chicago heyday, with its stomping pianists and blaring horns, would have been too strong a brew for audiences reared on the singalong folksong of Pete Seeger and the Weavers. So he allowed himself to be remade as a bard of the cotton fields, wearing overalls like the farmhands whose life he had long ago decided he never wanted to share. He played the role with innate dignity, and in doing so he helped to create a climate of blues appreciation. The countless musicians who sunned themselves in it years later, and the fans who gathered to hear them, owed him, perhaps, more than they realized.

But if there was something a little artificial about the concept of Big Bill, Folk Singer, there was nothing fake about the artist. He didn't write powerful songs like 'Looking Up At Down' and 'Just A Dream' to win the approval of politically progressive white listeners; they were addressed first to his own people:

> I dreamed I was in the White House,
> sittin' in the President's chair,
> I dreamed he was shakin' my hand,
> said, "Bill, I'm glad you're here" –
> But that was just a dream,
> just a dream I had on my mind,
> Lord, and when I woke up, baby,
> not a chair could I find.

True, he didn't record his most famous social song, 'Black, Brown And White', until he was in Paris and out of range of recrimination, but perhaps that was because he knew he could not be so explicit in his own country:

> If you's white, you's all right,
> If you's brown, stick around,
> But as you black, mmm, brother,
> get back, get back, get back . . .

Bill was not only a foreign ambassador for the blues. At home in Chicago he was one of the music's grand old men, encouraging younger men like J.B. Lenoir and Muddy Waters. After he died they went on singing his songs, and Muddy remembered him with an affectionate album of his best-loved numbers, *Muddy Waters Sings Big Bill*.

The Big Bill Europe saw in the 1950s, when he seemed like an elder statesman of the blues.

CARR WAS THE BLUES' FIRST GREAT POET OF THE NIGHT. IN SONGS LIKE 'MIDNIGHT HOUR BLUES', 'BLUES BEFORE SUNRISE' AND 'WHEN THE SUN GOES DOWN' ('IN THE EVENING') HE CONJURED UP THE IMAGE OF A DOUBTFUL LOVER, BROODING OVER AN EMPTY COFFEE CUP AND A BRIMMING ASHTRAY AS DAWN COMES UP ON BLUESVILLE'S RAIN-STREAKED STREETS. WITH HIS GENTLE TOUCH ON THE PIANO HE CREATED A MOOD OF AMBIGUITY.

Leroy Carr

half questioning, half resigned, Carr echoed the uncertainties of life facing Southern migrants in the urban North. His first recording, 'How Long – How Long Blues', came out in the economically untroubled climate of 1928, but the few years left to him were spent in the long shadow of the Depression. From time to time he cheered his listeners with an upbeat stomp, boasting "I'd rather be sloppy drunk than anything I know!" or wryly passing on a girlfriend's comment, "she said she liked my music, but my tune's too short". But most of his songs caught the mood of the times with their images of doubt and despair. In 'Hurry Down Sunshine' he mused:

Hurry down sunshine,
    see what tomorrow bring,
May bring drops of sorrow,
    and it may bring drops of rain.

Carr was born in Nashville, Tennessee, but grew up in Louisville and Indianapolis. After military service he worked as an itinerant pianist in the Midwest, then in 1928 began playing in the clubs and theatres of Indianapolis with the guitarist Scrapper Blackwell (1903–1962). The national success of 'How Long – How Long Blues', a gigantic record hit, made them one of the leading acts on the blues theatre circuit and set off a prolific recording career. Other well-received numbers, amidst regular remakes of 'How Long' under slightly different titles, were 'Prison Bound Blues' (1928), reportedly based on Carr's own stretch of time for bootlegging, 'Mean Mistreater Mama' (1934) and 'Blues Before Sunrise'

(1934). The duo moved to St Louis in the early Thirties, but were back in Indianapolis when Carr suddenly died at 30 from nephritis.

Carr and Blackwell were responsible for several momentous developments. Their way of integrating piano and pungent single-string guitar lines influenced virtually every piano-guitar partnership for the next 20 years: Big Bill Broonzy and Black Bob, Big Maceo and Tampa Red, Memphis Slim and Matt Murphy. Carr's studied compositions, which he is supposed to have written at the kitchen table with the help of Blackwell's sister Minnie, introduced into the blues a melancholic poetry of night thoughts. His wistfulness and clear diction, in sharp contrast with the self-confidence and rural accent of contemporaries like Charlie Patton or Texas Alexander, were imitated with passionate fidelity by many blues

A few weeks after Carr's death, his guitarist buddy Blackwell recorded a memorial, 'My Old Pal Blues'.

singers of the Thirties, especially Bumble Bee Slim and Bill Gaither, who recorded most of his work under the sobriquet "Leroy's Buddy".

At Carr and Blackwell's final session, a couple of months before Carr died, they recorded four duets and then the pianist, uncharacteristically, moved to the studio next door and did four more songs on his own. It has been suggested that the two men fell out, perhaps over what Blackwell perceived as his junior role in their partnership. Blackwell was a sensitive blues singer himself, who had made some attractive records, but after Carr's death he quickly disappeared from the recording scene. Twenty-odd years later, still living in Indianapolis, he made some autumnal recordings deeply in the spirit of the old duo, but hopes of a revived career were dissolved by his death in a street shooting.

KEY recordings

Leroy Carr 1930–1935,
Magpie. Includes several of the finest Carr-Blackwell sides such as 'Midnight Hour Blues', 'Blues Before Sunrise' and Carr's deeply moving last recording, 'Six Cold Feet In The Ground'.
Leroy Carr Vol. 2 1929–1935,
Magpie. Twenty more beautiful performances, among them 'Rocks In My Bed', 'Ain't It A Shame' and a pretty pop-blues hybrid, 'You Left Me Crying'.
Hurry Down Sunshine,
Indigo. Inexpensive compilation with 'Prison Bound Blues', 'Hurry Down Sunshine' and the original 'How Long – How Long Blues'.
Scrapper Blackwell, The Virtuoso Guitar Of Scrapper Blackwell,
Yazoo. Accompaniments and duets with Carr intersperse lean solo blues by the sharpest guitarist of his day.

Calling the tune at the swing cats' ball.

With experience in jazz and swing, a front-rank role in the jump-blues movement and an eerie foreknowledge of rock 'n' roll, Jordan had unmatched qualifications for leading an advance party into the future of American music.

Louis Jordan was born in Brinkley, Arkansas, where as a teenager he joined his father in the town band. He gained valuable experience in travelling shows like the famous Rabbit Foot Minstrels, where he developed a habit which he never lost of watching and learning from other acts. His idols were Louis Armstrong, Cab Calloway and Fats Waller. He learned to play clarinet and all the saxophones, and by 1936 was good enough to get a job in New York with the Chick Webb band, where he shared singing duties and romantic exchanges with

Louis

"HIGHBROW, LOWBROW, ALL AGREE – THEY'RE THE BEST IN HARMONY." WHAT LOUIS JORDAN SANG IN 'FIVE GUYS NAMED MOE' HIS PUBLIC ECHOED ABOUT THE FIVE (OR SIX, OR SEVEN) GUYS IN HIS TYMPANY FIVE, THE LIVELI- EST COMBO IN BLACK MUSIC OF THE FORTIES AND ONE OF THE MOST INFLUENTIAL BANDS OF THE CENTURY.

Musicians who worked with Jordan credit him with anticipating rap. B.B. King and Fats Domino name him as a formative influence. Chuck Berry says he identifies with him more than any other artist. To James Brown, "He was everything." They are responding not just to a man who led a swinging band, played elegant alto and tenor sax and sang with unquenchable bonhomie, but to a cultural hero whose music expanded the possibilities of enjoying life. Jordan presided not just at the 'Saturday Night Fish Fry' he sang about but also over a decade-long party of wartime and post-war optimism. Anyone with 75 cents for a record could be there in spirit, but it was essentially a community affair, a block party for black America – "ain't nobody here but us chickens."

KEY recordings

Let the Good Times Roll,
Bear Family. Milestone Recording.
Let The Good Times Roll!,
Coolnote. A garland of hit tunes in their original versions, plus amusing duets with Ella Fitzgerald and Louis Armstrong. An excellent introduction.
G.I. Jive 1940–1947,
Somebody Done Hoodooed the Hoodoo Man,
Jukebox Lil. Well-chosen selections from Jordan's glory years: blues, small-group swing, secular sermons, calypsos and some sheer, delightful nonsense.
No Moe!: The Greatest Hits,
Verve. Spirited 1956–57 recreations, with jazz sidemen, of hits like 'Saturday Night Fish Fry', 'Let The Good Times Roll' and 'Caldonia'.

the teenaged Ella Fitzgerald. Within two years he was confident enough to leave Webb and form his own group, the Tympany Four (later Five), naming it after the timpani (tuned percussion) that he featured for a while as a novelty.

The big-band era was not yet over, and music-business wisdom held that a small group like Jordan's couldn't fill a large ballroom with either music or customers, but by 1942 the Tympany Five was among the nation's top half-dozen bands, playing to white audiences as well as black and consis-

tune from an oil strike (shades of *The Beverly Hillbillies*!) His records frequently topped the R&B charts for months on end, and 'Choo Choo Ch'Boogie' sold a million.

But 1950 saw Jordan's last major hit, 'Blue Light Boogie'. He fought his declining popularity by experimenting – with a big band, with novelty tunes like calypsos or the mock-Balkan 'Tamburitza Boogie', and with new managers and record labels. Nothing really worked. Rock 'n' roll had ridden into town, though Jordan could have pointed out that he had trained the horse. He got by,

playing in resort hotels. Supposedly there's a time capsule buried in Las Vegas containing one of his horns.

In the Sixties and Seventies, out of step with contemporary black music, he nevertheless appealed to jazz fans overseas and made several trips to Europe. Even at his most optimistic he couldn't have predicted the revival of his music after his death: the hit show based on his songs, *Five Guys Named Moe*, and a generation of young musicians rediscovering the joys of jump 'n' jive and letting the good times roll.

Jordan

In a promotional shot for the Monogram movie *Swing Parade Of 1946* Jordan fronts a line-up of Josh Jackson (tenor sax), Wild Bill Davis (piano), Jesse Simpkins (bass) Aaron Izenhall (trumpet) and Eddie Byrd (drums).

tently racking up hits like 'What's The Use Of Getting Sober (When You're Gonna Get Drunk Again)' and 'Five Guys Named Moe'. Jordan's three-horn, three-rhythm combo generated all the rhythmic pep of a band twice its size, a technique pursued by later groups like Joe Liggins' and Roy Milton's, other style-setters of jump blues.

Jordan's records sold so well that Decca promoted him out of the "sepia" (black) catalogue into the mainstream pop list, on a par with stars like Bing Crosby, Louis Armstrong and Ella Fitzgerald, who all joined him for disc duets. He broke into movies, both the three-minute shorts that were the period's equivalent of music videos and full-length features like *Look Out Sister*, where he played a singing cowboy who makes his for-

Howlin' Wolf

HOWLIN' WOLF LOOKED EXACTLY THE WAY HE SOUNDED. HE WAS BUILT LIKE A BRICK BARRELHOUSE, AND WHEN HE STAMPED HIS FOOT THE STAGE ROCKED – LITERALLY. BUT IT WASN'T ONLY HIS PHYSIQUE THAT MADE HIM ONE OF THE BIG MEN OF MODERN BLUES.

h e had seen Charlie Patton and played with Robert Johnson, and however long he might live in Chicago, he never lost his fondness for the raw blues he grew up with. For a generation of Chicago residents who had been born like him in the Deep South, the Wolf was a custodian of downhome memories.

> "Well, I tell you about this. See, I got a different sound in the blues field."

Whether the memories were warm or not so welcome, they were a past his listeners might have walked away from but could never wholly forget. His most famous song, 'Smokestack Lightnin'', was not only a recovered fragment of an old Charlie Patton blues but an evocation of rural landscape, blues-remembered hills. At the same time, its guitar hook and galumphing rhythm reshaped it as a rhythm 'n' blues stomp that hip white teenagers could groove to.

This is the secret of Wolf's continuing success in the early Sixties, when most of his Chicago blues contemporaries had stopped having hits or even making records that might be hits. Wolf, backed by Willie Dixon, who produced him and wrote or revised his material, and by the slashing guitar of Hubert Sumlin, kept on coming up with great records. No other artist can match his amazing run of

"I'm built for comfort," Wolf sang. "I ain't built for speed."

and his 1971 meeting with Eric Clapton and the Rolling Stones' rhythm section for the *London Sessions* album was successful – fortunately, since Wolf had not been lucky with recent recording projects. The 1969 freak-out *The Howlin' Wolf Album* was roundly described by its subject as "electric dogshit", and *Message To The Young* (1971) went unappreciated by fans of all ages.

His energy depleted by illness, Wolf worked less in the Seventies, but pilgrims who found their way to the Blue Flame or the 1815 Club could still see him warming to the fire of his own enthusiasm for performing. As he said, "If there wasn't any people listening, there wouldn't be no Wolf."

singles from 1960–64: 'Spoonful', 'Wang Dang Doodle', 'Down In The Bottom', 'The Red Rooster', 'Goin' Down Slow', 'Three Hundred Pounds Of Joy', 'Tail Dragger', 'Killing Floor'. Blues in form and subject and style, they had the bounding exuberance of rock 'n' roll. All this from a man in his early fifties.

Howlin' Wolf was born Chester Arthur Burnett in West Point, near Tupelo, Mississippi. Before he was 20 he was on the road with his guitar and harmonica. He ran across Robert Johnson, Elmore James, Sonny Boy Williamson II and a young admirer, Johnny Shines, who recalled the aura around this singular figure. "I was afraid of Wolf, I mean to walk up and put your hand on him, no, I didn't touch him. Well, it wasn't his size. I mean what he was doing, the sound that he was giving off."

Another man who remembers Wolf with awe is Sam Phillips of Sun Records, who recorded his first sides in 1951. "When I heard him, I said, 'This is for me. This is where the soul of man never dies.' He was about six foot six, with the biggest feet I've

ever seen on a human being. Big Foot Chester is one name they used to call him. He would sit there with those feet planted wide apart, playing nothing but the French harp [harmonica], and I tell you, the greatest show you could see today would be Chester Burnett doing one of those sessions in my studio. God, what it would be worth to see the fervor in that man's face when he sang. His eyes would light up and you'd see the veins on his neck, and buddy, there was nothing on his mind but that song. He sang with his damn soul."

Wolf's early Memphis sides brim with energy, his harmonica ripping into the music like a buzz-saw while Willie Johnson's guitar leaps and sizzles like a firecracker. His gritty voice is reminiscent of Patton, while his yodel-like whoop came from another Mississippi predecessor, Tommy Johnson. Little of this was lost when he moved to Chicago, where he had long-term residencies at the 708 Club and Sylvio's Lounge.

The Wolf that European audiences witnessed in the Sixties was just as imposing,

KEY recordings

The Genuine Article,
MCA/Chess. Milestone Recording.
Ain't Gonna Be Your Dog,
MCA/Chess. Attractive double CD of alternative takes and other collectibles, with some informal, rather moving tapes of Wolf singing old blues with just his acoustic guitar.
Memphis Days – The Definitive Edition, Volumes 1 & 2,
Bear Family. Sam Phillips' 1951–52 Sun recordings, licensed to Chess: 'Saddle My Pony', 'Moanin' At Midnight', 'How Many More Years'. Many alternative takes and unissued sides.
Rides Again,
Ace. More early 1950s sides cut for RPM under Ike Turner's direction: 'House Rockin' Boogie', 'Riding In The Moonlight' and explosive guitar solos by Willie Johnson.
Live And Cookin' At Alice's Revisited,
MCA/Chess. Satisfying Chicago club date with Hubert Sumlin (guitar) and Sunnyland Slim (piano).
The Back Door Wolf,
MCA/Chess. Wolf's last studio album (1973), with new material by his bandleader and tenor saxophonist Eddie Shaw. A dignified bowing-out.

WITH HIS CONFIDENT SWAGGER, HIS DEVIL-MAY-CARE MOUSTACHE AND HIS BEEN-THERE, SEEN-IT-ALL LYRICS, T-BONE WALKER WAS A FAVOURITE PIN-UP OF CALIFORNIA'S BLUES-LOVING LADIES DURING THE FORTIES AND FIFTIES. IMAGE ASIDE, IT HELPED THAT HE COULD EFFORTLESSLY BEND A GUITAR TO HIS WILL.

delicate as a zookeeper brushing flies off a sleeping lion, he shuffled lightly around the beat, raising blues guitar-playing to a new level of rhythmic and chordal sophistication. Meanwhile he beguiled his listeners with wry, soft-spoken observations on life in the City of Angels. T-Bone was way cool.

More than anyone else, Walker created the modern blues guitar. You can trace the line of his influence through Gatemouth Brown, Pee Wee Crayton and practically every other picker in the South-West or West, onwards to B.B. King and from B.B. outwards in all directions: Buddy Guy, Eric Clapton, Stevie Ray Vaughan . . . . "He was the first electric guitar player I heard on record," said B.B. "I knew I just had to go out and get an electric guitar." That was around 1946 or 1947, when amplified blues guitar

was still in an experimental stage. T-Bone transformed it. "The sound of guitar today," said producer Ralph Bass, "everything that has happened to it since, came from T-Bone."

So would you believe T-Bone started out picking banjo and ukulele? It was the early Twenties, and the teenaged Aaron Thibeaux Walker was learning his craft among the street-strolling stringbands of Dallas. His mother and stepfather both played, and Blind Lemon Jefferson sometimes dropped in for dinner. By the age of 19 he had made his first record, under the billing of "Oak Cliff T-Bone" ("Oak Cliff" from the section of town he lived in, "T-Bone" from his middle name), and by 26 he was working the clubland strip of Los Angeles' Central Avenue, sometimes as the featured singer and guitarist with Les Hite's orchestra.

'Mean Old World'/'I Got A Break Baby', which he cut in 1942, has a strong claim to

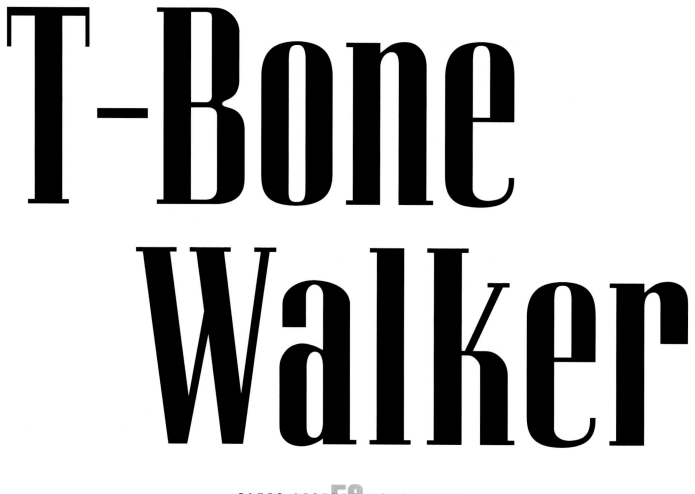

T-Bone Walker

be called the first modern blues record, but what with the war and a union-imposed recording ban, Walker was unable to push ahead with disc-making until 1946, when his 'Bobby Sox Baby' gave the new Black & White label its first hit. Over the next few years he used his frequent studio bookings to develop a new blues dialect, not only on guitar but in that's-life lyrics like 'Love Is Just A Gamble' –

Love is just a gamble,

say just what you want to say,

It's nice and sweet if you're a winner,

if you lose it's a debt that's hard to pay

– while across the studio the horn section droned a response that seemed to say "damn right, buddy".

In 1947–48 he had hits with 'Call It Stormy Monday', now an imperishable blues classic, and 'T-Bone Shuffle'. He moved from Capitol (who had bought up the Black & White sides) to Imperial and promptly scored with 'Glamour Girl' (1950). Here too

he recorded with horn sections, under the direction of the arranger and tenor player Maxwell Davis, but much of the time he was on the road with R&B package shows, sharing buses and rooming-houses with fellow stars like Wynonie Harris or Lowell Fulson.

After the mid-Fifties, sidelined by rock 'n' roll, Walker cooled his pace. A jazzy album for Atlantic, *T-Bone Blues*, brought him some kudos, but during the Great Blues Enlightenment of the mid-Sixties he was left somewhat in the shadows, and though he made several overseas tours he didn't have much going on record. In the last few years of his life he found a warm reception in Continental Europe, while at home he occasionally joined his old road-rivals Joe Turner or Cleanhead Vinson in genial "Battles Of The Blues". "They were all great men," band-leader Johnny Otis remembers fondly, "loving and respecting one another . . . and all three would be arguing about who'd best close the show."

Years before Jimi Hendrix, T-Bone Walker was playing guitar with his teeth or in strange positions.

KEY recordings

The Complete Capitol/Black & White Recordings,
Capitol. Milestone Recording.
The Complete Imperial Recordings, 1950–1954,
EMI. Double CD with 'Glamour Girl', 'The Hustle Is On', 'Cold, Cold Feeling'. Another model collection.
T-Bone Blues,
Sequel. The 1960 Atlantic album, with spots for jazz guitarist Barney Kessel and pianist Lloyd Glenn.
I Want A Little Girl,
Delmark. Mellow Paris-recorded set with Hal Singer on tenor.
Good Feelin',
Verve. Also from Paris, 1968, and rather more revolutionary, with boogaloo keyboard-playing by Manu Dibango. Shows its age but wears it vivaciously.

Robert Johnson

ALL HIS MUSIC CAN BE FITTED ON TWO CDS, YET THIS SMALL COLLECTION OF SONGS HAS MOVED MORE LISTENERS AND INSPIRED MORE MUSICIANS THAN ANY OTHER BLUES LEGACY. CREATED IN THE SOUTH OF THE THIRTIES, THESE INTIMATE, PASSIONATE NARRATIVES OF LOVE AND LOSS SEEM TO STAND OUTSIDE PLACE AND TIME.

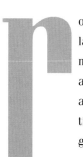obert Johnson's private landscape of dream and nightmare, of crossroads and hellhounds, has been absorbed into the imaginative worlds of singers and guitar-players, composers and novelists, painters and film-makers. For years Johnson was wrapped in a deliciously romantic fog of mystery and legend. Nobody even knew what he looked like, and in desperation researchers asked a police artist to sketch a hypothetical portrait from the descriptions of men who'd met him. He had died in his twenties, murdered, it wasn't clear how or where, and the site of his grave had been forgotten. He seemed to float through blues history like a ghost, often glimpsed but never really tangible.

Now we know more, but a few illusions still need to be dispelled. He was extraordinary, but not extraterrestrial. There is a place for him in the stylistic genealogy of the blues, between the musical generation of Charlie Patton and Son House and that of Muddy Waters and Elmore James. He was an original, but many of his ideas were borrowed from other artists. 'Walkin' Blues' came from House, '32–20 Blues' from Skip James. The sweet-and-sour flavour of 'Malted Milk' and 'Drunken Hearted Man' belongs to Lonnie Johnson, and the regretful cadences of 'Love In Vain' were inspired by Leroy Carr's 'When The Sun Goes Down'.

Still, being able to trace his sources does nothing to weaken Johnson's standing as a remarkable singer-guitarist. Note the hyphen: it carries a lot of weight. What strikes every listener is how organic Johnson's music is,

The photograph of Robert Johnson that took 50 years to surface.

how the vocal and guitar lines echo each other. It's hard to imagine him singing with a band, but tempting to try. Would he have sounded like Muddy Waters? Elmore James? Maybe: he wasn't much older than either.

Robert Johnson was born in Hazlehurst, Mississippi, from a brief union between his mother and a farm-worker, and used several surnames before choosing that of his natural father. As a teenager in Robinsonville he learned harmonica and guitar and hung round Patton, House and Willie Brown. He returned to Hazlehurst for a year or two, and when he came back to Robinsonville he showed the older men how he'd improved. "When he got through", House remembered,

"all our mouths was open." He would sometimes add, "He sold his soul to the devil to get to play like that." People often said that about blues guitarists. It was widely believed that if you suddenly acquired a skill or wealth or sexual success, you had made a deal with the Devil at a crossroads at midnight.

Johnson was notoriously restless. "If you'd wake him up in the middle of the night", said Johnny Shines, "and tell him there was a freight train coming through, why, he'd say, 'Well, let's catch it,' and he'd take hold of his guitar, and off he'd go." Shines travelled with him to Canada and New Jersey, and Johnson went alone to Texas on at least two occasions for recording sessions, cutting 16 numbers in San Antonio in 1937 and 13 in Dallas the following year. The sexy 'Terraplane Blues' was a good seller, but other songs seem more doubtful commercial propositions,

particularly 'Hell Hound On My Trail', which bears out Shines' description of Johnson as "close to a split personality":

> I got to keep movin', I got to keep movin',
> Blues falling down like hail . . .
> And the day keeps on worryin' me,
> There's a hellhound on my trail.

Johnson sounds ill-at-ease and his playing is peculiar, but perhaps these are deliberate devices to create a totally absorbing performance which, as Alexis Korner wrote, "communicates the kind of delirious vision one associates with William Blake".

One summer Saturday night in 1938, Johnson was playing at a juke-joint outside Greenwood, Mississippi. The proprietor, whose wife he was having an affair with, gave him poisoned whisky. He died in great pain some days later and was buried in the graveyard of a small church in a nearby town. A few months later the record producer John Hammond looked for him for his *Spirituals To Swing* concert in New York. Learning of his death he booked Big Bill Broonzy instead. It's endlessly fascinating to wonder what would have happened if Hammond had been in time, how different the entire future of the blues might have been had Johnson survived to sing 'Cross Road Blues' in Carnegie Hall.

KEY recordings

The Complete Recordings, Columbia. Milestone Recording.
King Of The Delta Blues Singers, Columbia. Historically an equally important milestone, this 16-track album, first released in 1962, gave Johnson to the world. Now available in a Mastersound Collector's Edition with original artwork. If any blues record should be sent into deep space in a time capsule, this is it.
The Roots Of Robert Johnson, Yazoo. Instructive, sometimes contentious compilation of recordings Johnson may have learned from, by Patton, House, Skip James, Lonnie Johnson, Hambone Willie Newbern and others.

Sonny Terry

THEY WERE AROUND FOR SO LONG THAT THEY BEGAN TO BE OVER-LOOKED OR UNDERESTIMATED. THEIR BLUES STORIES, ONCE NEW AND FASCINATING, WERE STILL WORTH LISTENING TO, BUT THEY HAD TOLD THEM TOO OFTEN AND LIKE PUB BORES THEY HAD LOST THEIR AUDIENCE.

S till, for a generation they had been despatch riders of the blues, delivering the music's messages to listeners from San Francisco to St-Germain-des-Prés. And who could count the blues harmonica wa-wa-wannabes that Sonny Terry taught to wail?

Sonny Terry (1911-86) and Brownie McGhee (1915-96) first met in North Carolina in 1939. In their twenties, they were already experienced musicians despite disability: Terry (born Saunders Terrell in Greensboro, North Carolina) had been blind since childhood, while McGhee, from Knoxville, Tennessee, had suffered from polio and had only recently given up walking with a stick. They had both been attracted into the orbit of the famous Blind Boy Fuller and worked with him before his death in 1941, after which McGhee was briefly touted on records as "Blind Boy Fuller No. 2".

His singing and guitar-playing were certainly Fullerish, but he possessed a suavity that would later prove invaluable in attracting listeners unprepared for more rugged performers. Terry's singing, by comparison, was rough and unsubtle, but he played with the mouth and hands of a musical athlete. Harmonica phrases, whoops and cries exploded in a firework display so packed with effects that it seemed beyond the powers of just one man.

Personable, musically expert yet never hard to follow, McGhee and Terry offered audiences an easy first experience of the blues.

& Brownie McGhee

In the early Forties they settled in New York and into a partnership that would become the longest-lasting double act in blues history. They fell into the same musical/political circles as Leadbelly and Woody Guthrie and performed on radio and stage, Terry playing in the New York production of the musical *Finian's Rainbow* and both of them appearing in Tennessee Williams' play *Cat On A Hot Tin Roof*. On disc they made singles for the black record-buying market, accompanied other blues artists like Champion Jack Dupree, Ralph Willis and McGhee's brother Stick, and were among the first blues musicians to record LPs, on Folkways and other labels, for white folksong devotees.

By the late Fifties, thanks to their widely circulated recordings, Terry and McGhee were perhaps the best-known active blues artists in the world, a position they strengthened over the next decade with further LPs and overseas tours. They first visited Britain in 1958, at the instigation of the jazz bandleader and blues-lover Chris Barber, and left behind them several guitar-and-harmonica duos faithfully modelled on theirs. Later visits continued to draw audiences, but the Terry-McGhee sound was too discreet and conversational to compete with the assertive and sexy Chicago blues that dominated most European fans' interests in the Sixties.

At home, though, they continued to make a living on the festival and coffeehouse circuits. They also added several movie credits to a list begun in 1958 with McGhee's playing on the soundtrack of *A Face In the Crowd*: *Buck And The Preacher* and *Book Of Numbers* in 1972, *Leadbelly* in 1976.

By then the strain of more than 30 years in each other's company had turned their stage act from a collusion into a pair of parallel performances, and at the end of the Seventies they separated for good. Of their individual careers thereafter Terry's was the more visibly successful. His collaboration with Johnny Winter on the album *Whoopin'* revealed that even as late as that he could produce surprising as well as rewarding music. McGhee's last recordings, however, sometimes reflect the weariness of a man who has said all he has to say.

LIGHTNIN' HOPKINS WAS EVERYBODY'S IDEA OF A BLUES SINGER. SURVEYING THE WORLD IMPASSIVELY THROUGH HIS DARK GLASSES, HE NOTED THE GAMES MEN AND WOMEN PLAY, PICKED UP HIS GUITAR AND SPUN OUT HIS THOUGHTS WITH THE SLEEPY WATCHFULNESS OF A FISHERMAN LAZILY CASTING HIS LINE.

Hopkins with bassist Big Will Harvey at the 1977 New Orleans Jazz & Heritage Festival.

h e accompanied his half-sung, half-narrated stories with lean single-string guitar lines that slid alongside the vocal melody, stretching and curling like a rattlesnake or a hoochie-coochie dancer. Lightnin' was laddish, even by bluesmen's standards, and he sang a lot about gals 'n' cars – often about gals *in* cars – but he had a deep dark side that he showed in blues about death and disaster. And through all the thousands of playlets he unfolded, he seldom needed more, by way of a supporting cast, than his guitar. He was the archetypal go-anywhere blues singer, equipped only with his box and his restless imagination. He "is the embodiment of the jazz-and-poetry spirit," said Mack McCormick, a folklorist who knew him well, "representing its ancient form in the single creator whose words and music are one act."

Some of Lightnin''s stories were about national or international events: hurricanes, floods, the war in Korea and later Vietnam, the conquest of space. He knew about them because they were in the papers and people in his own East Texas world talked about them, but he didn't have much information about other ways of life. Once, when he was making an LP for a UK label, he had second thoughts about a song that began "Buses

Lightnin' Hopkins

stopped running, trains won't allow me to ride no more", and had to ask McCormick, "Do they have buses and trains over there?"

Sam Hopkins was born near Centerville, Texas, midway between Dallas and Houston. His older brothers and sister played guitar, and he also hung out with Blind Lemon Jefferson and his cousin Texas Alexander. As a young man he tried farmwork, but realizing what it was like, he concentrated on music as his ticket out of wage-slavery. "I didn't have to fool with any boss-man, not so long as I could get my guitar going."

By 1946 he had enough of a reputation in the clubs along Houston's Dowling Street to win him an audition with Aladdin Records in

---

Houston's Poet in Residence for 35 years, Hopkins recorded more albums than any other bluesman.

L.A. Over the next three years he cut dozens of sides for Aladdin and the Houston label Gold Star. He was pliant about contracts: in the early Fifties he also recorded for RPM, Sittin' In With, Mercury, Decca, Herald and other labels. Few of these sides are less than gripping, and some of the Aladdin and Gold Star work is magnificent, such as the savage 'Tom Moore's Farm', an attack on a brutal landowner, or songs of warning and sour prediction like 'Fast Life Woman':

> You may see a fast life woman
>   sittin' round a whiskey joint,
> Yes, you know, she'll be sittin' there
>   smilin'
> 'cause she knows some man gonna
>   buy her half a pint.
> Take it easy, fast life woman,
>   'cause you ain't gon' live always. . . .

When rock 'n' roll came in, Lightnin' went

KEY recordings

The Gold Star Sessions, Vols 1 & 2, Arhoolie. Milestone Recording.

The Complete Aladdin Recordings, EMI. Scrupulously well-done double CD of late-1940s sides like 'Katie May' and 'That Mean Old Twister' (his first release), 'Shotgun' and 'Fast Mail Rambler'.

Lightnin' Hopkins, Smithsonian/Folkways. The unplugged 1959 set that put Lightnin' on the world stage: 'Penitentiary Blues', 'Bad Luck And Trouble', 'See That My Grave Is Kept Clean', 'Reminiscences of Blind Lemon'.

Lightnin' Hopkins, Candid. Impeccably recorded late-night studio date from 1960. Lightnin' accompanies himself on guitar or piano (or, briefly, both at once), sings blues and favourite jive pieces like 'Ain't It Crazy' and tells a long amiable story, 'Mr Charlie'.

Blues In My Bottle/Walkin' This Road By Myself, Ace. Two excellent early-1960s Bluesville LPs on one CD: 'Baby Don't You Tear My Clothes', 'DC-7', 'Coffee Blues' and the astronautical 'Happy Blues For John Glenn'.

Morning Blues, Charly. Jewel sides from 1969 with rhythm and Houston pianist Elmore Nixon: 'Rock Me Mama', 'Wig Wearing Woman', 'Lonesome Dog Blues' and the intense title song.

out, until the blues historian Sam Charters tracked him down in Houston in 1959 and recorded an acoustic set (most of his previous recordings had been with amplified guitar) which became one of the key documents of the blues revival. The following year found Lightnin' playing in folkclubs in L.A. and New York and initiating a marathon programme of recording. By the end of the Sixties he had 35 new albums to his name, not counting reissues of his earlier singles. He travelled widely in the United States, and overcame his fear of flying just twice to join the 1964 American Folk Blues Festival and to visit Germany and the Netherlands 13 years later. He died of cancer in Houston, his home for most of his adult life.

Muddy Waters

MUDDY WATERS WAS A KEY FIGURE IN THE HISTORY OF MODERN BLUES, CREATING A TEMPLATE FOR CHICAGO'S BAR-BAND MUSIC THAT WOULD LONG OUTLAST HIM. AN AUTHORITATIVE LEADER. A NOTABLE SINGER AND SLIDE-GUITAR PLAYER. AND THE BLUES' GIFT TO WOMEN, THE ORIGINAL HOOCHIE-COOCHIE MAN.

ost people remember Muddy as an elder statesman, taking things carefully, especially after the road accident that forced him to bring a chair on stage. But a piece of film survives from the 1960 Newport Jazz Festival, where a young, slim Muddy stalks the stage as restlessly as a leopard. Watching it, you realize how physical his act was, how little you get of the true man when he's reduced to a voice on a record.

Some of Muddy's cyclonic force comes across on one of his late singles, 'I Got A Rich Man's Woman', where he opens and closes the song with passages of vocal barnstorming. "But OHHHHHH mmm yeeaaah. . . ah ha ha HMMMM . . . WOAH yha ha ha ha

. . . hey WOAH yeah, WOAH yeah, WOAH yeah, the woman she's livin' on a poor man's pay. . . ." Now imagine Muddy doing that in front of you.

He grew up near Clarksdale, Mississippi, learned harmonica and guitar and played in a stringband with the fiddler Henry "Son" Sims, who had recorded with Charlie Patton. He cut some records for the folklorist Alan Lomax in 1941–42, including 'Country Blues' and 'I Be's Troubled', potent slide-guitar blues in the spirit of Son House and Robert Johnson.

Shortly afterwards he migrated to Chicago, where he pursued his music with the encouragement of Big Bill Broonzy and Sonny Boy Williamson I. Early recordings for Aristocrat and Chess like 'I Can't Be Satisfied' and 'Rollin' Stone' find him still hollering across the cornfields, though his amplified slide guitar and the bass player

roll the sound up to city levels, reenergizing Chicago's formula-bound music with a waft of soul from the Mississippi bottomlands. Hard practice with guitarist Jimmy Rogers and harmonica player Little Walter laid the foundations of a band idea realized on record in 1952–53, the core trio augmented by drummer Elga Edmonds and pianist Otis Spann.

The songs recorded by this band and its successors over the next seven years became the anthems of Chicago blues – songs such as 'I'm Your Hoochie Coochie Man', 'I Just Want To Make Love To You' (both 1954), 'I'm Ready' and 'Got My Mojo Working' (both 1956). Waters' LPs *The Best Of Muddy Waters* (1959) and *At Newport* (1960), with their potent repertoire like 'Rollin' Stone' and 'Tiger In Your Tank', would be much plundered sourcebooks during the Sixties blues renaissance.

Now practically unchallenged as Chicago's leading bluesman (though you wouldn't say that when Howlin' Wolf was in earshot), Muddy held court at Pepper's Lounge or Smitty's Corner when he wasn't on the road. Or abroad – he made his first visit to Britain in 1958 and to continental Europe in 1963 with the American Folk Blues Festival, and thereafter was quite a frequent visitor, even recording an album in England in 1971,

The London Muddy Waters Sessions, with local R&B heroes Georgie Fame and Rory Gallagher.

By then he had to live up, or down, to the experiments Chess had urged upon him in the late Sixties like the half-baked psychedelic rock settings of *Electric Mud* or the more judicious *After The Rain*.

By the mid-Seventies, Muddy was firmly established on the domestic circuit of blues festivals and college-town clubs. He had separated from Chess, but with Johnny Winter as producer made four sturdy albums between 1977 and 1981 for CBS/Blue Sky. The band's line-up, with the guitarists Luther Johnson Jr and Bob

"Name, McKinley Morganfield. Nickname, Muddy Waters. Stovall's famous guitar picker", Waters proudly told Alan Lomax in 1941.

Margolin, pianist Pinetop Perkins and harmonica player Jerry Portnoy, remained steady for much of the Seventies but was dissolved in 1980 after a dispute with Waters' management, It quickly reformed as the Legendary Blues Band, one of many groups that would carry Muddy's legacy in the years after his death.

Mr Lucky, a 1990s album called him, and by then he was. But in his 50-year career Hooker has often been Mr Unlucky, too.

now and then the performance would seem to change gear, as the singer deserted his muttered rhymeless monologues to deliver a clanging guitar solo. Amidst the automobile production lines of late Forties Detroit, John Lee Hooker offered blues that were unmistakably handmade.

What Hooker learned as a boy at home in Clarksdale, Mississippi, or later in Memphis or Cincinnati, can only be guessed at. The man who broke into the recording scene in the winter of 1948 with 'Boogie Chillen' may have seemed weird and wilful, but it would soon be apparent that this was not the effect of youth (he was 28, after all) or inexperience. John Lee Hooker was a fully-formed musician. Almost 50 years on, he has hardly progressed an inch.

At first his music was so captivating that everyone wanted a piece. Ostensibly an exclusive Modern artist, he moonlighted for

John Lee

FROM THE FIRST IT WAS OBVIOUS THAT THERE HAD NEVER BEEN A BLUESMAN LIKE THIS. 'BOOGIE CHILLEN', 'CRAWLING KING-SNAKE', 'NIGHTMARE BLUES' – NOT SONGS BUT VOODOO CHANTS, UNDERSCORED BY A STAMPING FOOT AND THRUMMING REPEATED RIFFS ON AN OPEN-TUNED GUITAR.

KEY recordings

The Legendary Modern Recordings 1948–1954,
Ace. Milestone Recording.
Boogie Awhile,
Krazy Kat. Early small-label rarities.
Don't You Remember Me,
Charly. Murky recordings but almost overbearingly intense performances like 'Late Last Night', 'Wandering Blues' and 'Stomp Boogie'.
This Is Hip,
Charly. The rocking band-backed Hooker of the Vee Jay years in 'Boom Boom', 'Dimples', 'This Is Hip' and 'It Serves Me Right To Suffer'.
Sings The Blues, The Country Blues Of John Lee Hooker,

Original Blues Classics. Unplugged coffeehouse Hooker, but just as mesmerizing.
Endless Boogie,
BGO. Powerful and surprisingly undated jam with Steve Miller, Mark Naftalin. Includes 'Kick Hit 4 Hit Kix U (Blues For Jimi And Janis)' and the outstanding 'Sittin' In My Dark Room'.
Free Beer and Chicken,
BGO. Typical 1970s session with heavy friends, reportedly Hooker's own favourite album.
The Healer,
Chameleon (US)/Silvertone (UK). Milestone Recording.
Mr Lucky,
Silvertone. A rewarding get-together with Albert Collins, Ry Cooder, Keith Richards and Van Morrison.

any company that knocked on his door, masking his identity with pseudonyms – a laughable subterfuge, given the singularity of his style. So he was Delta John on Regent, Birmingham Sam & His Magic Guitar on Savoy, Johnny Williams on Staff, The Boogie Man on Acorn and, flimsiest of all, John Lee Booker on Chess, a label for which he made some particularly compelling sides in 1950–51. His work for King (as Texas Slim) was even better, the misty acoustic of a back-of-the-store recording lending a disturbing Stephen King ambience to 'Moaning Blues' and 'Late Last Night'.

Meanwhile he launched a parallel career, unplugged, as a "folk blues" soloist with albums for Riverside, and as early as 1960 he was on the bill of the Newport Folk Festival. Two years later he toured Europe for the first time with the first American Folk Blues Festival, and in 1964, encouraged by 'Boom Boom' showing up on the pop charts there, he made the first of many trips to Britain. By the late Sixties, the folk-blues venture over; he was swimming in the electric blues mainstream, composing songs about Vietnam and miniskirts.

Next, with the prescience of an instinc-tive survivor, Hooker fell in with younger white musicians like Canned Heat, Elvin Bishop and Van Morrison, whose admiring collaboration kept him in the blues vanguard throughout the Seventies. But in the follow-ing decade he virtually vanished, till sup-porters like his agent Mike Kappus and guitarist/producer Roy Rogers conceived the fanfest *The Healer* (1989), the best-selling blues album ever. Ever since then Hooker's darkly murmuring voice and throbbing guitar, whether on disc, movie soundtrack or TV ad, have been an internationally recog-nizable soundbite of the blues.

Hooker

For Ry Cooder Hooker is "the last of those unstructured, free players … The real deal, ultimately, is the sound of his voice, that deep, well-like sound." To Bonnie Raitt, his music is "one of the saddest things I've ever heard".

While most of the freelance recordings quickly disappeared, Hooker's Modern discs were better distributed and some reached the R&B charts, like 'Hobo Blues' (1949), 'Crawling Kingsnake' (1949) and 'I'm In The Mood' (Modern, 1951). In 1955 he signed with the Chicago label Vee Jay and recorded – not for the first time, but now as a matter of policy – with supporting groups. The other musicians flattened his more baroque rhythmic contours and some of the hectic excitement departed for ever, but commer-cially the move was astute, as was proved by the enormous, and seemingly everlasting, appeal of songs with strong rhythmic hooks like 'Dimples' (1956) and 'Boom Boom' (1961).

MIDWAY THROUGH THE FORTIES, EVERY BLACK JUKEBOX WOULD HAVE HELD CHARLES BROWN'S 'DRIFTING BLUES' – "I'M DRIFTING AND DRIFTING, LIKE A SHIP OUT ON THE SEA". THE AMBIENCE OF THE MUSIC WAS AS ELUSIVE AS A WAFT OF CIGARETTE SMOKE: A LAZY PIANO, DISCREET BASS AND DRUMS, A VOICE WITH THE BLEAK TENDERNESS OF A LAST GOODBYE KISS.

i t was a new blues for new times – urban, sophisticated, free of nostalgia. Yet as it stood on the brink of a glowing post-war future, it voiced black America's uncertainty about what that future would bring. Charles Brown was born in 1922 in the Gulf Coast town of Texas City, Texas, and raised by his grandparents. He learned the rudiments of piano from his grandmother and when she was around he dutifully played the light classical pieces she liked, but alone in the house he began to investigate blues and boogie-woogie. "Back in the old days when honky tonk dives with piano players were popular," he recalls, "I would sneak to the back of the place and listen to the music of Ivory Joe Hunter and many others . . . I was so touched by the blues that I would go home humming and trying to remember some of the words."

Leaving college with a chemistry degree, he wound up in Los Angeles, where he won a talent contest and was hired as a dinner-time pianist at the Chicken Shack club, playing polite music – as his employer put it, "nothin' degrading like the blues." Soon he joined guitarist Johnny Moore and bassist Eddie Williams in their popular nightclub group The Three Blazers, and in September 1945 they began recording for the new Philo label. 'Drifting Blues' was one of the blues hits of 1946.

The trio made records for several companies, most of them labelled as by Johnny Moore's Three Blazers with perhaps a small-print credit "vocal by Charles Brown". "I enjoyed a good two years of success travelling with the Three Blazers," Brown remembers, "when suddenly money and misunderstanding came into the picture. I had to start all over on my own. Only a few people knew that I was one of the main attractions in the trio because the group was considered as The

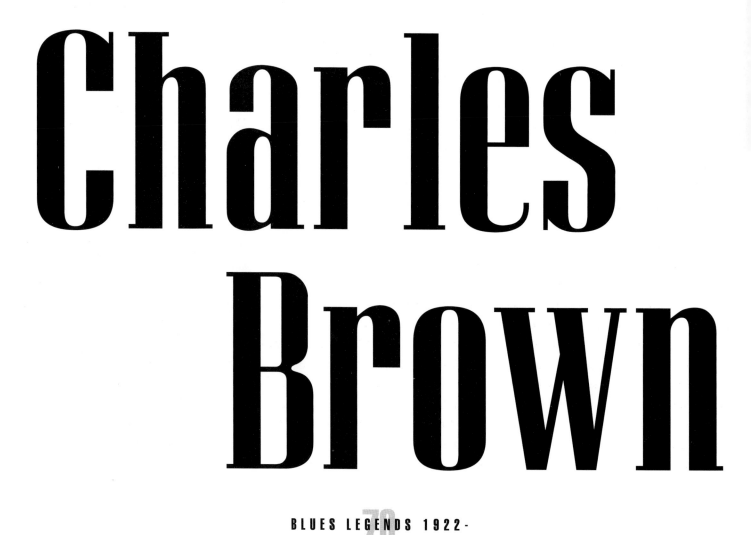

Charles Brown

Following his 1996 album *Honey Dripper*, Brown and his combo did supporting work, the year afterwards, on John Lee Hooker's *Don't Look Back*.

he says bluntly. "Couldn't get no money. I did window washing and little janitorial things."

His admirers' refusal to forget him and his own determination to keep on playing kept him afloat. No one could have been more unhip, in those days of Chicago blues worship, than a West Coast piano-playing blues-crooner, but he got his deserts in the Eighties and Nineties: a Lifetime Achievement Award from the Rhythm & Blues Foundation and high-profile work with fans like Bonnie Raitt, backed by his steady group featuring veteran tenor saxophonist Clifford Solomon and a young guitarist, Danny Caron, who sounded uncannily like Johnny Moore. Brown continued to sing and play everything from blues to 'The Very Thought Of You' in a voice astonishingly unscathed by time.

Three Blazers featuring Johnny Moore. So I left and started on my own."

His first record, 'Get Yourself Another Fool', was a hit. Between 1947 and 1951 he scored chart-placings with 'Merry Christmas Baby', 'Trouble Blues', 'Homesick Blues', 'My Baby's Gone', 'Black Night' and 'Seven Long Days'. On the popular R&B package shows of the time he regularly headlined alongside Fats Domino or Ray Charles, whose own early records were imbued with Brown's style.

By the late Fifties, however, Brown was reduced to working as a backing pianist or in the mob-owned casinos of Newport,

Kentucky, the sleaze section of Cincinnati. "They kept me there for two years. The boss used to give me hundred-dollar tips, but when I talked about going back to California, he said, 'Charles, you're pretty and I love you, but you wouldn't look too good with a bullet in your brain.'"

In 1960 he regained his record-selling powers with 'Please Come Home For Christmas'. It has become a seasonal standard, recorded in every pop style, most recently by Bon Jovi, but at the time it didn't do much for his career. He passed the Sixties and Seventies in a variety of locations and jobs, not always musical. "I was strugglin',"

KEY recordings

Drifting & Dreaming,
Ace. Three Blazers sides from 1945–46, typical of the format in which Brown got his start, but much more pop than blues. Includes 'The Warsaw Concerto'.

The Complete Aladdin Recordings,
Mosaic. Currently the only point of entry to Brown's most varied body of work in the late 1940s and early 1950s. A beautifully put together five-CD boxed set, but expensive and hard to find.

One More For The Road,
Alligator. An important moment in Brown's 1980s comeback. Faithful to the spirit of the early days, yet still lively, thanks in part to tenorist Harold Ousley and guitarist Billy Butler. 'Travelin' Blues', 'Route 66', 'I Stepped In Quicksand'.

All My Life,
Bullseye Blues. Very fine 1990 set with guest appearances by Ruth Brown, Dr John. 'Bad Bad Whiskey', 'Seven Long Days', 'A Virus Called The Blues'.

Albert King

"I'll play the blues for you…" Albert King serenades New York at the last concert from the stage of the Fillmore East, June 1971.

AS GARRISON KEILLOR SAID, THE WORLD IS FULL OF RISKS FOR TALL PEOPLE. ALBERT KING STOOD 6 FEET 4 INCHES AND WEIGHED 250 POUNDS, AND HE DIDN'T MOVE AROUND MUCH ON STAGE.

e was just as economical in his guitar-playing, using a few notes to do a lot, twisting them with his stubby fingers into shouts and murmurs, cries and moans. They had to work doubly hard because they were also doing part of a singer's job. Albert was not a demonstrative vocalist like B.B. King. – he delivered a song matter-of-factly, like a man having the last word in an argument.

Born Albert Nelson, in Indianola, Mississippi, King grew up in Arkansas. There may have been some distant family connection with B.B. King, but B.B.'s reply when questioned about it – "he's a brother" – was surely a joke. By 16 he was playing guitar and listening to blues over the airwaves from station KFFA in nearby Helena, from artists like Howlin' Wolf and Elmore James. He formed his first band, the In The Groove Boys, in Osceola. "They were local yokels," remembers Jimmy Thomas, a younger musician, "but to me they were fantastic."

He cut his first record in 1953, calling himself Albert King, for Parrot in Chicago, but it made no impact. He didn't record again until 1959, for Bobbin in St Louis, where he was based. Despite a small hit with 'Don't Throw Your Love On Me So Strong' on the King label, several more years ensued scuffling round what he called "one-arm joints" before he made an indelible mark on the blues map with 'Laundromat Blues' (1966), his first single for Stax. Its opening line, "You been meeting your man, baby, down at the local laundromat," was a brilliant lyric hook – no one had thought of staging a blues situation in a wash 'n' wait setting before.

King's next couple of years with the Memphis label, working with its versatile house band of Booker T. & The M.G.s and the Memphis Horns (Wayne Jackson on trumpet, Andrew Love on tenor sax), produced a wonderful series of tough blues and funky instrumentals like 'Oh Pretty Woman' (the source of Cream's 'Strange Brew'), 'Crosscut Saw' and 'Cold Feet', culminating in the stunning 'Born Under A Bad Sign'. Their musical settings gave them an immediately recognizable kinship with the hugely popular R&B of Stax artists like William Bell (who wrote 'Bad Sign') or Sam & Dave. They were later paraded on the album *Born Under A Bad Sign*, which blues writer Robert Palmer has described as "probably the most important and certainly the most stirring hard blues LP of the 1960s". This and King's 1968 album

KEY recordings

I'll Play The Blues For You,
Stax. Not to be confused with other like-named albums, this is subtitled *The Best Of Albert King*, containing strong (though not the original) versions of 'Born Under A Bad Sign' and 'Crosscut Saw'.

Live Wire/Blues Power,
Stax. Milestone Recording.

I'll Play The Blues For You/Lovejoy,
Stax. Two early-1970s albums on one CD: some overlap with its namesake above, but worth getting for 'Breaking Up Somebody's Home' and 'She Caught The Katy And Left Me A Mule To Ride'.

Live,
Charly. Storming performance from the 1977 Montreux Festival: long versions of 'As The Years Go Passing By' (with fine guitar cameo by Rory Gallagher) and 'Blues At Sunrise'.

I'm In A Phone Booth Baby,
Stax. Decent 1984 studio set with enterprising material like the title song (part-written by Robert Cray) and Dennis Walker's 'Brother, Go Ahead And Take Her'.

Live Wire/Blues Power had wide and long-term influence – not only in the South, where soundalike bands could still be heard 20 years later, but also on musicians far away such as Jimi Hendrix, Eric Clapton and Robbie Robertson, and later Gary Moore and Stevie Ray Vaughan.

Albert's albums in the Seventies (*Albert, Truckload Of Lovin', The Pinch*, etc), like B.B.'s of that period, steered him into the quiet waters of soft soul music or the wave-machines of funk, a move he defended as a strategy to grab younger listeners: "If I came on with the lowdown blues like I've done in the past, the kids wouldn't dig that. But with the kind of things I'm doing now they'll accept it and I can come back later to the

lowdown blues." He eventually did so, though it took most of a decade. (The album *San Francisco '83* marks the turning-point.)

But all along King had been playing the lowdown stuff in concert, and that's probably the way most people remember him, wandering on stage puffing at a curly pipe as if he were Sherlock Holmes come to solve a mystery. There was no mystery about his music. On records it might sometimes sound glitter-sprayed and sequinned, but in person it was plain, hardwearing denim.

As he hit his mid-sixties King began to drop hints about retirement, not unreasonably, given that he had health problems. Nevertheless, when he died he was planning yet another of his overseas jaunts.

We see him here, in glossy magazines, advertising Cutty Sark Scotch. We hear him there, on movie soundtracks or in TV ads for Pepsi or Levi's. B.B. King is presented as a man of taste and authority, someone whose opinion we can trust. His music, solid and seasoned like fine timber, conveys the same message.

The Pepticon Blues Boy, 1950.

blues-preaching of Junior Parker and Bobby Bland. Separate all the ingredients of B.B.'s style and you have a tableful of tasty and distinctive regional specialities. Let him mix them up again and turn on the heat, and they blend magically into something unique, the B.B. stew.

Born in Itta Bena, Mississippi, B.B grew up by the sunup-till-sundown calendar of a poor black farming family. In his teens, discovering his voice through church, he joined a local gospel quartet. He took up guitar and by his early twenties was playing in Memphis, where he secured a sponsored spot

B.B. King

FOR 40 YEARS B.B. KING HAS BEEN THE STYLISTIC PACE-SETTER IN BLUES. FOR AT LEAST HALF THAT TIME HE HAS ALSO BEEN THE INTERNATIONAL FACE OF THE MUSIC, A GLOBETROTTING AMBASSADOR FOR THE BLUES AS LOUIS ARMSTRONG WAS FOR JAZZ.

Imagine the history of blues guitar-playing as a railroad map, criss-crossed with lines of development and influence. B.B. King is a major junction, the Grand Central Station of post-war blues. Here the West Coast tracks of T-Bone Walker and Lowell Fulson meet the Chicago lines of Buddy Guy and Magic Sam and the Southern railway that stretches north from Memphis and Mississippi, carrying the musical freight of Elmore James and Muddy Waters.

It isn't only with his guitar that B.B. epitomizes the pan-American blues. His singing and material evoke, by turns, the dry wit of T-Bone Walker and Louis Jordan, the tear-stained melodrama of Roy Brown, the soulful

as "The Pepticon Blues Boy" on the new black-owned radio station WDIA, and then as a disc-jockey. Shortening "Blues Boy" to B.B., he embarked on a life of one-night stands, the "chittlin circuit" of mainly Southern black clubs and theatres, always described as "gruelling". Learning that B.B. once played 342 of these one-nighters in a year, you feel that "killing" might be a better word.

After a couple of singles for Bullet he signed with Modern and had a succession of hits on their RPM label: 'Three O'Clock Blues', 'You Didn't Want Me', 'You Know I Love You' (all 1952); 'Woke Up This Morning' and 'Please Love Me' (1953); 'You Upset Me, Baby' (1954), 'Sweet Little Angel' (1956),

'Please Accept My Love' (1958) and 'Sweet Sixteen' (1960). The more than 200 sides he cut for RPM and Kent also stocked cheap, garish but musically rewarding LPs on the Crown label, like the outstanding *My Kind Of Blues* (1960).

In the early Sixties B.B. was commercially potent enough to move to a major pop label, ABC. These were not particularly happy or successful years, but in 1967, aided by his new manager Sidney Seidenberg, he began to claim his place on the rock-blues circuit of Fillmore Auditoriums and white blues bands. His records on ABC's Bluesway label were produced to new specifications, the big-band sound giving

way to crafted arrangements played by versatile session musicians. The policy was vindicated by the success, on pop as well as R&B charts, of the string-decked 'The Thrill Is Gone' in 1969 and the following year's acclaimed album *Indianola Mississippi Seeds*.

Throughout the Seventies B.B. and Seidenberg rebuilt B.B.'s blues platform, broadening his appeal and offering a musical policy that was responsive to changing fashions. Albums like *Guess Who* (1972), *To Know You Is To Love*

You (1973) and *Friends* (1974) alienated blues diehards without relocating B.B. in the pop mainstream. The next decade's work was just as mercurial: a flabby country set, *Love Me Tender* (1982), was succeeded by a vigorous nod to B.B.'s jump-jazz models like Louis Jordan in *Blues 'N' Jazz* (1983). Yet on the road – a better-paved one by now, with much better hotels – B.B. unfailingly satisfied the expectations of his worldwide fans, and continues to do so.

If the blues was a corporate company, King would be chairman of the board.

REED'S LAZY, SLACK-JAWED SINGING, PIERCING HARMONICA AND HYPNOTIC GUITAR PATTERNS WERE ONE OF THE BLUES' MOST EASILY IDENTIFIABLE SOUNDS IN THE FIFTIES AND SIXTIES, AND HE HAD MORE HITS THAN ANY OTHER CHICAGO-BASED BLUESMAN. THE STYLISTIC TREMORS CAUSED BY HIS BEST WORK LEFT PERMANENT MARKS ON BLUES TERRAIN.

he had a particularly ardent fanclub in South Louisiana, where singers or harmonica players such as Slim Harpo, Lazy Lester, Silas Hogan and Jimmy Anderson all wove their styles out of Reed's motifs.

You can hear Reed too in the young Mick Jagger. The utter simplicity of his music – it was blues stripped down to the basics, naked rhythm – made it an ideal learning exercise for the British musicians who discovered R&B in the Sixties. The young dude with the sharp suit and the blow-wave who sang with Long John Baldry's band at London's Marquee Club – he was a great Reed fan. "Rod The Mod" they called him then, plain Rod Stewart later.

Reed was born in Dunleith, Mississippi. One day in his mid-teens, as he would retell it years later, a white man he was working for "pushed me with his feet – just taked his feet and pushed me across the ditch, you know. And I left the mule standin' in the field and started walkin'. I walked all the way back to Leland, Mississippi, to my brother's house, and then he sent me to Chicago."

He didn't stay that time, but by 1946, after a year in the US Navy, he was back in Chicago working in a steel mill. Soon he was playing in bars there or in the nearby steel town of Gary, Indiana. He seems never to have planned a musical career, rather to have slipped into one by accident. When he met up with his childhood friend Eddie Taylor and started playing with him again, he found he had acquired just what he needed, a strong bottom-end to his music. "At that time he wasn't going nowhere," Taylor would recall. "Just rapping on the guitar and blowing on harmonica. So I just told him to lighten up off his guitar and blow his harmonica and I put the beat to it." Taylor's sinewy guitar and bass guitar glued together Reed's ramshackle rhythms.

Their first record together, 'High And Lonesome' in 1954, launched a new Chicago label, Vee Jay. Reed would stay with the company for 11 years, logging R&B chart entries with 'You Don't Have To Go' (1954), 'Ain't That Lovin' You Baby' (1956), 'Honest I Do' (1957), 'Take Out Some Insurance' (1959), 'Baby What You Want Me To Do' (1959), 'Big Boss Man' (1960), 'Bright Lights, Big City' (1961) and 'Shame Shame

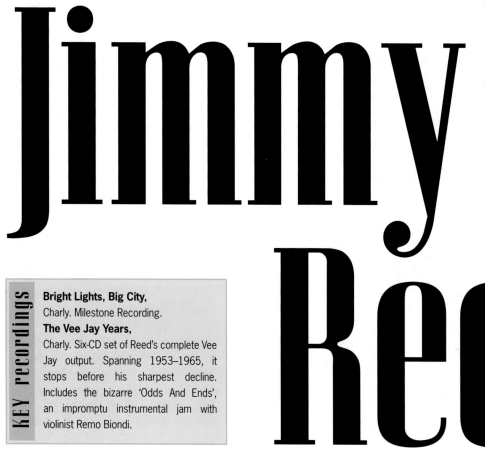

Jimmy Reed

*"Do you have any other songs you have composed?"
Reed was asked at his audition. "No, but I have
some that I writ."*

Shame' (1963). Practically all of these
became standards.

From 1955 until well into the Sixties
Reed was a major attraction in black clubs
across the US, earning two or three thousand dollars a week. Unlike some of his contemporaries he also got on to the white
college circuit, and his records found many
white purchasers. He visited England, where
the Rolling Stones had covered 'Honest I Do'
and 'Shame Shame Shame' had even
sneaked into the Top 50 pop chart for a
couple of weeks, and toured Europe with the
1968 American Folk Blues Festival.

By then, though, his appearances confirmed what his records had lately been
implying, that he was an artist, indeed a
man, in decline. His fans were used to him
sounding drunk – it was intrinsic to his style,
that shambolic air of a performance continuously on the verge of collapse – but it was
unsettling to find that he needed to be half-
cut to get on stage at all. His manager Al
Smith claimed "Jimmy could put on almost
as good a performance drunk as the average
artist could sober," but that was a manager's
"almost", not a critic's.

His association with Vee Jay, which had
yielded nearly 40 singles and a dozen LPs,
had terminated in 1965, and he went on to
make five albums for ABC-Bluesway and further sets for minor labels. Some of these
projects played up the rhythmic bias of his
music to an absurd degree, stacking the mix
with as many as four guitars. This lengthen-
ing discography did little more than document Reed's repeated failure to wring more
juice from a squeezed lemon. The recordings
of his last years border on travesty: his diction is almost impenetrable and his once
captivating rhythm sluggish.

FATS DOMINO'S MUSIC HAS AN OVERPOWERING PEPPER-SAUCE SMELL OF NEW ORLEANS. HIS RICH ACCENT AND BOUNCY PIANO, THE SPICY SAX SOLOS AND IRRESISTIBLE STRUTTING RHYTHM, CONJURE UP MARDI GRAS AND OYSTER BARS, THE CURLING IRONWORK OF THE BALCONIES AND THE TWIRLING BATONS OF THE PARADE DANCERS.

On top of all that, it's so good-humoured. Even in his bluest, bleeyooest songs, Fats sounds incorrigibly happy. Antoine Domino was born and grew up in New Orleans. Like so many there, he had family connections with music – a brother-in-law, Harrison Verret, played guitar and banjo in bands led by jazzmen Kid Ory and Oscar Celestin, and he taught Domino the rudiments of piano. As he put on weight in his teens, the youth began to be nicknamed "Fats", and it was under that moniker that he started to earn a local reputation as a singer and piano player. "Say Papa have you been to the Hideaway lately??" asked a columnist in a July 1949 local paper, "Fats Domino is out there making them holler!!!"

Within a year he would no longer be one of New Orleans' hidden talents. For his first recording he had taken a local favourite, an eight-bar blues called 'The Junker', and exchanged its drug theme for a personal ad:

They call, they call me The Fat Man,
    because I weigh two hundred pounds,
    All the girls they love me,
    'cause I know my way around.

It opened with several choruses of loping piano, and later there was a stretch of

Pop journalists in the 1960s unfailingly reported that Domino owned 600 pairs of shoes.

Fats Domino

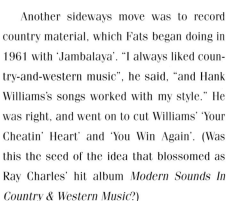

high-pitched waa-waaing. Strange! But potent: it sold 10,000 in 10 days in New Orleans, went into the R&B Top Ten and eventually dispersed three quarters of a million copies.

Domino's other early singles like 'Goin' Home' (an R&B No. 1 in 1952) or 'Going To The River' (1953) show where he was coming from. There were echoes of national blues stars like Charles Brown and Roy Milton, of regional figures like the Texas singer-pianists Amos Milburn and Little Willie Littlefield, and of the New Orleans piano "professors" Champion Jack Dupree and Professor Longhair. Dave Bartholomew, the trumpeter and bandleader who organized Domino's recordings, made simple arrangements with riffing horns, the rolling rhythm of drummer Earl Palmer and bassist Frank Fields and leathery tenor sax solos by Herb Hardesty or Lee Allen. The formula was durable and for the next ten years or so nobody messed with it – especially in 1955, when Domino scaled the charts with 'Ain't It A Shame', 'All By Myself' and 'Poor Me'. 'Ain't It A Shame' even reached the pop Top Ten despite a cover version by Pat Boone. In the next two years Domino went even higher in the pop charts with 'I'm Walkin'', 'Blue Monday' and others.

Occasionally Domino varied his blues and boogies with novelties like the old pop songs 'My Blue Heaven' and 'Blueberry Hill'. Bartholomew thought the latter was "no damn good – it took all day to record, and it still didn't sound right." Two weeks after it was released, Lew Chudd of Imperial Records called him up and said, "Dave, from now on, cut nothing but 'no-good' records. We just sold three million!"

Another sideways move was to record country material, which Fats began doing in 1961 with 'Jambalaya'. "I always liked country-and-western music", he said, "and Hank Williams's songs worked with my style." He was right, and went on to cut Williams' 'Your Cheatin' Heart' and 'You Win Again'. (Was this the seed of the idea that blossomed as Ray Charles' hit album *Modern Sounds In Country & Western Music*?)

Fats deserted Imperial in 1962 for ABC-Paramount but never recaptured either the sales or the spirit of his earlier work, and that applies to everything he has recorded ever since – not that there's a lot of it.

But in person he remains magnetic, and you can still hear what made Paul McCartney call him "an enormous influence" and Elton John "one of my musical heroes". In one of his crime novels set in New Orleans, James Lee Burke describes Domino entering a nightclub "like a Messiah

returning to his followers, his sequined white coat and coal black skin almost glowing with an electric purple sheen . . . [his] ringed, sausage fingers danced up and down on the piano keys and the saxophones and trumpets blared behind him . . . The place went wild."

Little Walter

KEY recordings

The Essential Little Walter, MCA/Chess. Milestone Recording. **The Blues World Of Little Walter,** Delmark. Eight early sides with singer Baby Face Leroy Foster and Muddy Waters on guitar, including a devastating two-part 'Rollin' And Tumblin''. Other tracks are by J.B. Lenoir and Sunnyland Slim.

THE HARMONICA IS THE POOR MAN'S BLUES HORN. IN CHICAGO THEY CALL IT "THE MISSISSIPPI SAXOPHONE". JUST FOUR INCHES OF TIN AND WOOD, BUT A SMART PLAYER CAN PRODUCE A YARD-WIDE SOUND THAT WILL CARRY FOR A CITY BLOCK. NOBODY BLEW MORE, AND MORE INVENTIVE, HARMONICA THAN LITTLE WALTER JACOBS.

laying deputy to sheriff Muddy Waters, he helped bring law and order to the Chicago-style blues band, and ever since then it's been virtually impossible to play amplified blues harmonica without acknowledging his influence. "You could always learn something from him," said the drummer Fred Below, "just by being around him. It was like Walter was running a school." "He was always thinking of something," echoed Muddy Waters. "His mind just kept going, learning more and more and more."

Maybe it's the nature of the instrument – it seems hardly more than a toy, really – that impels harmonica players to cheat their way beyond its limitations. Some soak it in water to make the wood swell and distort the sound. Others open it up and tinker with the reeds. Walter's trick was to devise a method of combining the harmonica with a hand-held microphone to create a hybrid instrument – electroharp in blue. "I snuggle up to that mike, see, 'cause I can keep a whole lot of wind in that harp. I don't have to do nothin' but navigate with it then."

Walter's voyage into blues history began when he started playing amplified on sessions with Muddy Waters. One of their early collaborations was 'Country Boy', but this was emphatically urban music, a kind nobody had heard before.

Walter had been around Chicago for almost a decade, playing on the streets and making a few records for fly-by-night labels, and he hadn't quite outgrown his first model, Sonny Boy Williamson I. Working with Waters during 1950–51 he finally broke with the old chugging, fill-all-the-spaces approach to harmonica-playing and began to blow like a jazz saxophonist, squeezing and stretching the notes, chopping up the rhythm, using dynamics with the delicacy of a lead singer in a gospel quartet.

In 1952 'Juke', a skipping instrumental cut at the end of a Muddy Waters session, turned into a runaway hit. Walter duly ran away, leaving his employer in mid-tour and rushing back to Chicago to pick up a band and capitalize on his chart success. But he continued to record with Muddy (interchangeably with Walter Horton and, later, Junior Wells) while producing lots of good sides in his own name, backed with unobtrusive skill by Fred Below and guitarists Louis and Dave Myers – The Aces. Some of his numbers were fiercely innovative instrumentals like 'Off The Wall', others vocals like 'Blues With A Feeling' or 'Mean Old World'. He's an underrated singer: his plain,

Walter played guitar on a few of Muddy Waters' records, such as 'Honey Bee'.

undramatic style frames a lyric very effectively. 'Last Night' (". . . I lost the best friend I ever had") is particularly touching.

Walter's best work was done in the first half of the Fifties. After that, Chicago blues rapidly lost ground to R&B and rock 'n' roll artists, Muddy hired James Cotton as his full-time harmonica man, and Walter took to drowning the dissatisfactions of his professional and personal life in several inches of whiskey. "That other stuff, that pot and stuff" too, according to Howlin' Wolf, who added

"I had the best harmonica player in the business", Muddy Waters often said.

sadly, "That boy could have been tops in the blues field." British fans remember him visiting in the Sixties, a sometimes morose and often irascible little man who didn't bother to hide his contempt for some of the musicians he found himself playing with. He died from the effects of a head injury sustained in a street fight.

Albert Collins

THROUGHOUT THE EIGHTIES THERE WERE FEW TO CHALLENGE ALBERT COLLINS FOR THE TITLE OF THE MOST EXCITING IN-PERSON ACT IN THE BLUES BUSINESS. ATHLETIC, DEMONSTRATIVE, SLYLY FUNNY, HE PUT ON A SHOW THAT WAS JUST AS RIVETING ON A FESTIVAL STAGE, IN A CONCERT HALL OR A BLUES CLUB, OR IN HIS JOKEY CAMEO IN THE MOVIE *ADVENTURES IN BABYSITTING.*

Collins made guest appearances on John Lee Hooker's *Mr Lucky* album and B.B. King's *Blues Summit.*

his use of minor-key tunings and high capo positions lent his guitar playing a supposedly "cold" edge, but beneath the icy surface moved the warm current of a Texas shuffle rhythm and the slow swell of a moody blues.

Born in Leona, Texas, he grew up in Houston, where he had a cousin to learn guitar from in Lightnin' Hopkins. He led his first band in his late teens but didn't record until 1958, when he had a regional hit with the instrumental 'Freeze', followed in the early Sixties by a succession of similar titles like 'Frosty' and 'Sno-Cone'. "Instrumentals sold in those days," Collins shrugged later, "so I wasn't doing too much singing." Encouraged by Bob Hite of Canned Heat, he moved to California in 1968, working in rock venues like the Fillmore West. His style at that time is captured on *Love Can Be Found Anywhere (Even*

Albert Collins on his last visit to London in March 1993.

In A Guitar) (Imperial), a mostly instrumental album with psychedelic cover art that gives off a smell of its era as pungent as patchouli.

There's Gotta Be A Change (Tumbleweed, 1971) put him in rock company, under the eye of the Eagles' producer Bill Szymcyzk. But he was still barely known to blues fans outside the United States. Jimi Hendrix had put in a good word: "There's one cat I'm trying to get across to people. His name is Albert Collins. He's good, really good." But it was difficult for Europe to see what had excited Collins' backers in California.

The Seventies were hard going, and he made most of his living in the building industry. One job he liked to recall was working on Neil Diamond's mansion. His fully realized talent was finally revealed in a series of albums for Alligator, beginning with *Ice Pickin'* (1978). Numbers like 'Avalanche', 'Ice Pick' and T-Bone Walker's 'Cold, Cold Feeling' brought the wintry motif out of cold storage, and subsequent albums were titled *Frostbite, Frozen Alive, Don't Lose Your Cool, Live In Japan* (some mistake here) and *Cold Snap.* The jagged instrumentals were

now carefully balanced with fervent slow blues like Freddie King's 'When The Welfare Turns Its Back On You' and guyish homilies about card-carrying shopaholic wives ('Master Charge', written by his wife Gwendolyn).

By the early Eighties he was a leading name on the international blues circuit, and in 1985 he was the only black blues artist to appear in the globally televised *Live Aid* concerts, making a guest appearance with the slide guitarist George Thorogood. That year he was united in a guitar summit-meeting with his Houston contemporary Johnny Copeland and the younger Robert Cray, who in earlier years had provided him with a

backing band whenever he worked in the Northwest. The album, *Showdown!*, won a Grammy award.

Collins also took part in an extraordinary variety of recording projects – with David Bowie, John Lee Hooker, B.B. King, Gary Moore and composer John Zorn, who wrote 'Two Line Highway' as a concerto for "the greatest living bluesman". His last album was a set of concert recordings, an appropriate exit by an artist who, in the words of his one-time producer Bruce Iglauer, "stalks the stage like some manic Western gunslinger, always in motion, guitar strap slung over his shoulder like an ammunition belt, blasting out spine-chilling barrages of notes."

Buddy Guy

Though he has given famous shows at the Montreux Jazz Festival and London's Royal Albert Hall, Guy is just as happy to play in a neighbourhood club: "Small places have kept me going pretty good over the years."

IT'S HARD TO BELIEVE THAT BUDDY GUY WON'T SEE 60 AGAIN. HE WAS FOR SO LONG THE YOUNG GUN OF CHICAGO BLUES. EVEN HIS PARTNERSHIP WITH JUNIOR WELLS, WHEN THEY WERE BOTH GROWN MEN WITH FAMILIES, HAD AN AIR OF TWO KIDS AT PLAY. PERHAPS IT WAS BECAUSE GUY WASN'T A LOT OLDER THAN THE FIRST GENERATION OF INTERNATIONAL BLUES FANS. HE WAS THE FIRST BLUESMAN WHO DIDN'T COME ACROSS AS SOBERINGLY SENIOR, WHO WAS YOUTHFUL ENOUGH TO JUMP ABOUT AND DO SEXY STUFF WITH HIS GUITAR.

Guy grew up in Lettsworth, Louisiana, stuck out in the country trying to learn John Lee Hooker tunes off the radio. At 21 he made the trip north to Chicago, where his first records would show that he had replaced Hooker as a model with B.B. King. But there nearly weren't any records, or any career in music at all. As he remembers, "I hadn't eaten for three days, and I was trying to borrow some money from someone to telephone my mother, to tell her I'd decided to come back to Louisiana. That was when Muddy Waters bought me a sandwich and told me to sit in the back of his Chevy station wagon. He said, 'You're hungry, I can tell.' But the fact

texas ALEXANDER (1900-1954)

Rolling and tumbling to their own inner rhythms, the blues of Texas Alexander take us back to the dawn of the music, the improvised field-hollers of working people singing to ease their boredom. He played no instrument but usually had a guitarist in tow; Lightnin' Hopkins and Lowell Fulson both served apprenticeships with him. His singing was difficult to follow, and on his records his accompanists can often be heard resetting their watches to Alexander Time. His finest collaborator was Lonnie Johnson, who devised free-form guitar melodies in counterpoint to the vocal lines.

Alger Alexander was born and died in Texas and probably spent most of his life there, singing on the streets or occasionally in the black theatres of Dallas or Houston. He recorded 64 sides between 1927 and 1934, a couple of them gorgeously accompanied by Johnson and jazz guitarist Eddie Lang, others with the guitarist Little Hat

Luther Allison
greeted 1997 with a
powerful new album,
Reckless (Ruf).

Jones or the Mississippi Sheiks. After a brief comeback on disc in 1950 he disappeared. (*Texas Alexander Vols 1–3* Matchbox)

luther ALLISON (1939–)

The molten intensity of his singing and guitar-playing locate Allison midway on the stylistic map between Albert King and Jimi Hendrix. Some of his live recordings tip into directionless swaggering, but more controlled studio performances like 'Big City' on 1995's *Blue Streak* reveal a thoughtful artist whose obvious powers are enhanced by being tightly reined. Quite why he is not better known after three decades puzzles him as much as it does his admirers.

In his teens he moved from Arkansas to Chicago, where he played in family groups. Following his first album, *Love Me Mama* (Delmark, 1969), his reputation grew fast and in 1972 he was the first blues artist signed by Motown Records. He first visited Europe in 1977, recording in France, and has had a large European following

ever since, much of his work and recording in the 1980s and 1990s being in Germany and France, where he lives. (*Blue Streak* Trip [Europe]/Alligator [US])

albert AMMONS (1907-1949)

Ammons' name is linked with those of Pete Johnson and Meade Lux Lewis in the Big Three of boogie-woogie piano. A native Chicagoan, he led his Rhythm Kings at Club DeLisa and other Windy City clubs in the 1930s, until the boogie-woogie craze at the end of the decade swept him and his two friends into New York nightclubs like Café Society and on to the stage of Carnegie Hall. The rhythmic solidity and intense blues feeling of his work was best displayed on solo recordings like 'Bass Goin' Crazy' and 'Boogie Woogie Stomp', while the rich texture of four collaborative hands has seldom been heard better than in his duets with Johnson. He returned to bandleading in the 1940s, though hampered for a while by paralysis in his hands, and recorded popular boogie-woogie settings of standards like 'Swanee River'. Occasionally he worked with his son Gene, an earthy tenor saxophonist who had a good career in jazz. His last years were spent mostly in Chicago. (*Albert Ammons 1936–39* Classics)

pink ANDERSON (1900-1974)

Anderson spent much of his life working on travelling medicine shows in his native South Carolina and elsewhere in the South-East. He recorded briefly in 1928 with a fellow singer-guitarist, the blind Simmie Dooley, but it was on four albums he made in later life that he revealed the depth of his repertoire: sturdy blues, rag songs like 'Chicken', 'I Got Mine' and 'He's In The Jailhouse Now' and the ballads 'John Henry', played with slide guitar, and 'Betty And Dupree'. Though in musical retirement fol-

A-Z Blues Artists

that I was talking to Muddy Waters took away all my hunger. It was enough just to have said 'Hello' to him. I was so happy I didn't feel the cramp in my stomach any more."

With Muddy's encouragement he played around the clubs until he was hot enough to conquer Magic Sam, Otis Rush and Junior Wells in a blues battle. In 1960 Willie Dixon got him on to Chess, where he cut 'First Time I Met The Blues', a song written years earlier by the singer and pianist Little Brother Montgomery, who played on the remake. The difference between Montgomery's meditative solo recording and Guy's full-out attack dramatizes the enormous changes in blues over a quarter of a century.

'Broken Hearted Blues' and 'Ten Years Ago', all screams and saxes, were just as stunning, but the heyday of Chicago blues was passing, and Guy's future lay elsewhere. In 1965 he visited Europe with the American Folk Blues Festival and was amazed to find himself a star. "A kid snatched a button off my suit. He said he wanted it for a souvenir. Back home I had a daytime job and nobody knew who I was, but these guys were shouting my name." Not only souvenir-hunters but musicians were hanging on to his coat-tails, guitarists like Eric Clapton and Jeff Beck. Thirty years later Clapton would call him "by far and without doubt the best guitar player alive".

At the end of the Sixties Guy teamed up with Junior Wells to form a sort of Brownie McGhee & Sonny Terry of electric Chicago blues – though their first joint album was the unplugged *Buddy And The Juniors*. Some of their performances were terrific – hear Wells' albums *Hoodoo Man Blues* and *South Side Blues Jam*, or the 1970 TV documentary *Chicago Blues* – while others, especially later, were mannered and self-parodying, full of interminable tributes to Muddy Waters or Sonny Boy Williamson II.

For a while Guy ran a Chicago club, the Checkerboard Lounge. He weathered the album, better bookings and a new club, Buddy Guy's Legends. His second son, who also plays guitar, used to say, "I'll jump on you out there!" When he turned 21 and could at last go into a bar and see his father on stage, he confessed, "I don't think I'm ready for you yet, Daddy."

Four hands in boogie-woogie tempo: Albert Ammons (rear) and Pete Johnson.

lowing a stroke, he continued to play in public until shortly before his death. (*Ballad & Folksinger Vol 3* Original Blues Classics)

billy boy ARNOLD (1935–)

Compared with the bossmen on the Chicago blues scene of the mid-1950s, Billy Boy Arnold sounded like a teenager. In fact he wasn't quite 20 when he recorded 'I Wish You Would', and soon after his birthday he added 'I Ain't Got You', both engaging pop blues with infectious rhythmic hooks. A decade on, they would catch the ear of British R&B groups like the Yardbirds.

The Chicago-born Arnold taught himself harmonica by listening to Sonny Boy Williamson I and by his mid-teens was working on the streets with Bo Diddley. Despite his promising start, his spell on the Vee Jay label was short (1955–57) and by the mid-1960s he was discouraged enough to quit music, though within a few years he was

back and touring and recording overseas. (*I Wish You Would* Charly; *Back Where I Belong* Alligator)

kokomo ARNOLD (1901–1968)

Arnold stood out among blues musicians of the 1930s as an eccentric slide guitarist who whipped his instrument into a rhythmic frenzy while delivering imaginative blues lyrics. Among his favourite tunes was the one he used for his 1934 hit 'Milk Cow Blues', a piece that has remained popular with both black and white musicians and was memorably recorded by Elvis Presley.

Little is known about his life. He was born James Arnold in Lovejoy, Georgia, and is thought to have moved to Chicago about 1929, though his first record, in 1930, was cut in Memphis. Released under the pseudonym Gitfiddle Jim, it was a bizarre blues treatment of the popular song 'Paddlin' Madeleine Home'. Music was always a sideline – Chicago knew him best as a bootlegger – but he cut several dozen records and did some studio work with Peetie Wheatstraw

before retiring from the business in 1941. When contacted by a researcher in 1959, he had no interest in playing again. (*Kokomo Arnold Vol 1 (1930–1935)* Document)

mickey BAKER (1925–)

McHouston Baker from Louisville, Kentucky, wound up in New York at 16, and at 19, attracted by the style of the jazzmen he hung around in pool-halls, decided to join their profession. He began playing guitar, discovering blues during a trip to the West Coast, when he heard Pee Wee Crayton. Returning to New York he immersed himself in the studio world, playing on innumerable blues and R&B sessions for Atlantic, Savoy and other labels. Observing the success of the pop duo Les Paul & Mary Ford he created an act with singer-guitarist Sylvia Vanderpool and had a hit with 'Love Is Strange' (1957). In 1961 he moved to France, working as a pop arranger, publishing guitar tutor books and playing unplugged gigs singing old blues learned from LPs. (*Mississippi Delta Dues* Verve)

long john BALDRY (1941–)

A generation of British blues converts remembers this rangy figure bellowing the blues from the stage of London's Marquee Club, now and then handing the microphone to his dapper deputy Rod (then "Rod The Mod") Stewart. Along with Alexis Korner and John Mayall, Baldry was a pace-setter and taste-maker in British blues of the 1960s. He sang with Korner's Blues Incorporated and with the harmonica player Cyril Davies' R&B All Stars before forming The Hoochie Coochie Men in 1964, followed by Steampacket (with Stewart) and Bluesology (with Elton John). After a hit with 'Let The Heartaches Begin' (1968) he no longer specialized in blues, and for years made his living on the club scene of Europe or, latterly, Canada. He became a Canadian citizen in

1980 and continues to work there. (*It Still Ain't Easy* Hypertension)

marcia BALL (1949–)

Ball is one of the *grandes dames* of the Austin, Texas music scene, having worked there since 1970 in blues, country and other settings. Her voice is not big but attractively husky, while she plays piano with more than a dash of Professor Longhair. In Austin in the early 1970s she sang country music with Freda & The Firedogs; later in the decade she recorded an album for Capitol, in the 1980s three more for Rounder, and in 1990 a joint album with fellow Austin troupers Lou Ann Barton and Angela Strehli, *Dreams Come True* (Antone's). (*Soulful Dress, Blue House* Rounder)

BARBECUE BOB (1902–1931)

One of the most approachable artists of his period, Barbecue Bob matched warm, communicative singing to vibrant and rhythmically firm 12-string guitar, often dusted with the glitter of his deft slide-playing. Though his chief success was with 'Mississippi Heavy Water Blues', a reflection on the dev-

astating 1927 floods, he brought great geniality to lighter material like 'Diddle-Da-Diddle', 'Yo Yo Blues' or 'Black Skunk Blues'. A popular disc artist, he recorded over 50 sides between 1927 and 1930 before dying of TB. His circle included his rougher and even more good-humoured brother Charley Lincoln, who also played 12-string. (*Chocolate To The Bone* Yazoo)

carey BELL (1936–)

Harmonica player and singer Bell is a blues conservationist, keeping alive the sound and spirit of the 1950s/60s Chicago dynasty while incidentally founding one of his own (see next entry). Born Carey Bell Harrington in Macon, Mississippi, he moved to Chicago in 1956 with his pianist stepfather Lovie Lee and immediately fell in with Little Walter, Sonny Boy Williamson II and Walter Horton, who passed on some of their harmonica learning. The heyday of Chicago blues harmonica was fading, and for survival Bell switched to electric bass, playing with Earl Hooker and other leaders. After his debut album *Carey Bell's Blues Harp* (Delmark, 1969) he worked in the 1970s with Muddy Waters and Willie Dixon's Chicago Blues All Stars. By 1990, when he recorded the album *Harp Attack!* (Alligator) with fellow blowers Junior Wells, James Cotton and Billy Branch, he was recognized as a senior partner in the company of blues harmonica players. (*Harpslinger* JSP; *Deep Down* Alligator)

lurrie BELL (1958–)

Bell's early promise has bloomed, but unpredictably and sometimes in corners. As a young lead guitar player and second singer with his father Carey's band, and even more in The Sons Of Blues with co-founder Billy Branch, he was capable of intense and inventive music that reminded some listeners of the young Otis Rush. Yet his career in the late 1970s and 1980s was a stop-and-start affair, suggesting some lack of focus or self-discipline, and he spent longer than an ambitious man might have done as the

Barbecue Bob was one of a circle of singer-guitarists in Atlanta, Georgia.

(hear him on classic Muddy Waters recordings like 'Hoochie Coochie Man' or 'I'm Ready') but tangential figures like Chuck Berry and Bo Diddley. (*The Essential Little Walter* MCA/Chess)

buster BENTON (1932-1996)

Singer and guitarist Benton was a likeable second-string artist, originally from Texarkana, Arkansas, but based in Chicago from the late 1950s. His slow-moving career received a fuel injection in 1970 when he had a minor hit with 'Spider In My Stew', an old-fashioned slow blues with a lyric that might have been written by Willie Dixon. This boost more or less sustained him for the next 25 years, which brought fitful work on the international blues scene and albums on Blue Phoenix and Ichiban. But he never found another money spider. (*Bluesbuster* Ronn)

BIG MACEO (1905-1953)

His output was meagre – 32 titles recorded between 1941 and 1947 represent all his significant work – but as both singer and pianist Maceo was hugely influential, his deliberate playing and quietly tragic story-telling in 'County Jail Blues' or 'Worried Life Blues' affecting a generation of singer-pianists like Otis Spann and Little Johnnie Jones. As his famous 'Chicago Breakdown' proved, he could deftly unroll a length of hard-wearing boogie-woogie as well.

Major Merriweather, as he was born in Atlanta, Georgia, grew up in Detroit and played there before moving to Chicago in 1941 and forming his richly rewarding partnership with Tampa Red, terminated after five years when Maceo suffered a stroke. He kept up his playing and even made a few more records, but he never regained his formidable powers. (*King Of The Chicago Blues Piano Players* Arhoolie)

Carey Bell greatly admires Walter Horton: "I liked that big tone he had. Nobody else had that."

guitarist in Koko Taylor's band. His reunions with his father produced satisfying music in a fairly conventional Chicago blues manner, captured on albums under both their names for JSP, particularly Lurrie's *Everybody Wants To Win* (1988). *Mercurial Son* (1995) revealed more of his musical personality, and his next move is sure to be interesting. (*Mercurial Son* Delmark)

fred BELOW (1926-1988)

The men who gave Chicago blues character in the 1950s were not all guitarists and har-monica players. Nobody laid more of the music's rhythmic foundations, particularly its archetypal backbeat, than the drummer Fred Below. A Chicagoan himself, he learned from the leading jazz drummers of his youth and initially worked in jazz, quitting in the late 1940s when he saw that blues offered more playing opportunities, though at first he had no idea how to satisfy the music's rhythmic demands and had to invent a *modus operandi*. Working with Louis and Dave Myers in The Aces, he recorded regu-larly with Little Walter, a roomy setting where he developed his ideas. (For a crisp demonstration of several of his techniques and a rare solo, listen to 'Off The Wall'.) From 1955, when he was Chess Records' house drummer, he accompanied almost everyone on the label, not only blues artists

Big Maybelle in the mid-1960s, when she was recording pop and soul for the Rojac label.

Sylvester replaced by Frank Mead and Steve Walwyn, the band proved with *Hip Joint* that it could play any kind of R&B, from Slim Harpo's 'Shake Your Hips' to the Charles Brownish 'Kiddio', with gleeful panache. The mid-1990s line-up included the singer and guitarist Andy Fairweather-Low. (*Hip Joint* Blue Horizon)

elvin BISHOP (1942–)

Joint lead guitarist with Mike Bloomfield in the Paul Butterfield Blues Band in the 1960s, Bishop spent most of the 1970s and 1980s on the fringes of rock before returning to the blues with *Big Fun* (Alligator, 1988). Equipped with a lively band fronted by sax and trombone that generates a lot of heat, he has a devoted following in the San Francisco area.

Originally from Tulsa, Oklahoma, Bishop fell in with Butterfield at the University of Chicago in 1959 and played in his band from 1963 to 1968. The next highlight was a pop hit with 'Fooled Around And Fell In Love' (1976). For some years afterwards his career was braked by business and personal problems, but the 1990s seem to have put a tiger in his tank. His Alligator albums are consistently well conceived and entertaining and demonstrate that Bishop can make his guitar talk idiomatically in almost any blues dialect. (*Ace In The Hole* Alligator)

paul BLACK (dates unknown)

Black underscores a snarling Dr Johnish vocal manner with serpentine slide guitar. A fixture on the Madison, Wisconsin, scene, Black previously lived and played in New York, in Louisiana, where he worked with the slide guitarist Sonny Landreth, and in San Francisco. Though he is hesitant about

BIG MAYBELLE (1924–1972)

Big Maybelle was a stentorian blues singer, popular in the 1950s with the same sort of material as Etta James or the young Esther Phillips: noisy blues, wide-screen ballads and dance anthems. Born Mabel Smith in Jackson, Tennessee, she learned her trade as a band singer with the all-women International Sweethearts Of Rhythm and Tiny Bradshaw's orchestra. Recording for OKeh (1952–56) she had hits like 'Gabbin' Blues' and established herself on the black club and theatre circuit, but her career was continuously at risk from her drug use. (*The Complete OKeh Sessions 1952–55* Epic)

BIG TOWN PLAYBOYS

Formed in 1984, the Playboys have long been acknowledged the best jump-blues combo in Britain, with few rivals anywhere else. Frequently called on to back visiting American artists, they have also made guest appearances on albums by Eric Clapton and Jeff Beck. Founder members included the singer and tenor saxophonist Ricky Cool, bassist Ian Jennings, guitarist Andy Silvester (previously with the blues band Chicken Shack) and pianist-singer Mike Sanchez, Amos Milburn reincarnated as a pencil-moustached smoothie from north London. Ten years on, with Cool and

Elvin Bishop: hard-wearing, all-weather, blue-denim bluesman.

claiming the title of a blues singer, his 1996 album *King Dollar* is an almost unbroken blues programme with three Robert Johnson numbers, a fierce Landreth-like solo on Pat Hare's 'Murder My Baby' and good harmonica by Andy Linderman. (*King Dollar* House Of Blues)

bobby "blue" BLAND (1930–)

Bland has been one of the most important artists in black music since the mid-1950s, and retains a loyal following amongst older black people that many blues artists might envy. Gifted with a voice that can plead more eloquently than a TV evangelist, he has sung blues, soul, country and pop, with results that are striking even when they are not flawless.

Born just outside Memphis, he hung out in his youth with Beale Street Kids like Junior Parker and B.B. King. His early recordings were undistinguished, and it took his long association with Duke Records and the arranger/bandleader Joe Scott to develop his skills as a boundary-rider on the border between blues and soul, in records like 'Farther Up The Road' (1957) and his early-1960s hits 'I Pity The Fool', 'Turn On Your Love Light' and 'That's The Way Love Is'. He also made a definitive recording of 'Stormy Monday Blues' with guitarist Wayne Bennett laying down what has become a statutory line. On his 1970s–80s albums like *Dreamer* he sometimes wandered more than two steps from the blues, but he filled a couple of recorded engagements with B.B. King, and his 1990s work for Malaco finds him once more with one foot in the blues and the other in deep soul. (*I Pity The Fool, Turn On Your Love Light* MCA; *Master Of The Blues* Nectar)

BLIND BLAKE (c1890–c1933)

He called himself Arthur Blake on one of his discs, and according to his record company he came from Jacksonville, Florida. That's his biography, more or less, to be fleshed out with sightings in the recording studio, where he cut about 80 sides for Paramount between 1926 and 1932, or outside it by admirers like the Kentuckian singer-guitarist Bill Williams. In his day he was as popular as Blind Lemon Jefferson, less for his greyish singing than for his unequalled command of rag and blues guitar-playing, displayed both in songs and, unusually for the time, in effervescent and technically demanding instrumentals with incidental talking, like his debut side 'West Coast

Bobby Bland's recent albums for Malaco like *Midnight Run, Portrait Of The Blues* and *Sad Street* maintain his position at the crossroads of blues and Southern soul.

Blues'. He also partnered the banjoist Gus Cannon, clarinettist Johnny Dodds and blues singers Elzadie Robinson, Irene Scruggs and, once or twice, Ma Rainey. Some of his pieces have drifted down into the repertoire of Ry Cooder ('Diddie Wah Diddie') and Leon Redbone. (MR; *The Best Of Blind Blake* Wolf)

rory BLOCK (1949–)

Blues enthusiasts first heard Block as a teenaged guitarist on Stefan Grossman's *How To Play Blues Guitar* album. She grew up in Greenwich Village, daughter of the musician and sandal-shop owner Allan Block, and hung out with blues students like Grossman and their main source, Rev. Gary Davis. All this tuition finally flowered (after a spell as a disco singer) when she recorded *High Heeled Blues* (Rounder, 1982), revealing that as well as a consummate guitarist in the styles of her spiritual grandfathers in Mississippi she was a singer with character and range. Of her many subsequent albums, *Turning Point* (1989), *Angel Of Mercy* (1994) and *Tornado* (1996) have featured her own songs, while *Mama's Blues* (1991), *Ain't I A Woman* (1992) and *When A Woman Gets The Blues* (1995) spend more time amongst her blues models like Tommy and Robert Johnson and the blueswomen Lottie Beaman and Mattie Delaney. (*Rhinestones & Steel Strings, When A Woman Gets The Blues* Rounder)

lucille BOGAN (1897–1948)

As tough a cookie as was ever heard on a record, Bogan sang straight-talking blues about drinking ('Sloppy Drunk Blues'), prostitution ('Tricks Ain't Walking No More'), gambling, lesbianism and other facets of what her generation called "the life". The jazz critic and sexologist Ernest Borneman grouped her with Ma Rainey and Bessie Smith in "the big three of the blues".

Born in Mississippi, she was raised in Birmingham, Alabama. She began recording in 1923, generally with a pianist. Most of her 1920s records were made in Chicago, where she was probably living. After a couple of years' silence she reappeared in 1933, using the name Bessie Jackson (nobody knows why), and recorded busily until 1935 with the pianist Walter Roland, also a Birmingham resident. Their most startling collaboration was an out-take of 'Shave 'Em Dry', a suggestive song already but in this version riotously obscene. (*Lucille Bogan & Walter Roland* Yazoo)

juke boy BONNER (1932–1978)

Few blues singers have had less truck with cliché than Bonner, a man of restless imagination and fearless plain speaking. He described the bleak prospects of black urban existence in songs like 'Life Is A Nightmare', 'Struggle Here In Houston' and 'Going Back To The Country' (". . . where they don't burn the buildings down"), accompanying himself on guitar, harmonica and drums in the self-sufficient one-man band mode of Joe Hill Louis and Dr Ross.

Raised in Houston, he drifted to the West Coast in his early twenties and made his first records there before returning to Texas. Some 1960 sides for the Louisiana label Goldband, when issued in Europe, stirred curiosity there and led to tours of Britain and the Continent. He recorded albums for Arhoolie (his best), Liberty, Sonet and other labels before his early death. (*Life Gave Me A Dirty Deal* Arhoolie)

james BOOKER (1939–1983)

A flamboyant pianist in the flamboyant city of New Orleans, Booker might have made a name even if his musical talents had been no more than ordinary. In fact he was a prodigious player, a legatee of Professor Longhair

but more versatile, though few of his recordings quite catch his magnificent oddity.

He was leading a band and working on sessions in his native New Orleans by the time he was 16, and at 21 had a hit with the organ instrumental 'Gonzo'. His career was upset by his drug dependency but revived in the mid-1970s by a well-received performance at New Orleans' Jazz and Heritage Festival and the album *Junco Partner*, followed by appearances and recordings in Europe. In the 1980s his physical and mental condition deteriorated, though he preserved till the end his capacity to surprise. (*Junco Partner* Hannibal; *Classified* Rounder)

eddie BOYD (1914–1994)

According to Willie Dixon, who produced him at Chess, the way to get something out of Boyd was to sit him at a piano with a bottle and wait for some alchemy of imagination and depression to produce a blues. Never were patience and whiskey so profitably expended: the process led to '24 Hours', 'Third Degree' and the evergreen 'Five Long Years', stories clipped from the daily paper of anybody's life and pasted on to deeply memorable tunes.

In the 1930s Boyd played in north Mississippi (he was born in Clarksdale) and Memphis, but by 1941 he was in Chicago, where he worked with Sonny Boy Williamson I. In 1947–48 he recorded with small bands in the manner of Memphis Slim, and it was with Slim's sidekick Ernest Cotton on tenor that he made his first, chart-topping recording of 'Five Long Years' (JOB, 1952). That led to a five-year spell on Chess, more hits and eventually an AFBF tour in 1965, when he recorded his first album, *Five Long Years*, with Buddy Guy. *7936 South Rhodes* (1968) had Peter Green on guitar. Boyd liked Europe and made his home there, first in Paris, then Helsinki, where he spent

Lonnie Brooks. "If my hands could get what my eyes see," he sings in 'Eyeballin'', "then my whole mind and body would be trouble-free."

the rest of his life. (*7936 South Rhodes* BGO; *A Sad Day* EPM/Blues Collection)

billy BRANCH (c1952–)

Blueswatchers looking for a new generation of harmonica players to succeed Little Walter and Walter Horton greeted Branch gladly when they first heard him in the 1970s in The Sons Of Blues, the band he formed with Lurrie Bell and bassist Freddie Dixon (son of Willie). In both technical range and feeling Branch stood in the great tradition.

After growing up in California, he returned to Chicago to go to college. By 1973 he was working in the clubs. The original SOB debuted on disc in 1978 in Alligator's *Living Chicago Blues* series. In 1983 Bell and Dixon left and Branch grafted with bassist J.W. Williams's Chi-Town Hustlers; the new SOB, with Carlos Johnson on guitar, cut *Where's The Money* (Red Beans, 1983). A decade on, Branch continued to lead the SOB, now with Carl

Weathersby on guitar. Meanwhile he had been chosen as the young gun amongst veteran harp-shooters James Cotton, Junior Wells and Carey Bell on *Harp Attack!* (Alligator, 1990). A pugnacious singer and occasional songwriter, Branch is also a dedicated promoter of the blues in educational programmes like Blues In The Schools. (*The Blues Keep Following Me Around* Verve)

john BRIM (1922–)

A supporting actor in the great drama of Chicago blues, singer and guitarist Brim played in a few 1950s scenes treasured by collectors like 'Rattlesnake' and 'Ice Cream Man' (Chess), with Little Walter on harmonica, or 'Tough Times' (Parrot) with Jimmy Reed – superb examples of small-band Chicago blues in its classic period. He left his native Kentucky in 1941 for Indianapolis, where he took up music, and then Chicago, where he and his wife Grace, who played drums, worked with Big Maceo. In 1953 they

moved to Gary, Indiana. It was probably the strength of his material that earned Brim his small but well-attended recording career, which concluded with a 1994 album featuring Bob Margolin and Jerry Portnoy. (*The Ice Cream Man* Tone-Cool)

lonnie BROOKS (1933–)

Lee Baker Jr (as he was born in Dubuisson, Louisiana) made a regional name in the late 1950s playing bluesy rock 'n' roll numbers like 'Family Rules' and 'The Crawl' as Guitar Jr. He had to drop the sobriquet when he moved to Chicago in 1960, since one of the two Luther Johnsons had first claim on it, so he issued himself the new identity of Lonnie Brooks. Over nearly 20 years he assembled a routine CV of club work, small-label singles and a lacklustre European-recorded album before remaking himself as a kind of Chicagoan Gatemouth Brown, mixing a cocktail of Windy City bar blues and New Orleans R&B which he has dispensed with verve and humour on a series of Alligator albums. Millions who have never heard his records have seen him playing the backporch bluesman who loses his wife but wins a recording contract in a sequence of TV ads for Heineken lager. (*Bayou Lightning, Satisfaction Guaranteed, Roadhouse Rules* Alligator)

clarence "gatemouth" BROWN (1924–)

A man who can handle several instruments and play anything from cajun music to jazz is a true vintage of the musical ferment that is Texas. Brown learned guitar and fiddle from his father, but began his professional career in the early 1940s as a drummer, before falling under the influence of T-Bone Walker

As well as guitar "Gatemouth" Brown plays a wild country fiddle, and, very occasionally, harmonica.

and concentrating on guitar. One of the hot musicians on the Houston scene, he had a regional hit in 1955 with 'Okie Dokie Stomp'. He spent part of the 1960s in Nashville, leading the house band for the TV show *The Beat*, and in the 1970s began to cultivate an audience in Europe, where he appeared at the 1973 Montreux Jazz Festival, and made several albums, juggling blues, cajun songs and country music, one with the country guitarist Roy Clark. His albums on Rounder emphasized his credentials as a guitarist – harsher and more forceful than T-Bone Walker, his playing has influenced Albert Collins and Lonnie Brooks – while those on Alligator and Verve have allowed him to be more eclectic. (*Peacock Recordings* Rounder; *Standing My Ground* Alligator; *The Best Of Clarence "Gatemouth" Brown: A Blues Legend* Verve)

roy BROWN (1925–1981)

Brown's original singing model was Bing Crosby and he started out as a pop balladeer, but the reception of 'Good Rockin' Tonight' (1947) and a story sequence of 'Fannie Brown' songs determined his career as a blues-singing party animal who occasionally, as in 'Hard Luck Blues' (1950), plunged into flamboyant confession. The tear-stained melodrama of his singing impressed artists both within his stylistic neighbourhood, like Bobby Bland and B.B. King, and beyond it (Johnnie Ray, Elvis Presley).

New Orleans-born, he tried gospel singing and boxing before going into music. His hits elevated him to the national R&B package-show circuit, where he sometimes contested Wynonie Harris in staged "Battles of the Blues". When his popularity ebbed in the rock 'n' roll era he tried teen-slanted songs like 'School Bell Rock', had little success and more or less retired, to return a decade later as a member of the Johnny Otis show, with a notable appearance at the 1970 Monterey Jazz Festival. He visited Europe in 1978 and at the time of his death was planning a US comeback. (*Good Rocking Tonight: The Best Of Roy Brown* Rhino)

ruth BROWN (1928–)

Ruth Brown was one of the most successful black artists of the 1950s on the borderline between R&B and rock 'n' roll. Her hits like 'Teardrops From My Eyes', 'Mama, He Treats Your Daughter Mean' and 'Lucky Lips' had an unthreatening appeal that gave her the edge over tougher-sounding contemporaries like Big Mama Thornton.

In her teens the Virginia-born Brown was hired by Lucky Millinder to sing with his band, and at 20 she was signed by Atlantic. After odd experiments like having her sing with Eddie Condon's Dixieland band, the label realized she was at her best with a small R&B line-up featuring tenor sax (usually Willis Jackson) and the guitar of Mickey Baker, and in the early 1950s she was one of the company's mainstays. Later recordings in pop settings have dated, but *Blues On Broadway* (Fantasy, 1989) finds her working happily with a jazz combo on blues standards and other vintage songs like a laid-back sister of Dinah Washington. (*Miss Rhythm: Greatest Hits And More* Atlantic [US]/Sequel [UK])

mojo BUFORD (1929–)

George Buford was a standby harmonica player for the Muddy Waters band, on and off, for 15 years or more. Born in Hernando, Mississippi, he grew up in Memphis and went to live in Chicago in 1952. Ten years later he shifted to Minneapolis, where he became a mainstay of the blues club world, leaving only when he got a call from Waters. Meanwhile he cut a few decent, unexceptional albums for labels in the US and Europe. (*State Of The Blues Harp* JSP)

BUMBLE BEE SLIM (1905–1968)

It's fitting that there should be few photographs of Bumble Bee Slim: how he looked was less important than how he sounded, and he sounded like a composite of several 1930s bluesmen, primarily Leroy Carr. A blunt indication of Carr's importance is the foot-high stack of discs by artists imitating him. Most of them were by Slim: some cover versions, others a touch more original, all sung in Carr's resigned tones and framed, like Carr's, by an unhurried piano and a clean-cut guitar.

His real name, which he sometimes used professionally, was Amos Easton, and he came from Georgia. In 1931–37 he cut about 175 sides, evidently not constrained by contracts, since he recorded simultaneously for Vocalion and Decca, and sometimes Bluebird as well. Bored by the repetitive work, he quit Chicago about 1937. After the war he made a few recordings on the West Coast that vindicated his adaptability, including an album, *Bee's Back In Town!* (World Pacific), with a

small jazz group. (*Bumble Bee Slim (1931–1937)* Story Of Blues)

R. L. BURNSIDE (1926–)

Burnside was musically active in his native north Mississippi, singing over repetitive guitar patterns in a style that sometimes suggested John Lee Hooker, sometimes Fred McDowell, for years before anyone outside heard him. He was exposed on some late-1960s field recordings, then at the 1971 Festival of American Folklife in Montreal and on a tour of Europe. Records for French and Dutch labels followed, one with his family group The Sound Machine. In the 1990s, albums for the local Fat Possum label showed that Burnside's personal sound machine was in excellent working order, but they hardly prepared amateurs of his juke-joint dance music for the dust-storm of *A Ass Pocket Of Whiskey* (1996), a rowdy, grungy and profane union with the Jon Spencer Blues Explosion. (*Mississippi Delta Blues Vol 2* Arhoolie; *Bad Luck City* Fat Possum; *A Ass Pocket Of Whiskey* Matador/Fat Possum)

GEORGE "WILD CHILD" BUTLER (1936–)

Butler arrived in Chicago from Alabama in 1966, tactically late for a singer and harmonica player of old-fashioned tastes, but was able to interest a label (though an outsider, Jewel Records in Shreveport, Louisiana) in recording him, with Willie Dixon as producer and Jimmy Dawkins, Cash McCall and Johnny Twist carving up the guitar territory. The results were very enjoyable, with the bubbling busyness of contemporary sides by Howlin' Wolf and Muddy Waters (evidently among Butler's singing models), but neither they nor albums for Mercury and other labels promoted him from

By the 1990s "Wild Child" Butler had relocated in Canada.

the second division. Undeterred, he continued to make sturdy music and thoughtful songs, and his 1990s albums are full of craftsmanlike straight-talking blues. (*The Devil Made Me Do It* Blue Horizon; *These Mean Old Blues* Bullseye Blues)

BUTLER TWINS (1942–)

Clarence and Curtis Butler played harmonica and guitar in their native Alabama when young, learning from their guitarist father Willie "Butch" Butler and his harmonica-playing friend Raymond Edwards. In their twenties they moved north to Detroit and have played there on and off ever since. Their music is deliberate, as thick and slow-moving as molasses and intensely Southern in character despite their years in the Motor City. *Not Gonna Worry About Tomorrow* (JSP, 1995) and the better-recorded *Pursue Your Dreams* (1996) both have lead guitar by Kenny Parker, a succinct player whose own debut album, *Raise The Dead* (JSP), with the Butlers and singer/harmonica player Darrell Nulisch, was released in 1996. (*Pursue Your Dreams* JSP)

paul BUTTERFIELD (1942-1987)

A native Chicagoan, Butterfield learned harmonica from Little Walter and was sitting in at blues clubs in his teens. In the early 1960s he began assembling a group and in 1965 an eponymous album introduced young America to the idiomatic but youthful and raw sound of the Paul Butterfield Blues Band: Mike Bloomfield and Elvin Bishop, guitars; Mark Naftalin, keyboards; Jerome Arnold, bass; and Sam Lay, drums. That year they played the Newport Folk Festival, incidentally assisting in the notorious first public unveiling of "Electric" Bob Dylan. *East-West* (1966), *The Resurrection Of Pigboy Crabshaw* (1967) and later albums progressively separated Butterfield from the

Chicago blues he played and sang with such understanding, and in 1972 the PBBB was dissolved. Butterfield went on to lead Better Days and work as a solo, while contending with the drug dependency that eventually killed him. (MR)

eddie c. CAMPBELL (1939–)

The West Side guitar sound of Magic Sam echoes in the playing of Eddie C. Campbell, a Chicago-raised singer-guitarist who learned firsthand from Sam, Otis Rush and Muddy Waters. His dry singing and agitated guitar-playing were presented on an excellently

produced album, *King Of The Jungle* (1977), with fine accompanying work by Carey Bell (harmonica) and Lafayette Leake (piano), and later recordings too are enhanced by a discipline not always evident in his life. To stay out of trouble he spent most of the 1980s in Europe, but felt able to return to Chicago at the beginning of the 1990s, and is reported to be faring well. (*King Of The Jungle* Rooster Blues)

Mike Bloomfield of the Paul Butterfield Blues Band studied guitar under Big Joe Williams (who once tried to knife him).

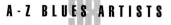

Canned Heat at Woodstock, 1969, with Bob "Bear" Hite centre stage.

CANNED HEAT

Of all the 1960s blues bands none was as stacked with record-collectors as Canned Heat. The group was founded in 1966 by Bob Hite (1945–1981) and Al Wilson (1943–1970), who sang and played harmonica (Wilson guitar too), and included Henry Vestine (guitar), Larry Taylor (bass) and Frank Cook (drums). They parlayed their popularity around L.A. into a major-label contract and festival appearances at Monterey in 1967 and Woodstock in 1969. 'On The Road Again', 'Going Up The Country' and 'Let's Work Together', all based on earlier blues records, reached the pop Top 40, and the band collaborated with John Lee Hooker in *Hooker 'N' Heat*. After Wilson's death there were personnel changes but Canned Heat never stopped their search for the transcendental boogie. The 1996 line-up on *Internal Combustion* (Connoisseur Collection) had Vestine and Fito De La Parra, drummer since 1970, with newer hands James Thornbury (vocal/har-

monica) and Junior Watson (guitar), but Heat were no longer quite so hot. (*The Best Of Canned Heat* EMI)

gus CANNON (1883–1979)

In the 1910s and 1920s the Mississippi-born Cannon worked on travelling medicine shows as a singer, banjoist and comedian. In Memphis in the late 1920s he formed his Jug Stompers: Noah Lewis (harmonica), Ashley Thompson or Elijah Avery (guitar) and later Hosea Woods (banjo/guitar). He himself picked banjo, sang and produced the jugband bass by blowing into an oil can hung around his neck. It was the sweetest-sounding yet also the bluesiest of the Memphis jug groups. Jugband music faded but Cannon remained in Memphis, occasionally performing on the streets or for civic events. In 1962 one of the Jug Stompers' songs, 'Walk Right In', became a Number 1 pop hit for the Rooftop Singers, and Cannon had a brief season of concert performances in Chicago and New

York with his Memphis acquaintances Furry Lewis and Willie Borum. As one of the oldest members of the Memphis music scene, he often featured in TV blues documentaries such as *The Devil's Music* (BBC, 1976). (MR)

bo CARTER (1893–1964)

The genial Carter coined, or at any rate circulated, some of the blues' more recherché sexual metaphors, like 'Banana in Your Fruit Basket', 'Pin In Your Cushion' and 'Cigarette Blues' ("draw on my cigarette, baby, till you make my good ashes come"). No doubt it was this facility with the nudging elbow that won him a long recording career – 110 songs in his own name between 1930 and 1940, and several more with the Mississippi Sheiks – but his reputation among blues enthusiasts rests equally on his fluid guitar-picking and graceful, unusual tunes like 'Some Day' or 'I Get The Blues'. He was born Armenter Chatmon into a large family of musicians – his brothers Lonnie and Sam played fiddle and guitar in the Mississippi Sheiks and

Bo Carter cultivated blue blooms in his garden of exotic metaphors.

allied groups – and took up guitar relatively late, having previously played bass or banjo in the family stringband. Unusually, he made the bulk of his musical income from records rather than dances. He lost most of his sight in the 1930s. (*Twist It Babe 1931–1940*, *Banana In Your Fruit Basket* Yazoo)

john CEPHAS (1930–)

If at first the singer and guitarist Cephas and his harmonica-playing partner Phil Wiggins (1954–) came across like a rejuvenated Brownie McGhee and Sonny Terry, almost two decades of refining their craft have established them not only as distinctive re-interpreters of East Coast blues styles that originated with Blind Boy Fuller or Rev. Gary Davis but as modestly experimental too: witness their original compositions and arrangements on *Cool Down* (1995). Nonetheless, they present their music, like McGhee, with a gentility that may not appeal to those who admire the blues in its most rugged forms.

Both men were born in Washington, D.C., but Cephas grew up in Bowling Green,

Virginia. He played for a few years with the pianist "Big Chief" Ellis before meeting Wiggins in 1976. The duo has covered thousands of miles touring under the sponsorship of the US State Department. (*Guitar Man* Flying Fish; *Cool Down* Alligator)

c.j. CHENIER (1957–)

C.J. Chenier saw little of his father Clifton when he was growing up in Port Arthur, Texas, and was just as unacquainted with his music; his own interests led him to play saxophone in funk bands, until his father invited him to join him in 1978, replacing the tenor-player John Hart. In the early 1980s, when Clifton's poor health was cutting down his accordion playing, C.J. took up the instrument, and after his father's death he stepped into his bandleading shoes. A gruff, muscular singer and efficient accordionist, C.J. tackles a more adventurous repertoire than his father, mixing old pop songs and soul numbers with zydeco dance tunes and blues in French. (*Too Much Fun* Alligator)

clifton CHENIER (1925–1987)

Clifton Chenier was the first musician to become internationally known playing zydeco, the dance music of black French Louisiana and East Texas. Zydeco originated as a fiddle and accordion music sharing repertoire with the parallel tradition of white Louisiana's cajun music, but by the 1950s the decline of the fiddle and the swamping influence of other black music, particularly from New Orleans, had practically converted zydeco into a regional genre of R&B. Chenier, who played the chromatic piano accordion rather than the diatonic button of his forerunners like Amédé Ardoin, led zydeco out of its homeland first to California, where there were enclaves of black migrants

C.J. Chenier, the new generation in zydeco.

from the South-West, then on to the international stage with singles and albums for Arhoolie, the 1969 AFBF and many other festivals and tours, and documentary films like Les Blank's *Dry Wood And Hot Pepper* (1973).

Chenier delivered a powerful blues when he chose, but zydeco is not a music that relies much on songs: the dance groove is everything, whether two-step or waltz, and Chenier's music never lacked rhythmic vitality, thanks to excellent sidemen like drummer Robert St Julien and his own brother Cleveland Chenier on the rub-board, a sort of corrugated metal pullover played with thimbled fingers or spoons. (*Louisiana Blues & Zydeco*, *Bogalusa Boogie* Arhoolie)

eric CLAPTON (1945–)

In the mid-1960s Clapton effortlessly outstripped every other guitarist playing blues in Britain. Since then he has taken his music in other directions, but the blues has been a constant influence, if not always an obvious one.

At 18 he joined the Yardbirds, a rising R&B band, but left after 18 months for the more blues-committed John Mayall's Bluesbreakers, where he became the nation's most revered blues guitarist. In 1966 he formed the supergroup Cream with Jack Bruce (bass) and Ginger Baker (drums) to give long, overwrought performances of numbers like Robert Johnson's 'Crossroads' and Skip James's 'I'm So Glad'. After spells in Blind Faith and with the American act Delaney and Bonnie he conceived Derek and The Dominoes and recorded his most enduring composition, the lovesong 'Layla'. During the 1970s and 1980s he overcame heroin dependency and in albums like *461 Ocean Boulevard* (1974) remade himself as a mainstream rock singer and songwriter. Late in the 1980s, however, stimulated by the arrival of new contenders like Stevie Ray

Vaughan and Robert Cray, he began to play more guitar and more blues, a decision reflected in *Unplugged* (1993) and the all-blues *From The Cradle* (1994), an almost pedantically faithful commemoration of Leroy Carr, Muddy Waters, Otis Rush and other models. (*Stages* Spectrum; *From The Cradle* Reprise)

william CLARKE (1951–1996)

The formative influence on Clarke's harmonica-playing was George "Harmonica" Smith, and the two men worked together for six years. The California-born Clarke also played with other L.A.-based bluesmen like Smokey Wilson and Shakey Jake and recorded five small-label albums before *Blowin' Like Hell* (1990). What distinguished him from most other harp-players of his generation was his bipolar allegiance to both Chicago and West Coast styles: if 'Cash Money' on *Blowin' Like Hell* might have been inspired by Little Walter, the adjoining 'Must Be Jelly' breathes California cool. *The Hard Way* (1996) affirmed Clarke's love of jazz with arrangements for chromatic harp of 'Moten Swing' and 'Walkin'' while not deserting the blues, whether Leroy Foster's 'Blues Is Killing Me' or Mercy Dee Walton's 'Five Card Hand' – choices that hint at his knowledge and taste. (*Blowin' Like Hell, The Hard Way* Alligator)

doctor CLAYTON (1898–1947)

Clayton's braying vocals are not to every listener's liking, but his songs have penetrated many other artists' repertoires, in particular Sunnyland Slim (whose first recordings were as "Dr Clayton's Buddy") and B.B. King, who has recorded 'I Need My Baby' and 'Hold That Train Conductor'. Born in Georgia, he began recording in Chicago in 1930 (as Jesse Clayton) but waxed his best compositions in

1941–46 with Blind John Davis on piano, including 'Angels In Harlem' and 'Pearl Harbor Blues'. He used to perform barefoot, wearing comically large, round spectacles. (*Dr (Peter) Clayton (1935–1942)* Document)

eddy CLEARWATER (1935–)

Clearwater (his real name is Harrington and he is related to Carey Bell) is a versatile guitarist at the modern end of Chicago style and a serviceable singer, but he's probably better heard live than on records, which require either more originality or more projection than he seems able to muster. He left Mississippi at 13, settled in Chicago a few years later and took up guitar, listening with special attention to Magic Sam and Chuck Berry. Since the beginning of the 1960s he has cut a pile of singles and some half dozen albums without proving that his skills go any

Eddy Clearwater has been nicknamed "The Chief" and sometimes wears Native American headdress.

farther than reheating tried blues and R&B recipes and sprinkling them with a pinch of personalized spice. (*A Real Good Time – Live!* Rooster Blues)

gary b.b. COLEMAN (1947–1994)

"B.B. is B.B. and should not be compared to any other B.B.'s who may be out there" a 1990 album note cheekily remarked, though Coleman himself would readily have admitted that Mr King was a model. This versatile Texas-born musician spent his youth in the South-West, playing in blues clubs and booking other artists. In 1985 he recorded his composition 'One Eyed Woman' and the album *Nothin' But The Blues*, first issued on his own label, then licensed to Ichiban, one of the few companies selling to the Southern black market that had any truck with blues. For the next decade Coleman was a pillar of the Atlanta-based label, producing albums by Buster Benton (*Money's The Name Of The Game*, 1989), Blues Boy Willie, Little Johnny Taylor and others. He also contributed songs and sometimes played guitar or keyboards. Meanwhile he made half a dozen albums of his own, featuring original material like 'I Fell In Love On A One Night Stand' and 'If You Can Beat Me Rockin' (You Can Have My Chair)'. (*The Best Of Gary B.B. Coleman* Ichiban)

johnny COPELAND (1937–)

Copeland's career is a lesson in patience. For 25 years he scuffled in East Texas, the homeboy that Albert Collins and Gatemouth Brown left behind. Then he went East and threw his hat into the ring with the album *Copeland Special* (Rounder, 1981), an explosive introduction to his gravelly singing and dramatic guitar-playing.

He spent his teens in Houston, where he met Joe Hughes and began to dabble in music. By 20 he was playing regularly and

doing a little recording and songwriting. For the next two decades he remained in Houston, having a few regional hits, satisfied with being as big as you could get there. "I always thought locally", he says. "I was making a living." Driven by disco to rethink his future, he moved to New York in 1979. The 1980s took him all over the world, and in West Africa he conceived the Afro-American-African fusion of *Bringin' It All Back Home* (1985) – a joyful experiment which he conducted again 10 years later in *Jungle Swing*, one of several sturdy albums for Verve that reunited him with old Houston friends. (*Texas Twister*, *When The Rain Starts Fallin'* Rounder; *Catch Up With The Blues*, *Jungle Swing* Verve)

elizabeth COTTEN (1895–1987)

Libba Cotten learned on a guitar belonging to one of her brothers. She spent her working life in domestic posts, first in Chapel Hill, North Carolina, where she was born, then around Washington, D.C., where she was housekeeper in the 1950s and early 1960s to Charles and Ruth Seeger, whose musician children Peggy and Mike introduced her to the coffeehouse and festival circuit. Her guitar and banjo repertoire was drawn almost entirely from idioms older than the blues: ragtime, common-stock songs like 'Ruben', hymns, instrumental band-music and children's songs like 'Shake Sugaree'. She picked both instruments left-handed without changing the stringing, this upside-down method lending depth to her sound. On guitar she commanded several picking styles, including three- or four-finger patterns on complex material like the three-part rag 'Washington Blues'. Her singing, husky and wayward, has some charm. Her best-known song was 'Freight Train', a favourite study among folk-club guitarists. (*Freight Train & Other North Carolina Folk Songs & Tunes* Smithsonian/ Folkways)

james COTTON (1935–)

Growing up in Mississippi, Cotton was intrigued by the harmonica-playing of Sonny Boy Williamson II and spent much of his youth learning from him. In the early 1950s he played harmonica with Howlin' Wolf and cut his first records, for Sun, before leaving for Chicago and a job in the Muddy Waters band, which he held for 11 years. In 1966 he put together a band of his own and found a place on the rock auditorium circuit, playing support to rock acts. Meanwhile he recorded several albums for Verve and Buddah. *High*

Robert Cray signalled a new direction in 1997 with his soul album *Sweet Potato Pie*.

Compression (Alligator, 1984) revived a flagging career, which was sustained by albums for Antone's and the harmonica summit meeting *Harp Attack!* (Alligator, 1990). Though unquestionably a leader in the company of blues harmonica players, Cotton as a singer is somewhat hard to take, since his voice is coarse-grained, fuzzy and limited in range. Yet that didn't spoil – in fact it enhances – his fascinatingly archaic acoustic album *Deep In The Blues* (1996) with Joe Louis Walker and bassist Charlie Haden. (*100% Cotton* Sequel; *Mighty Long Time* Antone's; *Best Of The Verve Years*, *Deep In The Blues* Verve)

ida COX (1896–1967)

Cox was one of the most successful blues artists of the 1920s, her recordings of 'Graveyard Dream Blues' and 'Chicago Bound Blues' selling in hundreds of thousands and her travelling shows visiting every centre of black life. Born in Georgia, she learned her trade in vaudeville. Between 1923 and 1929 she recorded 80-odd songs for Paramount, which billed her as the "Uncrowned Queen Of The Blues". Her collaborators were usually small jazz groups led by the pianist Lovie Austin or her husband, the pianist Freddie Crump. A decade's obscurity was ended in 1939 with an appearance at the *Spirituals To Swing* concert in New York and some stately recordings featuring an astounding assortment of jazz players like Red Allen, Hot Lips Page and Charlie Christian. At a final, frail

Ida Cox was billed "The Uncrowned Queen Of The Blues".

album session near the end of her life she sang once more her composition 'Wild Women Don't Have The Blues', now treasured as an early feminist text. (*Ida Cox Vols 1–4* Document; *I Can't Quit My Man* Affinity)

robert CRAY (1953–)

More than a decade on, Robert Cray's extension of the blues vocabulary in the mid-1980s can be seen to have been far-reaching. Though not the first, he was certainly the most charismatic figure to handle predominantly non-blues material with a kind of blues sensibility, though it was an unconventional one, developed as much from the naked emotion of Southern soul as from the more taciturn blues of Albert King. The genesis of his guitar-playing was equally

Arthur Crudup. "Do what you can do," Tampa Red told him. "What you can't do, forget about it."

complex: in his youth he had listened to rock bands like the Eagles before coming across Jimi Hendrix on record and Albert Collins in person.

The Robert Cray Band of the 1970s had a solid reputation in the North-West (Cray's family had settled in Tacoma, Washington) which earned them an album debut, *Who's Been Talkin'* (Tomato, 1980), but it was their connection with the producing and songwriting team of Bruce Bromberg and Dennis Walker at Hightone Records that helped to

create the mould-breaking music of *Bad Influence* (1983) and *False Accusations* (1985). Cray's participation with Collins and Johnny Copeland in *Showdown!* (Alligator, 1985) and his own *Strong Persuader* (Mercury, 1986) and *Don't Be Afraid Of The Dark* (Mercury, 1989), which all won Grammy awards, not only put him among the most bankable blues performers but gave him a standing in the larger world of rock, affirmed by regular appearances at Eric Clapton's annual London concerts. While the effect of his innovations continued to be widely visible in the 1990s, his own progress seemed a little less sure-footed. (MR; *The*

Score Charly; *False Accusations, Strong Persuader* Mercury)

pee wee CRAYTON (1914–1985)

An ardent disciple of T-Bone Walker, Crayton found himself in possession of a Number 1 R&B hit with his sleepy instrumental 'Blues After Hours' (Modern, 1948). Its flipside, the sleek pop ballad 'I'm Still In Love With You', and the livelier 'Texas Hop' indicate his range, but this was music very much of its place and time, California in the late 1940s, and he never managed to break that mould. He toured and recorded fitfully over the next

three decades, not an original artist but a likeable one. (*The Modern Legacy Volume 1* Ace)

arthur "big boy" CRUDUP (1905–1974)

Crudup's music is lean, sparse, his vocals like field-hollers, their edges buffed by a crooning sweetness. His guitar, often sourly tuned, puts the song in a plain frame. Even when competing with the dense band sound of Chicago, he rarely added anything to his own except a pulse on bass and drums. Perhaps he felt his songs were attractive enough unadorned. The list of artists who have sung them, including B.B. King, J.B. Lenoir, Jimmy Rogers and Elvis Presley, suggests he may have been right. Presley's choice of 'My Baby Left Me' and 'So Glad You're Mine' led to Crudup being called "The Father of Rock 'n' Roll". Ungratified (there was a matter of lost royalties), he would refer to his admirer as Elvin Preston.

The Mississippi-born Crudup took up music seriously in his mid-thirties, and in the early post-war years was popular in the South with records like 'Mean Old 'Frisco Blues', 'Who's Been Foolin' You' and 'That's All Right'. After a long break he resumed playing in 1965. On a 1970 trip to Britain he cut *Roebuck Man* with local musicians. His last engagements were with Bonnie Raitt. (*That's All Right Mama* RCA/Bluebird)

rev. gary DAVIS (1896–1972)

You could almost say that Davis was the greatest blues guitarist never to play blues. His religious beliefs forbade his singing secular material, and in a long and very prolific life he yielded only so far as to record one blues coupling (in 1935) and a couple of albums' worth of instrumental blues and rags like 'Candy Man' and 'Cincinnati Flow Rag'. These prove what would be evident anyway from his playing on gospel songs,

that he was technically equipped far beyond most blues guitarists of his or any era, capable of improvising tirelessly in several keys, always with a brusque touch that was instantly recognizable.

Growing up in South Carolina, he learned from the blind guitarist Willie Walker. He himself taught Blind Boy Fuller, and at some time in the 1930s was ordained as a Baptist minister. He moved to New York in the early 1940s, making his living as a street-singer until his fame brought him a regular supply of guitar students and record dates for Prestige-Bluesville and other labels. His influence on the New York folk scene of the 1960s was immense. Stefan Grossman, Rory Block, Woody Mann, David Bromberg and Dave Van Ronk are just a few of the guitarists whose playing he moulded. (*The Complete Early Recordings* Yazoo; *Harlem Street Singer* Original Blues Classics; *Blues & Ragtime* Shanachie)

blind john DAVIS (1913–1985)

Blind John Davis was not a career bluesman but a versatile pianist and singer who could just as comfortably earn a living playing standards, boogie-woogie or jazz. Though born in Hattiesburg, Mississippi, he grew up in Chicago, losing his sight at the age of nine. He was attracted to the piano by hearing men playing it in his father's club and

Rev. Gary Davis was not only a brilliant guitarist but skilful on banjo and harmonica.

discovering that they earned money that way. By his mid-twenties he was known on the Chicago scene as a reliable pianist for a blues date, and between 1937 and 1942 he must have played on several hundred sides by Big Bill Broonzy, Sonny Boy Williamson I, Merline Johnson, Tampa Red and other singers. He cut a few blues of his own, singing in a light, unemphatic voice.

After the war he worked with Lonnie Johnson, made a few more singles – 'No Mail Today' (1949) was a small hit – and in 1952 travelled with Broonzy to France. He continued to scrape a living in Chicago's clubs for the next 30-odd years, strangely ignored by the city's new blues fans and promoters. (*Blind John Davis (1938)* Story Of Blues)

larry DAVIS (1936–1994)

Fate was not fickle to Larry Davis so much as downright treacherous. A blues singer with the soulful ear of a Junior Parker, he originated 'Texas Flood', an album-title song 30 years later for Stevie Ray Vaughan, and won four W.C. Handy Awards in 1982, yet, a decade on, he was still known only to specialists.

He was born in Kansas City and raised in Little Rock, Arkansas. With his fellow band-member Fenton Robinson he was signed to Duke Records and promptly had a regional hit with 'Texas Flood' (1958), which he followed the next year with 'Angels In Houston'. At the time he was playing bass – Robinson played the guitar on 'Texas Flood' – but he took up guitar in the late 1960s, only to be invalided successively by a motorcycle accident and a stroke. He returned to music in 1981 and made a very fine debut album, *Funny Stuff* (Rooster Blues), but his career lost momentum and, despite further albums for Pulsar and Bullseye Blues, never got back on track again. (*I Ain't Beggin' Nobody* Evidence)

walter DAVIS (1912–1963)

Sobriety is what chiefly distinguishes Walter Davis's work: a well-mannered touch on the piano, and lyrics pitched in the keys of uninsistent seduction or quiet desperation. You feel, as with Tampa Red, that away from the club or studio he would be found not fighting or philandering but fishing.

A Mississippian by birth, he settled in St Louis in the 1920s, a contemporary and associate of Roosevelt Sykes, Henry Townsend and Peetie Wheatstraw. Sykes accompanied him on his first records (1930–33) – thereafter he had the ability or confidence to play for himself – and Townsend played guitar with him, on and off, for almost 20 years. He was among the most productive and popular recording artists in blues, cutting about 180 sides between 1930 and 1952, several of which – 'M&O Blues', 'Angel Child', 'Come Back Baby' – have been taken up by other singers. He retired after suffering a stroke and became a preacher. (*Walter Davis Vol 1 (1933–1935), Vol 2 (1935–1937)* Document)

jimmy DAWKINS (1936–)

Not unlike his contemporary Luther Allison, Dawkins has never quite realized, to his own or his fans' satisfaction, the promise he displayed so prodigally at the start of his career. His debut album *Fast Fingers* (Delmark, 1970) announced the arrival of a frighteningly quick-thinking player in the hard-edged West Side style of Magic Sam (with whom he'd played), and was duly honoured, not in Chicago, where he had been living since he left Mississippi in 1955, but in France, where he was given the Hot Club's Grand Prix for the record of the year. Though not ignored at home – he cut two further albums for Delmark and worked assiduously on the Chicago club circuit – he retained a keen European following for years, touring

Willie Dixon. Near the end of his life he was awarded a Grammy for *Hidden Charms*.

with the AFBF or Chicago blues troupes and recording albums for several French and British companies. In the 1980s he diversified into management and running his own label. He was still in there pitching in the 1990s, evidently a musician for whom there is no alternative to the blues. (*All For Business* Delmark; *Tribute To Orange* Black & Blue [Europe]/Evidence [US]; *B Phur Real* Wild Dog)

floyd DIXON (1929–)

Floyd Dixon's singing and piano-playing were originally modelled on the approach of Charles Brown, though he also resembled more exuberant artists such as Amos Milburn in his fondness for partying songs like 'Hey Bartender'. Born in Texas, he grew up in L.A. and began to work in the clubs there in the late 1940s. He first recorded at 18, in the small combo format popular on the West Coast. When Charles Brown left Johnny Moore's Three Blazers in 1950 to go

solo, Dixon replaced him as pianist and singer and recorded with the band for Aladdin. Staying with the label, he had a small hit under his own name in 1952 with 'Call Operator 210'. Work fell off in the 1960s and he left music for a time, but reappeared in the mid-1970s in San Francisco. Since then he has enjoyed a busy career, touring overseas and adding several albums to his prolific discography. (He had previously recorded singles for about 20 labels.) (*Marshall Texas Is My Home* Ace; *Wake Up And Live!* Alligator)

willie DIXON (1915–1992)

For over 30 years Willie Dixon was the most prominent producer, composer and general fixer on the Chicago scene. His genius as a songwriter, his most enduring gift to the blues, lay in refurbishing archaic Southern motifs, often of magic and country folkways and sometimes derived from earlier artists like Charlie Patton, in contemporary arrangements, to produce songs with both the sinew of the blues and the agility of pop. British R&B groups of the 1960s constantly drew on the Dixon songbook.

Born in Vicksburg, Mississippi, he sang and played bass in the 1940s with the Five Breezes and the Big Three Trio before becoming house producer for Chess in 1952. He supervised sessions by Muddy Waters, Howlin' Wolf, Little Walter and many others, often playing bass on them, and wrote such enduring numbers as 'Hoochie Coochie Man', 'I Just Want To Make Love To You', 'I'm Ready' (Waters), 'Spoonful', 'Wang Dang Doodle', 'Little Red Rooster' (Wolf) and 'My Babe' (Walter). Freelancing in 1956–60 he produced Otis Rush and Magic Sam for Cobra before returning to Chess. He also helped to organize and joined most of the AFBF tours and put together all-star Chicago groups for European work. He recorded albums with Memphis Slim and

later under his own name. (*The Willie Dixon Chess Box* MCA/Chess)

thomas a. DORSEY (1899–1993)

Son of a Baptist minister and an organ-playing mother, Dorsey grew up in Atlanta, learning piano from musicians at the 81 Theater. Moving to Chicago in 1916, he studied music and worked in jazz bands. In 1924–28 he was Ma Rainey's bandleader on her touring shows. As staff arranger for the Chicago Music Publishing Company he became connected with Brunswick Records and set up and played on many sessions. As Georgia Tom he partnered Tampa Red in personal appearances and on records; their enormous success with 'It's Tight Like That' (1928) initiated a genre of suggestive chorus songs to which Dorsey further contributed on discs with the Hokum Boys and other groups.

In 1932 he quit the blues to work purely in gospel music, directing choirs and touring and broadcasting with them. In 1933 he founded the National Convention of Gospel Choirs and Choruses, which he served until the 1970s; he also engaged in pastoral and lecturing work. He composed several hundred gospel songs, drawing on white as well as black strains of American music. Among the most famous are 'Precious Lord Take My Hand', 'Peace In The Valley', 'He Knows How Much You Can Bear', 'If You See My Saviour' and 'A Little Talk with Jesus'. In 1982 he was the subject of the film *Say Amen Somebody*. (*Come On Mama Do That Dance* Yazoo)

champion jack DUPREE (c1909–1992)

Dupree was an amiable entertainer who came over well on stage, but he could also play by the rules of the recording studio, and there are great rewards in his large output of piano-accompanied blues, boogies and storytelling. He played in his native New Orleans before going north and spending

most of the 1930s in boxing. He first recorded in 1940 and soon after moved to New York, where he fell in with Brownie McGhee and Sonny Terry and often worked with them in public and on records for many small labels. His excellent 1958 album *Blues From The Gutter* (Atlantic) revived his song 'Junker's Blues', the inspiration for Fats Domino's debut recording 'The Fat Man'.

He settled in Switzerland in 1960, afterwards moving to Denmark, England, Sweden and finally Germany. This prolonged European stay made him one of the most recognized of blues emigrés, and he worked and recorded prolifically. Sidemen on his album dates included Alexis Korner and the young Eric Clapton. He could produce new

Champion Jack Dupree. "I'd rather have that piano than a wife. 'Cause that piano ain't goin' to leave me."

songs to order, both on current events such as the Vietnam War and the assassination of Martin Luther King, and more general reflections on the world he hoped to see, like his 1961 composition 'Free And Equal'. (*New Orleans Barrelhouse Boogie* Columbia; *Trouble Trouble* Storyville; *Back Home In New Orleans* Bullseye Blues)

big joe DUSKIN (1921–)

Though he had played piano since his childhood, the Cincinnati-based Duskin was unknown to blues fanciers until he was nearly 60, but not for the usual kind of rea-

son. He promised his father, a minister then in his eighties, that he would refrain from playing the blues during his lifetime; the old man lived to be 104. Free at last, Duskin displayed on *Cincinnati Stomp* (1979) a mature command of piano blues and – a rarer skill by then – boogie-woogie, which he had absorbed at first hand in the 1940s from masters like Albert Ammons and Pete Johnson. He was enthusiastically received in Britain, where he made *Don't Mess With The Boogie Man* (Special Delivery, 1988) and was featured in a TV arts documentary on boogie-woogie. (*Cincinnati Stomp* Arhoolie)

Big Joe Duskin was inspired to play boogie-woogie by Pete Johnson's '627 Stomp'.

snooks EAGLIN (1936–)

A New Orleans cat with at least three blues lives, Eaglin was first heard of outside his native city as a street-singing human jukebox. Grabbing blues, pop songs and anything else in the air, he reworked them into a highly personal music, his thick, brooding delivery set against rich, almost orchestral acoustic guitar playing. Next he returned to the R&B haunts of his youth and recorded a handful of singles in the New Orleans style of

Snooks Eaglin's 'St James Infirmary' was featured in a 1997 Budweiser ad.

the period (1960–61). Then, after a couple of long spells of obscurity, he re-emerged in the late 1980s, once again an eclectic artist but drawing on more recent R&B, funk and jazz developments in his city's music. (*New Orleans Street Singer* Storyville; *Baby, You Can Get Your Gun, Out Of Nowhere* Black Top [US]/Demon [UK])

ronnie EARL (1953–)

The only guitarist to offer a serious challenge to Earl's chops and versatility is his predecessor in Roomful Of Blues, Duke Robillard. (Now there's a Battle of the Blues Guitars worth staging.) The New York-born Earl didn't begin playing until his twenties, inspired by a Muddy Waters show. He was a member of ROB in 1980–88, contributing to Muse albums by Joe Turner and Eddie "Cleanhead" Vinson as well as the band's records. Meanwhile he worked with his own group, the Broadcasters, cutting several albums for Black Top, and continued to do so into the 1990s. A full CV would also list dozens of appearances on other people's

records (Hubert Sumlin, Snooks Eaglin etc). Basically a West Coast stylist in the tradition of T-Bone Walker, he can play virtually anything, as could be guessed from his lyrical lines on the jazz-tilted instrumental set *Grateful Heart* (1996). (*Test Of Time* Black Top; *Grateful Heart: Blues & Ballads* Bullseye Blues; *Blues Union* [with Joe Beard] Audioquest)

david "honeyboy" EDWARDS (1915–)

By the 1990s Edwards was living history, one of the few men still around with first-hand memories of Robert Johnson. Not that he was ready for the chair by the fireside: as his public appearances and recordings showed, he could still sing and pick his guitar with great spirit, if no longer with the zip of the 27-year-old who sang 'Wind Howlin' Blues' and 'The Army Blues' into a Library of Congress microphone for Alan Lomax (*Delta Bluesman*).

"There are more colors in my blues today," Ronnie Earl said proudly in 1993.

Nearly another decade would go by before the Mississippi-born Edwards recorded again, and his entire discography for the 1950s and 1960s amounts to no more than nine songs from seven sessions – perhaps because he always preferred interpreting other people's blues to creating his own. (*Delta Bluesman* Indigo; *White Windows* Evidence)

tinsley ELLIS (1957–)

Blues guitar fanciers were alerted to Ellis when he was playing with the Heartfixers, an Atlanta-based blues band he led jointly with the singer and harmonica player Chicago Bob Nelson. The group made three hearty albums for the small Landslide label, one with the singer Nappy Brown, before breaking up in 1988. Ellis, himself a native Atlantan, then formed a new band and signed with Alligator. The price you pay for his tempestuous guitar work is listening to sludgy singing and songs with a short shelf-life. (*Storm Warning* Alligator)

sleepy john ESTES (1899–1977)

Estes used blues as a medium for journalism. Sometimes the stories were national, like the poverty described in 'Need More Blues', but more often they were local-colour pieces about characters in the town where he lived, Brownsville, Tennessee: 'Martha Hardin', 'Lawyer Clark Blues'. Whatever the story, he filed it in a broken-down, lugubrious voice to a jerky guitar backing often smoothed and adorned by the harmonica of Hammie Nixon (1908–1984), his colleague for many years.

Estes spent most of his life in western Tennessee, often in Memphis, where he first recorded in 1929 with the mandolinist Yank Rachell. His partnership with Nixon was first documented on songs like 'Drop Down Mama' and 'Someday Baby Blues' in 1935; later sides replaced the harmonica player with the guitarists Son Bonds or Charlie

Pickett. In the 1940s and 1950s Estes virtually disappeared and was presumed dead until he reappeared in 1961, not nearly as old as he had sounded, and began a second career, reunited with Nixon, that took him to Europe (several times) and Japan, and produced a clutch of albums, mostly for Delmark. (MR; *Legend Of Sleepy John Estes* Delmark)

FABULOUS THUNDERBIRDS

In the late 1970s and 1980s the university town of Austin, Texas, became a leading blues centre. One reason for that was the club Antone's; another, the resident band. The original T-Birds – guitarist Jimmie Vaughan, harmonica player Kim Wilson, Keith Ferguson (bass) and Mike Buck (drums) – came together in 1974, but it took a dozen years of backing other artists, making albums noticed only by their fans and going through personnel changes before the band hit paydirt with *Tuff Enuff* (Epic), whose title track was a Top 10 pop hit. In the late 1980s Vaughan left to work with his brother Stevie Ray and was replaced by Duke Robillard. Wilson works in his own name with

the guitarist Rusty Zinn and has recorded *That's Life* (Antone's, 1994). (*Tuff Enuff* Epic)

sue FOLEY (1968–)

Singer-guitarist Foley was born in Ottawa and played in bands there and in Vancouver before joining the Austin, Texas, blues community at the beginning of the 1990s. Her 1992 debut *Young Girl Blues* revealed a guitarist equally skilful with the self-willed rhythms of John Lee Hooker ('Gone Blind', 'Time To Travel') and the happy swing-blues of Memphis Minnie ('Chauffeur Blues') or Tampa Red ('But I Forgive You'). Its successors continued to mix familiar blues themes and original material, until *Walk In The Sun* (1996) presented a repertoire virtually all her own, a garland of flowers grown from the seeds of her blues training like 'Give It To Me', 'The Wind' and the Broonzyesque 'Train To Memphis'. Whether playing electric or acoustic, Foley is a guitarist with chops and character. (*Young Girl Blues* Antone's)

robben FORD (1951–)

Ford was the prodigious teenage guitarist in a band with his brothers Mark (harmonica) and Patrick (drums) that made some impact around San Francisco in the early 1970s and a striking album, *The Charles Ford Band* (Arhoolie), named after their father. After that Robben and Pat played with Charlie Musselwhite and Robben put in a couple of years with Jimmy Witherspoon. Since then both Mark and Pat have continued to head blues bands but Robben has gone much farther afield, working with Miles Davis and co-founding the jazz-funk band The Yellowjackets. In the 1990s, heading the trio The Blue Line, he circled back to the blues. (*Handful Of Blues* Stretch)

The Fabulous Thunderbirds, with Kim Wilson at the microphone.

An unknown fan attains tattered immortality as he is photographed meeting "Baby Face" Leroy Foster.

"baby face" leroy FOSTER (1923–1958)

Foster was unlucky to hitch up, around 1949–50, with Muddy Waters and Little Walter – unlucky because the smoke of their trajectory into the blues bigtime has all but blotted out his far from minor talent. A warm, confiding singer who sounded rather like Willie Nix or a more expansive Sonny Boy Williamson II, he was also a busy but unfussy drummer and a guitarist whose allegiance was less to Robert Johnson than to the West Coast sound of, say, Johnny Moore. This unusual combination of skills did not prevent him making at least one record that can be called a classic of its time and place, the 1950 coupling with Snooky Pryor of 'My Head Can't Rest Anymore'/'Take A Little Walk With Me'. His early death

Frank Frost's Jelly Roll Kings may be the longest-standing blues band in the business.

robbed the Chicago scene of one of its quirkiest characters. (*The Blues World Of Little Walter* Delmark)

frank FROST (1936–)

Frost's selling-point is that he didn't go to Chicago, like so many of his blues contemporaries, but remained in the South, playing in juke-joints in Mississippi and his native Arkansas with fellow-minded stay-at-homes Sam Carr (drums) and singer-guitarist Big Jack Johnson, the long-term members of his Jelly Roll Kings. Competent on guitar, harmonica and keyboards, Frost has an affinity for the lazy, nasal sound of Jimmy Reed and Slim Harpo – he had a small hit with 'My Back Scratcher' on the back of Harpo's big seller 'Scratch My Back' – but has survived by keeping not too far behind the fashion in

R&B. He had a satisfying cameo in the 1986 movie *Crossroads*. (*Jelly Roll King* Charly)

blind boy FULLER (1908–1941)

One of the few regional blues artists to challenge the Chicago-based oligarchy of Big Bill Broonzy, Tampa Red and their friends, Blind Boy Fuller was the most prolific and best-selling recording artist in the South-East in the 1930s. His clean-fingered guitar-playing, clear diction and catchy songs formed a stylistic model that was copied by many younger or lesser figures, white as well as black.

He learned guitar in the mid-1920s and after losing his sight about 1928 became an itinerant musician, playing his loud steel-bodied National guitar on the streets of North Carolina cities like Winston-Salem, Durham, Burlington and Raleigh, where large black workforces served the warehouses and factories of the tobacco industry. In the mid-1930s he was the centre of a circle that included Gary Davis (who gave him some elements of his guitar style), Sonny Terry and the washboard and guitar player Bull City Red (George Washington). He was also a formative influence on Brownie McGhee. (MR; *Trucking My Blues Away* Yazoo)

jesse FULLER (1896–1976)

With its jolly, raggy tune and upbeat lyrics, 'San Francisco Bay Blues' ought to be the city's unofficial anthem. It was created by a singular figure, a musician for whom the description "one-man band" seems hardly adequate. Fuller played guitar (12-string, at that) with harmonica and kazoo on a neck rack, one foot operating a hi-hat cymbal and the other an ungainly sort of upright bass with pedals, which he called a fotdella. He trained this battery of instruments on every kind of music within his range, from blues and rags to hymns and antique pop songs.

Fuller left his native Georgia young and finally wound up in California, where he used to play outside the Hollywood film lots. The success of his big money song, which was covered by folkclub artists like Ramblin' Jack Elliott, led to TV appearances, a European tour and several delightful albums. (*San Francisco Bay Blues* Original Blues Classics; *Frisco Bound* Arhoolie)

lowell FULSON (1921–)

After T-Bone Walker, the most important figure in West Coast blues in the 1940s and 1950s is Lowell Fulson. His synthesis of south-western guitar blues and Californian jump music made a template for Ray Charles (who once played piano in his band) and B.B. King. But unlike some pioneers he con-

tinued to make fresh discoveries and adapt to other people's.

He grew up in southern Oklahoma and as a boy played in a local string band. By his late teens he was singing and playing guitar in small-town gambling joints, and for a while he travelled as guitar player to Texas Alexander. After army service he found his way to California and recorded busily for several labels, murmuring his blues while untwirling guitar phrases like smoke-rings, generally in a small-group setting with piano, bass and drums, occasionally in a guitar duet with his

Firing on five, the multiskilled minstrel man Jesse Fuller.

brother Martin. 'Three O'Clock Blues', the original of B.B. King's hit, came from this period, along with 'Guitar Shuffle', 'Everyday I Have The Blues' and 'Blue Shadows'. 'Reconsider Baby' (Checker, 1954), his biggest hit, has become a standard.

In the 1960s he made a painless transition to the soul-blues idiom of Bobby Bland and was successful with 'Black Nights', 'Tramp' and the mildly freaked-out sound of *In*

A Heavy Bag (Jewel). He kept active in the 1980s and 1990s and made workmanlike albums for Rounder and Bullseye Blues, where he displayed attractive new songs by himself and associates like Jimmy McCracklin. (*San Francisco Blues* Black Lion; *Tramp/Soul* Ace; *It's A Good Day* Rounder)

anson FUNDERBURGH (1954–)

Guitarist Funderburgh from Plano, Texas, leads one of the South-West's hardest-working blues bands, the Rockets, founded in 1978 with singer and harmonica player Darrell Nulisch but since 1986 featuring Sam Myers in those roles. Unhampered by the creativity of contemporaries like Stevie Ray Vaughan and Ronnie Earl, Funderburgh plays as if flipping through the pages of a blues guitar lexicon, offering on-the-spot demonstrations of the playing of Freddie King, Elmore James or B.B. King. (*Thru The Years: A Retrospective* Black Top)

bill GAITHER (1910–1970)

After the death of Leroy Carr in 1935, the singer Bill Gaither from Louisville, Kentucky, took it on himself to invest the late star's stylistic legacy in a series of thoughtfully written slow and medium-paced blues evocative of twilight brooding. Under the billing "Leroy's Buddy" and with the unemphatic but attractive piano playing of Honey Hill, he recorded over 100 sides between 1935 and 1941. By the end he was able to peel off the Carr mask, though sometimes only to replace it with a different one such as Peetie Wheatstraw's. Nevertheless, his best sides are very engaging. (*Bill Gaither (Leroy's Buddy) Vol 1 (1935–1936), Vol 2 (1936–1938)* Document)

cecil GANT (1913–1951)

Though not a dedicated blues artist, Gant played a pivotal role in the revival of the record industry in the mid-1940s, which had far-reaching effects on the blues business. His meandering pop ballad 'I Wonder' was so popular that independent labels sprang up everywhere to exploit black music, seizing the initiative from the slow-moving major record companies.

Hardly anything is known about his early life. He was serving in the army in L.A. when he made 'I Wonder', and was billed on many of his records as "Pvt. Cecil Gant, The G.I. Sing-sation". As well as singing in the dreamy vein of his hit, he could deliver a pleasant blues and an energetic boogie, versatility shared by West Coast contemporaries like Charles Brown and Ivory Joe Hunter. Leaving the army he returned to the city of his birth, Nashville, where he launched the blues list of the Bullet label in 1946 and later recorded for Decca. Some of his last sides were rockabilly boogies with a Nashville studio guitarist, only a few breaths away from the rock 'n' roll of Bill Haley.

terry GARLAND (1953–)

One of the more individual interpreters of early blues, this Tennessee-born singer and guitarist entertainingly rehashes ingredients of Robert Johnson, Blind Willie McTell and Muddy Waters while concocting similar-tasting recipes of his own devising, such as 'Good Time Blues' and the title track of *The One To Blame*, his 1996 successor to two albums on BMG/First Warning. The versatile harmonica player Mark Wenner from the Nighthawks contributes valuably to his records. (*The One To Blame* Demon)

larry GARNER (1952–)

Singer-guitarist Garner delighted many blues fans in the early 1990s with his beguiling blend of rootsiness and inventive songwriting, first exposed on a custom-made tape and then more widely on the self-produced *Double Dues* and *Too Blues*. He grew up in Baton Rouge, Louisiana, his first inspiration the guitar-playing preacher Rev. Utah Smith, and hung out with local musicians such as Lonesome Sundown, Silas Hogan, Guitar Kelley and Tabby Thomas, whose club, Tabby's Blues Box, was his playing base in the 1980s and gave him the subject matter for the strongest song on *Double Dues*, 'No Free Rides'. The larger budgets available for his Verve albums didn't materially alter his music, though 'The Haves And The Have Nots' on *Baton Rouge* suggests that if there were ever a blues recession he could take his portfolio down Nashville's Music Row. The same album's 'Go To Baton Rouge' offers a tourist's guide to Louisiana music spots. You might guess that routine blues subjects don't interest Garner very much, and you would be right. (MR; *Too Blues* JSP; *You Need To Live A Little, Baton Rouge* Verve)

jazz GILLUM (1904–1966)

Gillum's casual, chatty singing and squeaky harmonica make one of the most recognizable combinations in 1930s and 1940s blues. Any record from his heyday gives much the same flavour as any other: he hardly changed at all between the mid-1930s and 1949, though the later sides have rather more emphatic backings, and the fluent guitarist Willie Lacey strikes a more modern note than Big Bill Broonzy, who accompanied Gillum on earlier recordings like 'Key To The Highway' (1940). Gillum also originated 'Look On Yonder Wall' (1946, with Big Maceo on piano), which was later popularized by Elmore James. Overtaken by the generation of Muddy Waters and Howlin' Wolf, he faded into retirement in the 1950s. His last, slightly sad recordings were on a couple of 1961 albums with Memphis Slim and the singer-guitarist Arbee Stidham. (*Key To The Highway 1935–1942* EPM/Blues Collection)

lloyd GLENN (1909–1985)

A gifted pianist, writer and arranger, Glenn contributed tasteful, economic playing to many of Lowell Fulson's records in the 1950s and 1960s. He also wrote Fulson's only Number 1 hit, 'Blue Shadows'. He was born in San Antonio, Texas, played with jazz bands in the 1920s and 1930s and found his way to L.A. in 1941. Before joining Fulson in 1949 he had played on T-Bone Walker's 'Call It Stormy Monday'. While with Fulson he cut some small-group instrumentals featuring his piano like 'Old Time Shuffle' and 'Chic-a-Boo'. In the 1960s he played on B.B. King's *My Kind Of Blues* (Crown) and *Lucille* (Bluesway) and worked with Walker again on album dates. He was active into the 1980s. (*Chic-a-Boo* Night Train)

rosco GORDON (1934–)

A Memphis riposte to Fats Domino, with a strong hint of Little Richard, singer-pianist Gordon was one of the early-1950s blues gang known as the Beale Streeters, with Bobby Bland and Johnny Ace. 'Booted' (RPM/Chess, 1952) gave his disc career a kick-start, followed in the same year by 'No More Doggin" (RPM). There were no further hits, despite a lot of time in the Sun studios, until 'Just A Little Bit' (Vee Jay, 1960). Thereafter, despite his youth, talent and exuberant if oddball personality, Gordon made no lasting mark on the blues canvas, either in person or with his records, though the dragging rhythm of 'No More Doggin" is said to echo in the bluebeat music that preceded reggae.

otis GRAND (1950–)

The name sounds too good to be true, and is: O.G. was born Fred Bishti, in Beirut, though he has spent much of his life in the United States. He played with local blues names at Eli's Mile High Club in Oakland, California, and made contacts that would later prove handy, such as Joe Louis Walker, who produced his debut album *Always Hot* (1988). By then Grand was based in Britain, where

Otis Grand furthered his association with Joe Louis Walker by playing on his 1997 album *Great Guitars*.

he and his Dance Kings quickly became a popular club act. Walker also played on *He Knows The Blues* (1992), alongside the trumpeter and arranger Calvin Owens, tenor saxophonist Pee Wee Ellis and singer Jimmy Nelson. *Nothing Else Matters* (1994) involved singer-harmonica players Curtis Salgado (from the original Robert Cray Band), Sugar Ray Norcia and Kim Wilson, while Walker and Salgado returned for *Perfume And Grime* (1996), which also called on Luther Allison and singer Darrell Nulisch. These layers of collaborators are not added to muffle any shortcomings in the leader: Grand is an incisive guitarist, and his material is knowledgeably selected (when he doesn't write it himself) and imaginatively arranged. (*He Knows The Blues, Nothing Else Matters, Perfume And Grime* Sequel)

lil GREEN (1919–1954)

Though Green recorded numerous blues, she was popular in the 1940s, and is remem-

bered today, for her bluesy pop song 'Romance In The Dark' and her lingering rendition of Joe McCoy's minor-key lament 'Why Don't You Do Right?' She also handled riper material like the drug song 'Knockin' Myself Out' or the big-band-accompanied 'Blowtop Blues' with lip-smacking relish. Her style was knowing, somewhat in the manner of Billie Holiday or the young Dinah Washington. Born in Mississippi, she spent most of her life in Chicago, working in the clubs and recording with Big Bill Broonzy and the flowery pianist Simeon Henry. (*Why Don't You Do Right? 1940–1942* EPM/Blues Collection)

GUITAR SLIM (1926–1959)

"He was the performinest man I've ever seen", said his contemporary Earl King, winding up a story of a gig where Slim dyed his hair blue and was carried through the crowd on his valet's shoulders, playing guitar non-stop. Records seldom convey more than

Eddie Jones, alias Guitar Slim.

a shadowy outline of such occasions, but songs like 'The Story Of My Life', 'Sufferin' Mind' and 'The Things That I Used To Do', Slim's gigantic hit of 1954, do evoke a vivid personality.

Born Eddie Jones in Greenwood, Mississippi, Slim was fascinated by Clarence "Gatemouth" Brown and began by borrowing his style and material. After a few singles for Imperial and Bullet, he signed with Specialty and cut 'The Things That I Used To Do' with Ray Charles playing piano (and allegedly shouting the "yeah!" at the end). Specialty's boss Art Rupe hated it, but it lodged at the top of the R&B chart for six weeks and set Slim off on a hectic touring schedule that lasted for years and probably contributed to his early death from pneumonia. (*The Things That I Used To Do* Ace)

John HAMMOND (1942–)

The son of the famous jazz and blues producer John Hammond, J.H. Jr began playing in New York in the early 1960s and was soon recording for Vanguard. Initially an inter-

preter of acoustic guitar blues, he also worked with The Band and Charlie Musselwhite on *So Many Roads* (Vanguard, 1965), with the Nighthawks and in other group settings, but he never deserted the earlier blues forms that had been his first love, continuing to play them with unswerving commitment throughout the 1970s and 1980s. His 1990s albums for Pointblank, especially *Found True Love* (1995), reveal a mature performer, no longer in thrall to early models like Robert Johnson but commanding a variety of styles, both acoustic and electric. (*Big City Blues* Vanguard; *John Hammond* Rounder; *Found True Love* Pointblank)

HARLEM HAMFATS

The Hamfats were a studio creation, put together by Decca Records' blues producer Mayo Williams to record novelty and blues numbers with a jazzy, almost Dixieland line-up of Herb Morand (trumpet), Odell Rand (clarinet), Horace Malcolm (piano), Charlie McCoy (mandolin), Joe McCoy (guitar), bass and drums. It was no coincidence that their first session, in April 1936, fell less than three weeks after the recording debut of Tampa Red's similar group, the Chicago Five, for the rival Bluebird label. What couldn't

Liz Green and her orchestra – maybe the line-up on her 1946 recording of 'Blowtop Blues' (left). Right, John Hammond.

Corey Harris's second album, *Fish Ain't Bitin'*, appeared in 1997.

have been planned was the hit the Hamfats scored with that first record, 'Oh! Red'. The band cut 75 sides in three and a half years, several written by Joe McCoy like 'Weed Smoker's Dream', which he later turned into 'Why Don't You Do Right?' for Lil Green. Joe was the chief singer, occasionally relieved by his brother Charlie or Herb Morand. There were personnel changes towards the end of the group's life, but nothing affected the consistency of this formulaic but well-played and very jolly music. The band also accompanied fellow Decca artists like Johnny Temple, Frankie Jaxon and Rosetta Howard. (*Harlem Hamfats Vols 1–4* Document)

james HARMAN (1946–)

The Alabama-born Harman had exercised his lungs as a blues harmonica player and singer in Chicago, New York and elsewhere before he chose the air of southern California in the 1970s and became known as a skilled, reliable musician, whether for a backing job or leading his own band, which recorded several albums for this label and that during the 1980s before settling in 1990 on Black Top. Harman is an amusing songwriter and an excellent, unfussy harp player. (*Do Not Disturb, Black And White* Black Top)

corey HARRIS (1969–)

Corey Harris is one of several young black musicians (others include Keb' Mo' and Alvin Youngblood Hart) who raised the flag of acoustic guitar blues in the mid-1990s. He grew up in Denver, Colorado, spent time in linguistic research in North Africa in his early twenties and came home to a teaching post in Louisiana. On his debut solo album *Between Midnight And Day* (1995) he investigates the repertoire of Charlie Patton,

Booker White, Fred McDowell, Muddy Waters, Sleepy John Estes and others. The results are occasionally a little pallid, but his live performances are more red-blooded. (*Between Midnight And Day* Alligator)

wynonie HARRIS (1915–1969)

Wynonie Harris had a voice as wide as the Midwestern prairie and as loud as the harvesters that rolled across it. In the late 1940s and 1950s he was one of the most bankable acts in black music, earning $1,000 a week and defeating Joe Turner and T-Bone Walker in staged "Battles of the Blues". If he couldn't outsing them, he outdid them with dancing and prancing.

His first job was as a dancer in the clubs of his home town, Omaha, Nebraska. In 1944, now a singer too, he joined Lucky Millinder's orchestra and recorded the mock sermon 'Who Threw The Whiskey In The Well'. On the King label in 1945–52 he sent 16 singles into the R&B Top Ten (three to the top), including the party anthem 'Good Rockin' Tonight' (a cover of Roy Brown's hit that did even better) and the hillbilly-blues crossovers 'Good Morning Judge' and 'Bloodshot Eyes', accompanied by musicians from the ranks of Millinder, Todd Rhodes and Duke Ellington. By 1955 it was all over: rock 'n' roll bankrupted him and perhaps broke his heart. He scuffled for gigs and made a few unimportant records before throat cancer robbed him first of his voice, then his life. (*Bloodshot Eyes: The Best Of Wynonie Harris* Rhino)

alvin youngblood HART (1963–)

Though born in Oakland, California, Hart had family connections with Carroll County, Mississippi, and spent time there in his childhood, hearing his relatives' stories of Charlie Patton, "being around these people who were there when this music was going on." He took up guitar seriously in his mid-teens and played "Hendrix and the Stones and all the good garage band stuff." Later he infiltrated blues circles in Chicago and L.A., discovered he wasn't really interested in playing band blues and in 1984 decided to concentrate on acoustic guitar. "I guess my big break came when I opened for Taj Mahal for four nights at [San Francisco club] Yoshi's." In 1996 he made a powerful and individual album debut, playing steel, slide and standard guitars and banjo on a mixture of dug-up and new-grown blues. (*Big Mama's Door* OKeh)

bertha "chippie" HILL (1905–1950)

With her deep voice, trenchant delivery and clear preference for slow blues, Hill stands alongside Sippie Wallace at the other end of the line of early female blues singers from the suave vaudeville-trained artists like Ethel Waters or Alberta Hunter. In 1925–29 she recorded a couple of dozen blues, often with Louis Armstrong on cornet; his accompaniments to 'Pratt City Blues' and the lovely eight-bar melody of 'Trouble In Mind' are judged to be among his finest. She then devoted herself to raising seven children, before making a splendid return to performing and recording in the late 1940s. (*Bertha "Chippie" Hill (1925–1929)* Document)

michael HILL (1952–)

Hill came to the blues from the untypical social/musical background of the South Bronx and the Black Rock Coalition, and just as his tense guitar-playing reflects Hendrix more than B.B. King, so his songs like 'Hard Blues For Hard Times' and 'Bluestime In America' spring not from blues commonplaces but from the dislocations of contemporary city life. As the notes to *Bloodlines*, the startling 1994 debut album by Hill's Blues Mob, drily remark, "folk who'd rather not hear about the country's social problems when they listen to the blues may find some discomfort here." The Mob's members include Hill's brother Kevin (bass) and his singing sisters Wynette and Kathy. (*Bloodlines, Have Mercy!* Alligator)

Z.Z. HILL (1935–1984)

A soul-blues singer in the vein of Bobby Bland or Johnny Taylor, Hill is a crucial figure in recent blues history: his record 'Down Home Blues' was the best-known blues song of the 1980s, and the album *Down Home* (1981) sold strongly for years. Hill was a good, seasoned performer rather than an exceptional one, but he was exceptionally lucky in his access to good songs like 'Cheatin' In The Next Room', 'I'm A Blues Man' and 'Shade Tree Mechanic'. Before his hit and the resulting firm association with the Malaco label in Jackson, Mississippi (where Bland, Taylor and Little Milton also found a base), the Texas-born Hill had been quite well known on the Southern soul circuit and had made many singles. He died after a road accident. (*Greatest Hits* Malaco)

smokey HOGG (1914–1960)

For a long time Hogg was almost as much of a mystery as Robert Johnson. Many of his Texas contemporaries remembered him, but there was no reliable photograph and no clue about what had happened to him after he wound up his amazing recording career in 1958. Amazing, because as virtually every one of his more than 150 sides attests, he couldn't play in time and was often unable, or didn't bother, to tune his guitar. He didn't even have an early hit to explain why 15 labels gave him a whirl, though 'Little School Girl', a loose version (what else?) of Sonny Boy Williamson I's song, is said to have sold quite well in 1948. Evidently there was something appealing in his ramshackle

often with Junior Wells; they recorded together for Chief (1960), Hooker playing on Wells' hit 'Messin' With The Kid'. The 1960s brought a couple of European tours and albums for Arhoolie, Blue Thumb and Bluesway. The tune 'Two Bugs And A Roach' was sardonically named for the tuberculosis that killed him. (*Sweet Black Angel* One Way; *Two Bugs And A Roach* Arhoolie)

walter HORTON (1917–1981)

If Little Walter was the Charlie Parker of blues harmonica, "Shakey" Horton was perhaps its Art Pepper: less of an innovator, but gifted with graceful ideas and a golden tone. He sounded huge in his famous 'Easy' and his commanding duets – they are more than accompaniments – with Johnny Shines on 'Brutal Hearted Woman' and 'Evening Sun'. Whether it was Little or Big Walter (as Horton was also known) on classic 1950s Muddy Waters sides like 'Hoochie Coochie Man' is still uncertain: some accounts put them both in the studio, playing by turns.

Later on, Earl Hooker would take up a twin-necked Gibson model.

music, though blues enthusiasts have reserved most of their approval for his two-part 'Penitentiary Blues' (1952), a powerful retelling of the old Texas prison song 'Ain't No More Cane On The Brazos'. The older man who appeared in New York about 1970 claiming to be Hogg was an impostor. (*Angels In Harlem* Specialty [US]/Ace [UK])

earl HOOKER (1930–1970)

Perhaps there isn't room in the public memory for two bluesmen with the same last name. At any rate, few artists have been so casually consigned to the minor league as Earl Hooker. (Try finding some of his records.) Circumstances were never much in his favour: he was often ill, wasn't a gifted singer and no record company persevered with him. On the other hand, he was a slide guitarist of wayward brilliance, expanding the legacy of Tampa Red and Robert Nighthawk into an electric slide style of shimmering clarity.

When he was a boy his family moved from Clarksdale, Mississippi, to Chicago, where he met Nighthawk and learned 'Anna Lee' and 'Sweet Black Angel'. From 1949 into the early 1950s he worked in the Memphis area with Ike Turner and on radio with Sonny Boy Williamson II. Recordings for Sun with Pinetop Perkins were never issued. Back in Chicago he plied the club circuit,

Walter Horton's much-admired instrumental 'Easy' was based on Ivory Joe Hunter's 'I Almost Lost My Mind'.

Son House. "Blues, the way it started, is something comes between man and woman."

He grew up around Memphis, a shy boy, seldom seen without a harmonica. In the early 1950s he cut 'Easy' and other sides for Sun and Modern, and in Chicago recorded with Shines, Johnny Young and Otis Rush as well as obscurer singers like Tommy Brown. His accompaniment to Jimmy Rogers's 'Walking By Myself' (Chess, 1956) has been much copied, but his own sides like 'Hard Hearted Woman' (States, 1954) and 'Need My Baby' (Cobra, 1956) suffer a little from his foggy, unconfident singing. In the 1960s and 1970s he worked intermittently with Willie Dixon's Chicago Blues All Stars and made several albums, but he was never at his best as the front man in a group and will be remembered mostly for the intuitive brilliance of his responses. (*Mouth Harp Maestro* Ace; *Big Walter Horton & Carey Bell* Alligator; *Fine Cuts* Blind Pig)

son HOUSE (1902–1988)

As an old man, House had something about him of King Lear: hesitant, forgetful, at times pathetic, yet revealing in flashes a dignity and personal force that explained why, in his heyday, he had been a running mate of Charlie Patton and a model for Robert Johnson and Muddy Waters. Beside Patton he was a guitarist of rudimentary skill, but his voice had even greater richness, and though his repertoire was not large, it included 'Preachin' The Blues', a song that not only was personally important but epitomized a conflict of beliefs experienced by many blues singers.

He began playing guitar in Mississippi in the mid-1920s and soon afterwards met Patton and Willie Brown. In 1930 the three men recorded for Paramount. House also recorded for the Library Of Congress in 1941–42, then left Mississippi for Rochester, New York, where he spent two decades undisturbed before blues gumshoes knocked at his door. He sang at the 1964 Newport Folk Festival, recorded the fitfully powerful *Father Of Folk Blues* (Columbia, 1965) and other albums and made two trips to Europe, the second, in 1970, in a condition of advanced frailty. (*Masters Of The Delta Blues* Yazoo [MR]; *The Complete Library Of Congress Sessions 1941–1942* Travelin' Man; *Father Of The Delta Blues: The Complete 1965 Sessions* Columbia/ Legacy)

peg leg HOWELL (1888–1966)

Some of the earliest and most fascinating music recorded in Atlanta in the late 1920s was by the singer-guitarist Joshua "Peg Leg" Howell and his friends, particularly the fiddler Eddie Anthony, whose vigorous dance playing gives us a rare view of the black string-band music that was almost obliterated by the craze for recording blues guitarists. Howell himself, born in rural Georgia and disabled in his twenties by a shooting accident, had the strong delivery and ear-catching repertoire of the professional street-singer. As so often, we need to detach the obligatory "Blues" from song-titles like 'Coal Man Blues' and 'Skin Game Blues' and hear them as older rag songs. Though he lost his other leg in 1952 Howell survived long enough to make an album in 1963, though by then he was very frail. (*Peg Leg Howell/ Eddie Anthony Vols 1 & 2* Matchbox)

joe HUGHES (1937–)

Singer-guitarist Hughes is a Houston contemporary and friend of Johnny Copeland who was sold on the blues by local heroes like "Gatemouth" Brown and Johnny "Guitar" Watson – "anyone who had fire in their playing and a good shuffle". He played with the Dukes of Rhythm in the 1950s, on the road with Bobby Bland in the 1960s, and in soul bands in the 1970s. Like Copeland he couldn't see much of a future for the blues in Houston, but unlike him he stayed there.

Nevertheless the word was out and he was invited to several blues festivals in Europe. The Dutch label Double Trouble issued *Texas Guitar Master* (1986), which included a live "Battle of the Guitars" with fellow Texan bluesman Pete Mayes (1938–) that testified to the abiding influence on both men of T-Bone Walker. An inventive songwriter and versatile performer, Hughes is equally happy with slow blues, Texas shuffles and old R&B hits. (*If You Want To See The Blues* Black Top; *Texas Guitar Slinger* Me And My Records)

helen HUMES (1913–1981)

The versatile Humes was successively a teenaged blues singer, band vocalist with Count Basie, saucy R&B diva and a mature interpreter of the classy popular song. She grew up in Louisville, Kentucky, was spotted by the guitarist Sylvester Weaver and made her first records in 1927, her true young voice consorting oddly with bizarre material like 'Garlic Blues'. In 1938 she followed Billie Holiday into the Basie orchestra for a four-year stay, then went west and was next heard sounding very sprightly on the jump blues 'Be-Baba-Leba' (Aladdin, 1945) and 'Million Dollar Secret' (Modern, 1950). But all along she yearned to sing Broadway rather than blues, and in the 1960s and 1970s she had her wish, making many albums of pop standards with distinguished jazzmen. (*Helen Humes 1927–1945* Classics; *Be-Baba-Leba* Whiskey, Women And . . .)

alberta HUNTER (1895–1984)

No actuary would consider the blues life a good risk, yet this remarkable woman sang blues at the dawn of the music's commercial life in 1921 and was still

In the 1930s, Alberta Hunter appeared as far afield as Copenhagen and Cairo.

doing so with enormous elan 60 years later. Though she had great success with some of her blues sides like 'Down Hearted Blues' (1922) and 'Chirping The Blues' (1923), Hunter was equally adept with the suggestive material that vaudeville and cabaret audiences enjoyed, such as 'My Particular Man', and even as a conventional danceband vocalist, a role she filled for several months in the 1930s at London's Dorchester Hotel. While in Britain she made a luminous appearance in the film

Radio Parade Of 1935. She also sang elsewhere in Europe, and further afield for the USO during World War II. She tried retirement in the 1950s, returned to the profession for a while in the early 1960s and bowed out again, only to make a triumphant third entrance in 1977. During her final years she performed regularly at The Cookery in Greenwich Village, sang the title song in the movie *Remember My Name* and made three albums. (*Alberta Hunter Vols 1–4* Document; *Songs We Taught Your Mother* Original Blues Classics)

ivory joe HUNTER (1914–1974)

Hunter straddled blues, boogie-woogie, R&B and country music and seemed capable of making his name in any of them. Who else was honoured both at the Monterey Jazz Festival and on Nashville's Grand Ol' Opry?

Born in south-east Texas, he learned to play piano in his teens. Moving to Oakland, California, he recorded blues and boogies in the late 1940s on his own Ivory and Pacific labels. As a singer he sounded like a cross between Charles Brown and Nat "King" Cole. His disc of the country song 'Jealous Heart' (King, 1949) signalled a direction his music would eventually take, but in the meantime he had Number 1 R&B hits with the ballad-blues 'I Almost Lost My Mind' (MGM, 1949), the pop 'I Need You So' (MGM, 1950) and 'Since I Met You Baby' (Atlantic, 1956), a distant melodic relative of 'I Almost Lost My Mind' that went high in the pop Top 20 and is remembered affectionately by a generation that smooched to it as teenagers. All these were Hunter's work, like 'Empty Arms' (Atlantic, 1957), later a country hit – as was 'Since I Met You Baby', repeatedly. (*7th Street Boogie* Route 66; *Since I Met You Baby: The Best Of Ivory Joe Hunter* Razor And Tie)

mississippi john HURT (1893–1966)

Until early middle age Hurt was known only as a party songster around Avalon, in Carroll County, Mississippi. In 1928 he made some discs for OKeh but his recording career stalled after his second session and did not restart for 35 years, when blues enthusiast Tom Hoskins traced him from the lyrics of 'Avalon Blues'. He was introduced to the

East Coast coffeehouse circuit, recorded a pair of albums for Piedmont and played the 1964 Newport Folk Festival. He made further albums for Vanguard and personal appearances all over the US in the remaining two years of his life, though to their regret he never played for his fans overseas.

The numbers his devotees particularly liked were the rag songs 'Salty Dog' and 'Candy Man' and the blues-ballads 'Spike Driver Blues' (a variant of 'John Henry') and 'Frankie'. Hurt knew more of these songs than the other artists who had second careers alongside him, like Son House or Skip James, and in a way he was a Leadbelly for the 1960s. He sang in a kind of loud whisper, to a melodious finger-picked guitar accompaniment. (MR; *Today!* Vanguard)

j.b. HUTTO (1926–1983)

An ardent follower of Elmore James, Hutto transcended mere imitation to forge a convincing personal style. He was also one of the small band of blues artists whose music retains its strength and character over several decades.

He spent his first 20 or so years in Augusta, Georgia, only taking up the guitar when he came to Chicago at the end of the 1940s. Encouraged by James, he learned to use a slide, displaying his progress and his sawtooth-edged singing on a set of impressive 1954 sides for Chance such as 'Dim Lights' and 'Combination Boogie'. A decade later he reappeared at a South Side bar, often working with Walter Horton, and recorded for Vanguard, Delmark and Testament. For more than a decade he was a popular club and festival draw. He also recorded several more albums, the last, *Slideslinger* (1982), being his best yet. His nephew Lil' Ed Williams (1955–) and his Blues Imperials preserve Hutto's raw approach. (*Slidewinder* Delmark; *Slideslinger* Black & Blue [Europe]/Varrick [US])

"bull moose" JACKSON (1919–1989)

The nickname was only half appropriate: Bull Moose Jackson didn't bellow all the time. In his big 1948 hit 'I Love You, Yes I Do' he practically crooned. But some of his songs – and here 'Big Ten Inch' springs to attention – were undeniably horny.

He was born Benjamin Clarence Jackson in Cleveland, Ohio, and worked as a saxophonist with bands in Ohio and Buffalo, New York, before joining Lucky Millinder. From 1945 he recorded with Millinder under the leader's name for Decca or his own for King, but from 1947 he was on King exclusively with his Buffalo Bearcats. He toured extensively and made occasional appearances in movies and revues. By 1958 he was living in Philadelphia and working outside music, but he made a comeback in the mid-1980s as a sort of founding father of suggestive R&B. (*The King R&B Box Set* King [MR])

jim JACKSON (c1890–c1937)

Not much of a singer and hardly anything of a guitarist, Jim Jackson nevertheless had a resounding hit with the plodding, catchy 'Jim Jackson's Kansas City Blues' (1927). Born in Hernando, Mississippi, he got his grounding as an entertainer on minstrel and medicine shows, and often hung out in Memphis with Gus Cannon, Furry Lewis and Will Shade. Following his hit he recorded a series of 'Kansas City' follow-ups and soundalikes, interspersed with rather more interesting rag songs like 'Traveling Man', 'Long Gone' and 'I'm Gonna Start Me A Graveyard Of My Own', or the arresting hymn parody 'I Heard The Voice Of A Pork Chop' – numbers which he put over with heavy playfulness and an often inaccurately fingered guitar. His last recording was in 1930 and nothing is known of his later life. (*Jim Jackson Vols 1–2* Document)

john JACKSON (1924–)

Like Leadbelly, John Hurt or Snooks Eaglin, John Jackson confounds received ideas about Southern music. He will sing and play anything, from a common-stock banjo tune to a Blind Blake guitar rag to a hillbilly blues he learned off a Jimmie Rodgers disc. His work often puts him in front of blues audiences, which he can satisfy with his enormous stock of blues, but as a respected member of the Washington D.C. folk music set and popular festival performer, he often has the chance to solicit different listeners with other kinds of songs.

Jackson learned to play as a boy in rural Virginia before moving in his twenties to Fairfax, Virginia, where he had a day job as a gravedigger. His easy-swinging guitar and strongly accented singing were first heard outside his locality on early-1960s albums for Arhoolie. He visited Europe with the 1969 AFBF and several times later, and has also recorded for Rounder. (*Don't Let Your Deal Go Down* Arhoolie)

John Jackson at the 1971 Festival of American Folklife, Montreal.

lil' son JACKSON (1916–1976)

Lil' Son Jackson's lean, loping, undecorated guitar blues could not be anything but Texan. A contemporary of Lightnin' Hopkins, he first recorded, like him, for Gold Star in Houston, but was snapped up by Imperial in 1950 and promptly had a hit with 'Rockin' And Rollin'', a sedate but infectious rendering of 'Rock Me Baby'. Further sessions

sometimes involved horns and rhythm sections, without affecting Jackson's thoughtful approach and country-boy language ("I made a New Year revolution . . .").

After being injured in a road accident in 1954 he went back to his job as an automobile mechanic. He made a pleasant solo album, *Blues Come To Texas*, for Arhoolie in 1960, but no further return to the music business. (*Texas Blues* Arhoolie; *The Complete Imperial Recordings* Capitol)

papa charlie JACKSON (c1880s–1938)

Lodged in the history books as the first male blues singer to earn fame through records, which he began making in 1924, Papa Charlie Jackson was actually a stage entertainer whose output of blues (when they were blues: titles, as often, are deceptive) was matched by jolly renditions of vaudeville and rag songs like 'Alabama Bound' and 'Mama Don't Allow It'.

He may have been born in New Orleans. He is reported to have played on Chicago's Maxwell Street in the 1920s (he did record a 'Maxwell Street Blues'), and earlier he may have worked on travelling shows. As well as his 70 solo sides, accompanying himself on the six-string banjo-guitar, he sang with cornetist Freddie Keppard's Jazz Cardinals ('Salty Dog', 1926) and accompanied Ida Cox and, on her last recordings, Ma Rainey. In the 1930s he was based in Chicago, where he recorded briefly for OKeh (1934) and was associated with Big Bill Broonzy. (*Papa Charlie Jackson Vols 1–3* Document)

elmore JAMES (1918–1963)

Elmore James's career dramatically illustrates the potency of one good idea – the yammering slide-guitar figure that opens his many recastings of 'Dust My Broom'. With it he not only electrified the legacy of Robert Johnson: he created one of the basic riffs of modern blues. But James had more cards in his hand. His versions of Tampa Red's 'It Hurts Me Too' and 'Anna Lee', or the almost interchangeable blues 'The Sun Is Shining' and 'The Sky Is Crying', are epics of suspense, so slow-moving, so laden with the desperate intensity of voice and guitar that they seem about to collapse. Yet James could rock almost playfully, as in 'Shake Your Moneymaker' or his several 'Hawaiian Boogie's.

He returned from war-time navy service to his native Mississippi to lead a band. In 1951 he recorded his first 'Dust My Broom' for Trumpet with Sonny Boy Williamson II, a running mate from pre-war days, but it was his work on Flair and Meteor in 1952–56 that made him a blues star. Based by turns in Mississippi and Chicago, he retained a steady band with the pianist Little Johnny Jones (1924–1964), his bass guitarist cousin Homesick James Williamson and tenor saxophonist J.T. Brown, a group heard in excellent form on the Chief and Fire sides of 1957–60. His last recordings for Fire, with New York studio musicians, were ragged but fervent as ever. By one of fate's bitterest jests, James died as a generation of blues-lovers was on the brink of discovering him. (MR; *Let's Cut It: The Very Best Of Elmore James* Ace)

jesse JAMES (dates unknown)

A turbulent singer and pianist of unknown past and future, Jesse James bobs to the surface of blues history just once, at a recording session on 3 June 1936. He is supposed to have been a prisoner on parole for the day, who was so affected by his taste of freedom that he broke down after singing four numbers and was taken back to jail. That may be a tall tale, but his performances of 'Southern Casey Jones' and the defiant 'Lonesome Day Blues' are so full of concentrated energy that you could well believe they came from a man who thought he had only one chance to address the world beyond his prison cell. (*Piano Blues Vol 1* Document)

skip JAMES (1902–1969)

Skip James was such a singular musician that even among the often fiercely individual stylists of early Mississippi blues he seems a maverick. While you can discern common ground between, say, Charlie Patton and Tommy Johnson, the man whose voice arched high over a ghostly chiming guitar in 'Devil Got My Woman' appears to live on a different map.

Nehemiah James was born in Bentonia, Mississippi, a minister's son. In his youth he played with the unrecorded Henry Stuckey. Like Patton, Tommy Johnson and many other Mississippi blues artists, he got on record through the recommendation of the talent-scout H.C. Speir, who owned a music store in Jackson. Unlike his peers, Skip James was a commercial failure, a setback that soured him for the rest of his life. He pursued gospel music and the Baptist ministry, only returning to the blues, reluctantly, when some record collectors contacted him in 1964. He thrilled the audience at that year's Newport Folk Festival, but his albums for Melodeon and Vanguard, though magnetic at the time, now seem fragmentary and fitful. The Edsel recordings, made a little earlier, are more focused. (MR; *She Lyin'*, *Skip's Piano Blues* Edsel)

steve JAMES (1950–)

A Huck Finn of the blues, Steve James sings and picks his way amiably, sometimes cheekily, through decades of old music while devising jolly songs of his own. Based in Austin, Texas, he plays mandolin, with some of the flavour of Yank Rachell that Ry Cooder has also acquired, and several styles of gui-

Frankie "Half Pint" Jaxon

"FAN IT"

tar, assisted on his albums by the harmonica player Gary Primich and banjoist-guitarist Danny Barnes. The slide guitar maestro Bob Brozman guests on *Art And Grit*. (*American Primitive, Art And Grit* Antone's)

frankie "half-pint" JAXON (1895–)

A diminutive vaudeville entertainer with a perky way with a song, Jaxon recorded several dozen hokum blues and other jolly numbers between 1926 and 1940: 'Fan It' and 'Chocolate To The Bone' were two of his favourites. Originally from Montgomery, Alabama, he was prominent in vaudeville by the early 1910s, often working as a female impersonator, and became one of the first stars of the Apollo Theatre. He could thus call for superior accompanists on his sessions, like the cornetists Punch Miller and, allegedly, Freddie Keppard; his later recordings were with small jazzy line-ups like the Harlem Hamfats. Blues fans reserve a special place in their hearts for his orgasmic parodies of 'How Long How Long Blues' and 'It's Tight Like That', louche collaborations with Tampa Red, Georgia Tom and assorted jugbandsmen. Last heard of in L.A. in the mid-1940s, Jaxon also produced revues and sang on radio. (*Frankie "Half-Pint" Jaxon Vols 1–3, Tampa Red Vol 1* Document)

buddy JOHNSON (1915–1977)

Buddy Johnson was the leader, principal writer and arranger and joint vocalist, with his younger sister Ella and the crooner Arthur Prysock, of one of the premier black orchestras in the first decade after World War II. He left South Carolina for New York in 1938, formed a band the following year and had a hit in 1940 with 'Please Mr Johnson', sung by Ella, as were 'That's The Stuff You

"If this song's too hot," sang Frankie Jaxon, "Go out and buy yourself a five-cent fan ..."

jimmy JOHNSON (1928–)

In the mid-1970s Chicagoans saw a change in Jimmy Johnson. For years he had followed the soul road; now he was turning down the blues highway. He brought with him valuable experience, having played guitar behind demanding singers, but he surprised some blueswatchers with his intense singing. Enthusiasts beyond Chicago first heard the reborn Johnson on *Living Chicago Blues Vol 1* (Alligator, 1978), then on two quirky sets for Delmark. Later he acquired and retained a following in Europe: *I'm A Jockey* (Birdology, 1994) originated in France. The spaces between those dates reveal how slowly he has been able to capitalize on early gains.

Leaving Mississippi for Chicago at 22, he worked with various small-timers before forming a band to play blues and soul material. After a spell outside music, in 1974–75 he worked with Jimmy Dawkins and Otis Rush and recorded for the French MCM label – rough drafts compared with his mature and unhackneyed later recordings. His upward progress was stalled by a 1988 road accident in which two of his band were killed, but by 1994 he could look at his rivals and assert, "I can defend myself. I'm ready. I'm waiting for them!" (*Johnson's Whacks* Delmark)

lil JOHNSON (dates unknown)

The women singers of the 1930s occupy an almost unwritten chapter of blues history. Lil Johnson recorded more than 50 sides in Chicago between 1929 and 1937, achieving good sales with 'Get 'Em From The Peanut Man (Hot Nuts)' and 'Press My Button (Ring My Bell)', whose subject matter needs little guesswork, and other sprightly performances like 'Was I Drunk'. Yet no one seems to remember her, and no photograph has surfaced. Her abrasive voice was usually framed by combos that included Big Bill

"Personally, I like classics," Buddy Johnson told *Down Beat* magazine, "but our bread and butter is in the South. The music I play has a Southern tinge to it. They understand it down there."

Gotta Watch' (1944) and 'Since I Fell For You' (1945). The blend of pop ballads, jive novelties and occasional blues or boogies was typical of the era (compare Cecil Gant, Ivory Joe Hunter, Lucky Millinder or Louis Jordan), but Johnson could forecast trends as well as fall in with them. His harder sound of the 1950s, especially when he left Decca for Mercury and worked with studio musicians like guitarist Mickey Baker and tenor saxophonist Sam "The Man" Taylor, prefigured rock 'n' roll. Based on the East Coast, and for a time the resident band at Harlem's Savoy Ballroom, the Buddy Johnson orchestra also had a following in the South and Midwest. Johnson retired because of ill health in the early 1960s. (*Walk 'Em Ace; Buddy & Ella Johnson 1953-1964* Bear Family)

Broonzy, the pianist Black Bob and trumpeter Lee Collins, though her 1929 sides are distinguished by stout piano-playing by Charles Avery or Montana Taylor. (*Lil Johnson Vols 1–3* Document)

luther "guitar junior" JOHNSON (1939–)

Luther "Guitar Junior" Johnson made his name as guitarist in the Muddy Waters band from 1972 to 1980, succeeding another player of the same name, nicknamed "Georgia Boy" or "Snake" (1934–1976). Mississippi born, Johnson had been in Chicago since he was 16, learning from Magic Sam in particular. During his Waters period he recorded *Luther's Blues* (1976) in France; afterwards he formed the Magic Rockers, recorded for Alligator in the *Living Chicago Blues* series, and moved to Boston, where he cut the excellent *Doin' The Sugar Too* (Rooster Blues, 1984) with the horn section from the Roomful Of Blues band. While his years with Waters were reflected in selections like 'I'm Ready', the outstanding track, 'Hard Times (Have Surely Come)', redeployed a Magic Sam riff. He subsequently recorded albums for Bullseye Blues and Telarc. A third Luther Johnson (1939–), nicknamed "Houserocker", is a Georgia-based singer-guitarist who has recorded for Ichiban. (*Luther's Blues* Black & Blue [France]/Evidence [US]; *Doin' The Sugar Too, I Want To Groove With You* Bullseye Blues; *Slammin' On The West Side* Telarc)

"For Luther to have 50,000 miles on a two-year-old van is normal," reports his producer and ex-sideman Ron Levy. "He tours non-stop."

merline JOHNSON (dates unknown)

Almost as obscure as her contemporary Lil Johnson – though at least there are photographs of her – The Yas Yas Girl, as Merline Johnson was almost always billed on record, cut more than 70 sides in the late 1930s and early 1940s, accompanied by small groups with Big Bill Broonzy, Blind John Davis and the saxophonist Buster Bennett. Unlike Lil Johnson, she did not specialize in suggestive numbers, though she did not eschew them either; her métier was bar-room blues like 'New Drinking My Blues Away' and 'I Just Keep On Drinking', which she put over in a hard-edged, unwinsome style. (*The Yas Yas Girl (Merline Johnson) Vols 1–3* Document)

pete JOHNSON (1904–1967)

Pete Johnson shared with the other members of the "Boogie Woogie Trio" the technical virtuosity and melodic fertility that can make this the most exciting of all piano music styles, but he was more comfortable than Meade Lux Lewis in a band setting, and as an accompanist, unlike Lewis or Albert Ammons, he could sparkle but not outshine his singing partner.

He spent the first half of his life in Kansas City, where he was born, taking up piano at 22. In the mid-1930s his act with the singer Joe Turner caught the radio-bent ear of the producer John Hammond, who persuaded them to try their luck in New York. They had none until the 1938 *Spirituals To Swing* concert, after which both found club work, Johnson at the Famous Door on 52nd Street. He also worked with Ammons and Lewis at Café Society and on records; his 1941 duets with Ammons are exceptional. In the same year the three were featured in the movie short *Boogie Woogie Dream*. After the war Johnson worked in small groups and was repeatedly reunited with

Turner, for instance on his *Boss Of The Blues* album (1956) and a 1958 *Jazz At The Philharmonic* tour of Europe, despite losing part of a finger some years earlier while changing a tyre. His last years were troubled by illness and poverty. (*Pete Johnson 1938–39, Pete Johnson 1939–41* Classics)

tommy JOHNSON (c1896–1956)

A mere handful of discs made in 1928–29 is the tangible evidence of the reputation

Pete Johnson used to play at a nightclub in Niagara Falls where he had to climb a long ladder to the piano above the bar.

Tommy Johnson once enjoyed among Mississippi blues singers; that and the vigorous life of his songs in later hands. 'Big Road Blues', 'Maggie Campbell Blues' and 'Cool Drink Of Water Blues' have survived, whether under those titles or others, through two or three generations to become blues standards, while 'Canned Heat Blues'

has at least inspired the name of a band. Though a contemporary and acquaintance of Charlie Patton, Johnson handled his music quite differently, singing with the gentle, unflustered air of a man fishing on a summer evening. The effect is enhanced by Charlie McCoy's rippling second guitar and Johnson's quiet shifts into falsetto, like absent-minded yodels. (*Tommy Johnson* Document)

curtis JONES (1906–1971)

His voice was small and his piano-playing unshowy, so it was probably his songs that made Jones one of the better-selling blues artists of the late 1930s. 'Lonesome Bedroom Blues' (1937) was popular and much copied, but some of his later sides sug-

Curtis Jones recorded only a few songs with guitar, at 1960s sessions in London produced by Mike Vernon.

gest that he was poaching on the preserves of Roosevelt Sykes, then with a rival label. He had begun playing music in his native Texas and moved to Chicago about 1936 with his wife, whose departure soon afterwards inspired his hit song. His vogue faded after the war and he all but disappeared until the late 1950s.

After making albums for Bluesville and Delmark, in 1962 he emigrated to Europe, where he spent the rest of his life, except for a couple of years in Morocco. He made further albums in Britain, the last in 1968 when visiting with the AFBF. His first instrument had been the guitar, and he liked to play a number or two with it on his records and personal appearances. There too his approach was terse. (*Lonesome Bedroom Blues 1937–1941* EPM/Blues Collection)

floyd JONES (1917–1989)

Jones entered the Chicago blues scene in the late 1940s, a contemporary of Muddy Waters with some of the same musical affiliations to the past – his record of 'Dark Road' (JOB, 1951) was based on a song by Tommy Johnson. Born in Arkansas, he grew up in Mississippi, where he met Charlie Patton and Tommy as well as Robert

Born in Arkansas, Charley Jordan settled in St Louis in the mid-1920s. He was disabled in a 1928 shooting incident.

Johnson, and began playing guitar in his teens. From 1945 he was based in Chicago, where he cut 'Stockyard Blues' (Marvel, 1947) with his older brother Moody Jones, a skilful guitarist, and the harmonica player Snooky Pryor. It was one of the first recordings of the new Chicago combo style. In the early 1950s he wrote and recorded 'Big World', 'Ain't Times Hard' and 'On The Road Again'; their combination of bleak subject matter and doleful delivery was striking but markedly uncommercial, and for years afterwards Jones performed only fitfully. He remade some of his core songs with Walter Horton and Otis Spann on a 1967 Testament album. (*Floyd Jones – Eddie Taylor: Masters Of Modern Blues* Testament)

charley JORDAN (c1890–1954)

One of the leading guitarists in St Louis in the 1920s and 1930s, a stylistic brother to Henry Townsend and Hi Henry Brown, Jordan also had a gift for writing blues in fresh, vivid and humorous language, sometimes on unexpected themes ('Lost Airship Blues', 'Hell Bound Boy Blues'). His most appreciated number, however, seems to have been 'Keep It Clean', a selection of mildly suggestive traditional jokes strung on the melodic thread of a blues, to which he added several sequels. After a batch of quirky solo sides and six riveting guitar duets with Hi Henry Brown ('Titanic Blues' and 'Preacher Blues' are exceptionally fine), he recorded mostly with Peetie Wheatstraw, each accompanying the other's recordings. He wrote many blues for Wheatstraw and other St Louis artists, and acted as a local talent scout for both Vocalion and Decca. (*Charley Jordan Vols 1–3* Document)

KEB' MO' (1951–)

Spearheading the acoustic blues revival of the mid-1990s, Keb' Mo' is an imaginative guitarist with an attractively shop-worn voice somewhat reminiscent of Taj Mahal.

Born Kevin Moore in L.A., he started on guitar at 11. In the 1970s he played behind the singer and violinist Papa John Creach and worked as a studio picker, writer and arranger for A&M Records. Later he played with bandleader Monk Higgins. "At that point, I had a one-directional, blinkered view of blues. But Monk started pointing out all the different kinds of blues and I learned about Mississippi John Hurt and Blind Boy

Keb' Mo' played the Robert Johnson role in a documentary drama *Can You Hear The Wind Howl?*

Jo Ann Kelly tackled the material of artists as diverse as Charlie Patton, Jelly Roll Morton and Billie Holiday.

Fuller." Sure enough, you can hear touches of Fuller when Mo' plays his National steel guitar, while Hurt's velvet-voiced playfulness echoes in songs like 'Angelina' and 'Lullaby Baby Blues'. Although Mo' also admires Robert Johnson and has sung his songs on both his OKeh albums, the strongest flavour in his very catchy original pieces seems to be derived from the gently swinging, raggy guitarists of the South-East. But he is comfortable in more modern electric settings too ('Dangerous Mood'). (*Keb' Mo'*, *Just Like You* OKeh)

jo ann KELLY (1944–1990)

"To many American performers", an obituarist wrote, "Jo Ann Kelly was the only British singer to earn their respect for her development of what they would be justified in thinking of as 'their' genre."

The London-born Jo Ann Kelly and her brother Dave (1948–) became blues fans in their teens. Few women were then singing or playing blues in Britain, and none with her skill or understanding of early blues styles or her deep, thrilling voice, inspired by her teacher-in-spirit Memphis Minnie. At the end of the 1960s, with an album on a major label in the United States, it seemed that she might be spirited away there and moulded into another Janis Joplin, but her allegiance was to the English club scene, though in the 1970s and 1980s that failed to support her financially and she worked a good deal on the Continent, latterly with the guitarist Pete Emery or in bands. Dave Kelly served in the John Dummer Blues Band, Tramp and other groups before helping to found the Blues Band, with which he still plays. (*Just Restless* Appaloosa; *Women In (E)Motion Festival* Traditional & Moderne)

vance KELLY (1954–)

This Chicago singer-guitarist attracted a great deal of attention with his 1994 album *Call Me* and its 1996 successor *Joyriding In The Subway*, where he applied his heartfelt style to blues and soul standards – he obviously admires Johnny Taylor and Little Milton – and to original compositions, with solid support on both discs by John Primer. Like Primer, he combines an enquiring eye for a song with a moderately conservative taste in sound, producing music that lives by the principles of classic Chicago bar blues yet is not enslaved by the past. Kelly had been playing on the club scene since he was 15 and had learned from guitarist Buddy Scott, but his most demanding apprenticeship was a stint playing guitar with A.C. Reed in 1987–90. Kelly plays regularly at the 1815 and Checkerboard clubs. (*Call Me*, *Joyriding In The Subway* Wolf)

willie KENT (1936–)

Though he had been playing bass in Chicago clubs since the 1950s, the Mississippi-born Kent did not put his music first until he was past 50. Following major heart surgery, he reconsidered his life, quit his day job driving trucks, and formed a band. His impassioned singing and the overall feel of his music are reminiscent of Byther Smith or John Primer, and *Too Hurt To Cry* (1994) is among the finest albums of the 1990s in what has been called the Chicago Traditionalist style. (*Ain't It Nice*, *Too Hurt To Cry* Delmark)

junior KIMBROUGH (1930–)

Until the early 1990s Kimbrough lived quietly in the Mississippi hill country, a singer-guitarist known only to specialists for a couple of poorly circulated singles and an

informally recorded track, 'In The City', on the English rock compilation *The Honky Tonk Demos* (Oval, 1979). Then came *All Night Long*, recorded live at his local club. His raw, repetitive style suggests an archaic forebear of John Lee Hooker, a character his music shares with that of his fellow north Mississippian R.L. Burnside. (*All Night Long* Fat Possum [US]/Demon [UK]; *Sad Days Lonely Nights* Fat Possum)

earl KING (1934–)

The moment Earl King opens his mouth you hear New Orleans, the crumbling wail of Professor Longhair or Snooks Eaglin. You also hear one of the niftiest songwriters in present-day blues, though the forms he uses go beyond strict blues structures ('Time For The Sun To Rise') and conventional subject

Earl King's songs have been recorded by Stevie Ray Vaughan, the Neville Brothers and Dr John.

matter ('Medieval Days'). He was born Earl Johnson in New Orleans, began recording at 19 with Huey "Piano" Smith, changed his name to King and had his first success with 'Those Lonely Lonely Nights' (Ace, 1955), a classic example of the New Orleans pop ballad. In the 1960s he wrote 'Trick Bag' and 'Big Chief', the latter popularized by Longhair, recorded for Motown (though the material was never issued) and filed many hours as a session guitarist. His Black Top albums are attractive showcases for his wit and ingenuity. (*Sexual Telepathy* Black Top [US]/Demon [UK]; *Hard River To Cross* Black Top)

freddie KING (1934–1976)

Freddie King may have been, for a time, the most far-reachingly influential of the Gang Of Four who redirected blues guitar traffic in the 1950s. Other musicians copied particular recipes of Magic Sam, Otis Rush and

Buddy Guy but tried to absorb the whole stylistic flavour of King's playing, exemplified alike by finger-snapping instrumentals such as 'Hideaway' and 'San-Ho-Zay', the powerful blues 'Have You Ever Loved A Woman' and the cavernously echoing 'It's Too Bad Things Are Going So Tough' and 'The Welfare Turns Its Back On You'. He recorded these and many other sides for the King subsidiary Federal between 1960 and 1964, occasionally obeying the promptings of the teenage market with tunes like 'Surf Monkey' and 'The Bossa Nova Watusi Twist'. In the late 1960s King cut a couple of slightly over-produced albums for Cotillion, and in the 1970s several for Shelter, mixing blues with compositions by Don Nix ('Same Old Blues') and Leon Russell. None of these albums was negligible, but they generally lacked the crispness of his earlier work. His last work for RSO, which he put together at the suggestion of his admirer Eric Clapton, was even less blues-orientated, but the numerous compilations of concert material that have been issued since his death indicate that in public he drew from an older and bluesier repertoire. (*Blues Guitar Hero* Ace; *King Of The Blues* EMI/Shelter)

KINSEY REPORT

This family group works on the progressive wing of the blues, promoting a music that reflects its members' unusual mixture of experience. They came together in 1984: singer-guitarist Donald Kinsey (1953–), his brothers Ralph (1952–) on drums and Kenneth (1963–) on bass, and rhythm guitarist Ron Prince (1956–). Blues had not been their first goal: Donald had played and recorded in the 1970s with Bob Marley and Peter Tosh, and had run his own reggae-tinged band with Ralph and Prince, the Chosen Ones. But even earlier he and Ralph had played with their father Lester "Big Daddy" Kinsey (1927–), a competent blues singer and guitarist in the Muddy Waters

mould. *Bad Situation* (Rooster Blues, 1984) introduced the whole family, but further albums split the generations, Big Daddy recording a couple of workmanlike sets for Verve while the Kinsey Report took its loud, sometimes overwrought music and unmemorable songs to Alligator and Pointblank. (Big Daddy Kinsey: *I Am The Blues, Ramblin' Man* Verve; The Kinsey Report: *Midnight Drive* Alligator, *Crossing Bridges* Pointblank)

eddie KIRKLAND (1928–)

Kirkland belonged to the small 1950s community of Detroit bluesmen. His first recorded work was with John Lee Hooker, playing guitar and occasionally singing on numerous Modern singles and the album *Don't Turn Me From Your Door*. His own *It's The Blues Man* (Tru-Sound, 1961) revealed him as a sort of Detroit Magic Sam, but soon afterwards he left the city for Macon in south Georgia (Jamaican by birth, he had been brought up in Alabama). He renewed his association with Hooker on the latter's *Simply The Truth* (1969); Hooker responded by guesting on *All Around The World* (1992). Kirkland has not fulfilled the promise of his early work: his clogged singing aside, he seems unable to find attractive and memorable material.

(*It's The Blues Man* Original Blues Classics; *All Around The World* Deluge [US]/Sky Ranch [France])

alexis KORNER (1928–1984)

Korner was the bossman of British blues in the 1950s and early 1960s. Not only was he one of the first British musicians to study the techniques of blues guitar-playing, but as a record collector, journalist and fan he gath-

An early 1960s line-up – one of many – of Alexis Korner's Blues Incorporated, with tenor saxophonist Art Themen.

ered and shared information on what was then an obscure and unfashionable music. Above all, he left his mark on the scene as a bandleader, providing playing opportunities in his group Blues Incorporated for the younger men who would form the Rolling Stones, Free, Led Zeppelin and many other blues-derived bands.

In the mid-1950s he was involved in the skiffle craze, playing guitar and mandolin with the jazz bandleaders Chris Barber and Ken Colyer, but it was with Cyril Davies (1932–1964), a harmonica player, guitarist and singer totally committed to the blues, that he made his most telling music, crystallized on *R&B From The Marquee* (Ace Of Clubs, 1962). Never content to do one thing for long, he investigated the blues-jazz borderlands with forward-looking jazz musicians like the saxophonist Dick Heckstall-Smith, drummer Phil Seamen and bassist Danny Thompson, moves illustrated in *Alexis Korner's Blues Incorporated* (Ace Of Clubs, 1965). In the late 1960s, displaced from the centre of blues activity by his protégés such as the Stones and John Mayall, he worked mostly in Europe with New Church and formed alliances with the Danish guitarist Peter Thorup and bass player Colin Hodgkinson. He had unexpected pop success in 1970 with the blues-rock big band CCS, and there were more bands to come, like Snape and Rocket 88, but in his last years he was better known as a free-thinking radio-show presenter and a honeyed voice-over in TV ads. (*A New Generation Of Blues, I Wonder Who* BGO; *The BBC Sessions* Music Club)

smokin' joe KUBEK (1956–)

Kubek's Dallas-based quartet, fronted by the twin guitars of Kubek and the Louisiana-born singer Bnois King, has a loyal following in the South-West for its tightly strung blues-rock. The band's energy has been channelled

since 1991 into five albums for Bullseye Blues which feature the two front-men's songs. (*Got My Mind Back* Bullseye Blues)

paul LAMB (1955–)

Since the beginning of the 1990s Lamb has had an unbroken run of winning the British Blues Connection's annual award for the best local harmonica player, while his King Snakes have frequently taken the title of best band. Born in Northumberland, Lamb was a teenage devotee of Sonny Terry and played only acoustic blues until about 1980, when he began working with the guitarist John Whitehill in an electric band and extended his self-tuition programme to include Walter Horton. Lamb and Whitehill continued to play together; their partners in the King Snakes are the singer and rhythm guitarist Chad Strentz, Jim Mercer (bass) and Martin Deegan (drums). (*Fine Condition, She's A Killer; Shifting Into Gear* Indigo)

LAZY LESTER (1933–)

When Lightnin' Slim exhorted a collaborator to "play your harmonica, son!", he was usually addressing Lazy Lester. After accompanying Slim with dexterity and feeling on many of his best-known numbers, Lester made his own splash as a singer in 1958 with the brisk rocker 'I'm A Lover Not A Fighter'. The reverse side, 'Sugar Coated Love', with its Jimmy Reedish vocal and echo-treated harmonica, was more typical of his approach. Leaving Louisiana (where he was born Leslie Johnson) and the Excello label in the mid-1960s, Lester moved, like Slim, to Michigan, where he restarted his career in the late

1980s. (*I'm A Lover Not A Fighter* Ace; *Harp & Soul* Alligator)

j.b. LENOIR (1929–1967)

Lenoir stood out among Chicago artists of the 1950s and 1960s with his clear, high voice, somewhat reminiscent of "Big Boy" Crudup, and his versatility as both writer and performer. Nobody since Big Bill Broonzy (one of his models) had encompassed both rocking, horn-driven band music like 'Mama Talk To Your Daughter' and the moving solo performances 'I Don't Care What Nobody Say' or 'I Been Down So Long'.

Lenoir's early life was spent in Mississippi and New Orleans. He arrived in

As a young man J.B. Lenoir fell under the patronage of Memphis Minnie and Big Maceo.

Uncomfortable typecast as a boogie-woogie and blues pianist, Meade Lux Lewis spent his later years playing rags and old-time pop songs.

Chicago at 20, and over the next decade recorded frequently for JOB, Chess/Checker and Parrot, causing a stir with the lyrics of 'Eisenhower Blues' (1954), which is said to have been withdrawn under government pressure. Supported by Willie Dixon, he recorded, in 1965, the mesmerizing *Alabama Blues!* (CBS), with unflinching descriptions of Southern racism in the title song, 'Move This Rope' and 'Born Dead'. The album was issued only in Europe, where he appeared that year with the AFBF. A second visit in 1966 consolidated his reputation overseas. His death after a road accident robbed the blues of a bold and articulate spokesman for social justice. In 1970 a further collection of songs was compiled by John Mayall; this and the original *Alabama Blues!* album have been reissued on *Vietnam Blues*. (*Natural Man* MCA/Chess; *The Topical Bluesman* Blues Encore; *Vietnam Blues* Evidence)

furry LEWIS (1893–1981)

Unlike many of his Memphis contemporaries, Furry Lewis was a natural loner, his music individual rather than collaborative, aimed at passers-by on the street rather than dancers. He lived long enough to become one of the city's blues characters, an entertainer and storyteller as much as a blues singer. He appeared in the Burt Reynolds movie *W.W. & The Dixie Dance Kings* (1975), on the *Tonight* show, even in *Playboy* magazine.

Born in Greenwood, Mississippi, he came to live in Memphis at the age of six. He lost a leg at 23, jumping a freight train. No doubt this inclined him towards a career in music, and he fell in with Memphis types like Jim Jackson and Gus Cannon, playing with

them on Beale Street for the roustabouts off the riverboats. Between 1927 and 1929 he recorded a couple of dozen pieces for Vocalion and Victor, mostly blues but including two-part versions of the blues-ballads 'Casey Jones' and 'John Henry'. He sometimes fingerpicked, sometimes played with a slide.

After 30 years of menial work Lewis had a second chance in the music business. He recorded albums for Folkways, Bluesville and at least half a dozen other labels, and briefly joined a touring rock revue, the Alabama State Troupers. Yet although he was famous to blues fans across the world he seldom worked in Memphis, living on his wages as a trash-collector or on welfare. (*In His Prime 1927–1928* Yazoo; *Fourth And Beale* Lucky Seven [US]/Verve [Europe])

meade lux LEWIS (1905–1964)

If one tune captures the unstoppable momentum of piano boogie-woogie, it's Meade Lux Lewis's thrilling composition 'Honky Tonk Train Blues'. He would be remembered for that alone, but his career was a long and productive one. Inventive, too: he transferred his pieces to harpsichord and celeste and occasionally exercised the rare skill of whistling the blues.

Chicago-born, Lewis was inspired to play by Jimmy Yancey. In his youth he worked, like Albert Ammons, as a taxi driver. The first 'Honky Tonk Train' appeared in 1927, but it was the 1935 version, commissioned from the producer John Hammond by a British label, that became the best-known. Other popular compositions include 'Bear Cat Crawl' and 'Yancey Special', dedicated to Lewis's first teacher, which was arranged for big band and recorded in 1938 by Bob Crosby (as was 'Honky Tonk Train'). In the late 1930s he worked frequently with Ammons and Pete Johnson, then in 1941 moved to the West Coast. He made several

Soundies (early music videos) in 1944, and appeared in the movies *New Orleans* (1947) and *Nightmare* (1956). (*Albert Ammons & Meade Lux Lewis: The First Day* Blue Note; *Meade Lux Lewis 1927–39, 1939–41, 1941–44* Classics)

smiley LEWIS (1913–1966)

In the 1950s Smiley Lewis was the unluckiest man in New Orleans. He hit on a formula for slow-rocking small-band numbers like 'The Bells Are Ringing' and, his career's biggest hit, 'I Hear You Knocking', only to have Fats Domino come up behind him with similar music more ingratiatingly delivered. Lewis was practically drowned in Domino's backwash.

Having made a judicious name-change – he was born Overton Amos Lemons – Lewis launched himself on the New Orleans scene in the late 1930s as a strolling café singer with a guitar. He recorded for DeLuxe and Imperial, where he worked with the producer Dave Bartholomew, and wrote and recorded 'Blue Monday' and 'One Night', later taken on with more success by Domino and Elvis Presley respectively. (*Shame Shame Shame* Bear Family; *I Hear You Knocking* EMI)

joe LIGGINS (1915–1987)

Liggins's infectious shuffle blues 'The Honeydripper' blanketed black jukeboxes in the closing months of World War II, topped *Billboard*'s R&B chart for many weeks and logged a reported two million sales. It was enough to establish him, but 'Pink Champagne' (1950) proved almost as successful. With Roy Milton, he was an architect of the small-band jump blues of the first post-war decade.

The Oklahoma-born pianist grew up in San Diego, California, where he studied arranging, and moved to L.A. in 1939 to work with Illinois Jacquet and other band-

leaders. In the mid-1940s he formed a combo with the saxophonist "Little" Willie Jackson, began recording and, on the strength of 'Honeydripper', filled a busy schedule for the next ten years. After a long period of relative inactivity he began to appear on the blues circuit in the 1970s, still in cahoots with Jackson. His guitar-playing brother Jimmy (1922–1983) also led a band with some success. (*Joe Liggins And The Honeydrippers* Ace)

LIGHTNIN' SLIM (1913–1974)

Slim's stock-in-trade had mostly fallen off the back of other artists' trucks, but by the time he came to sell it he had added touches of his own. Imagine Lightnin' Hopkins' music

Lightnin' Slim on stage during one of his 1970s visits to England.

former at folk and blues festivals, though to his foreign admirers' sorrow he never played outside the United States. (MR; *You Got To Reap What You Sow* Arhoolie)

LITTLE CHARLIE & THE NIGHTCATS

This good-humoured quartet has been popular in the San Francisco Bay area since the mid-1970s. Twenty years on, three of its founder members were still there: guitarist Charlie Baty (1953–), harmonica player, singer and songwriter Rick Estrin (1950–) and drummer Dobie Strange (1948–). The band has formulated a distinctive mixture of Chicago bar-band blues and a more laid-back West Coast manner reflected in Estrin's sleepy singing and left-field compositions like 'Homicide' or 'Smart Like Einstein'. *Night Vision* (1993) was produced and played on by Joe Louis Walker. (*Captured Live, Straight Up!* Alligator)

LITTLE MILTON (1934–)

The conventional critical judgement locates Milton about midway between Bobby Bland and B.B. King, which implies the range of his material reasonably accurately but may not convey his appeal to older black listeners, who remember sides like 'Grits And Groceries' and the inspirational 'We're Gonna Make It', an R&B chart-topper in 1965. No doubt that audience contributed to the success, 20-odd years later, of 'The Blues Is Alright'.

His career has taken him from Mississippi, where he was born Milton Campbell, to Memphis, where he cut slashing guitar blues for Sun and Meteor in the 1950s, thence to East St Louis, and in the 1960s to Chicago, where he joined Checker and extended his range with sides like 'If

galvanized by some of the Chicago oomph of Howlin' Wolf and Muddy Waters.

Otis Hicks by birth, Slim grew up in southern Louisiana and began singing and playing guitar around the Baton Rouge area in the late 1940s. He debuted on Jay Miller's Feature label in 1954 with 'Bad Luck' ("if it wasn't for bad luck, I wouldn't have no luck at all"), graduated the following year to Excello, and spent the next decade being regionally famous for songs like 'Rooster Blues', accompanied by local harmonica players such as Lazy Lester. Slim often adapted other people's numbers: 'Just Made Twenty One' was his 'Boogie Chillen'; 'I'm Grown' grew out of Muddy Waters' 'Manish Boy' (or Bo Diddley's 'I'm A Man'), and so on. The guitar intros were lifted from the Hopkins folio. He was popular in Europe and toured there several times, recording the unexciting *Blue Lightning*. (*It's Mighty Crazy, Nothin' But The Devil* Ace)

mance LIPSCOMB (1895–1976)

Though Lipscomb was 65 before he made a record, he had been playing for dances and other local functions in Navasota, Texas, since his teens, developing a muscular and reliable dance-guitar style. His father was an ex-slave and a fiddler, and Lipscomb learned fiddle too, though he never played it on record. What spread his name outside his home patch was the encounter with a couple of visiting music fans that led to his first album and the first release on Arhoolie. *Texas Songster* (1960) revealed how broad and catholic his repertoire was, and further sets for Arhoolie made that point in greater detail, Lipscomb happily turning from a blues number to 'It's A Long Way To Tipperary'. A man of great dignity and integrity, he made a natural subject for documentaries like Les Blank's *A Well Spent Life* (1971). He was also a popular per-

Walls Could Talk'. By the 1970s he was a comprehensively accomplished singer whether viewed from a blues or soul standpoint, but his commitment since then to recording for labels like Glades and Malaco, which cater to a chiefly black market, has stood in the way of wider recognition. (*If Walls Could Talk* MCA/Chess; *The Complete Stax Singles* Stax; *Live At Westville Prison* Delmark; *Greatest Hits* Malaco)

little willie LITTLEFIELD (1931–)

Littlefield made his name in his teens as a Houston club pianist and singer chasing the stylistic trail of Amos Milburn. The similarity won him a contract in 1949 with Modern and a hit with 'It's Midnight'. In 1952 he switched to Federal and cut 'K.C.

Lovin", the original canvas that was lightly repainted by the songwriters Leiber and Stoller to make the blues standard 'Kansas City'. From the 1950s to the 1970s he was based in California, but then moved to the Netherlands, where he has built a considerable European reputation with his vigorous boogie-woogie piano playing and smoky singing, and has recorded some half a dozen albums. (*Going Back to Kay Cee* Ace; *Paris Streetlights* EPM/Blues Collection)

robert LOCKWOOD (1915–)

Lockwood is connected to Robert Johnson even more closely than Johnny Shines, for Johnson was his stepfather and first guitar teacher. Since he is as much of an individualist as Shines, he has dealt briskly, sometimes brusquely, with the Johnson legend. It's typical that when he gave one of his infrequent album recitals of Johnson songs for *Plays Robert & Robert* (1983), he puckishly chose to use a 12-string guitar.

Originally from Marvell, Arkansas, in the 1940s Lockwood played with Sonny Boy Williamson II in his *King Biscuit Time* slot on the radio station KFFA. His broadcasts and appearances at station-sponsored events quickly brought him the reputation of a man to watch on guitar, a kind of T-Bone Walker for the Delta. He spent the 1950s in Chicago playing and recording with Little Walter, Sunnyland Slim and other artists but made few records in his own name. In 1961 he moved to Cleveland (his home ever since),

Robert Lockwood's first guitar was a $2.98 Gene Autry model. "Robert Johnson and me made my second."

emerging from this relative seclusion at intervals to make an overseas tour or a quirky album for Delmark or Trix. In the 1980s he and Shines worked together, their Rounder albums showing both men determinedly playing the music they were interested in rather than the familiar requests of the blues audience – an attitude Lockwood maintains. (*Mississippi Blues (1935–1951)* Wolf; *Steady Rollin' Man* Delmark; *Contrasts* Trix; *Plays Robert & Robert* Black & Blue)

LONESOME SUNDOWN (1928–1995)

It's a better name for a bluesman than the one he was born with, Cornelius Green, and it fitted his rather melancholic style. He began playing guitar seriously in his mid-twenties and in 1955 joined Clifton Chenier's band, but what he really wanted was to sing:

he had a voice as warm and dry as Arizona. His first record, 'Lost Without Love', had a solemn guitar intro that he would repeat on 'My Home Is A Prison', 'I Stood By' and several later sides. Between 1956 and 1964 he recorded these and other tough slow blues ('Lonesome Lonely Blues', 'Hoo Doo Woman Blues') for Excello. His producer Jay Miller encouraged him to try different material but he lacked the light touch needed for jovial things like 'I'm A Samplin' Man'. As a session musician who worked with him recalled, "When he'd do a blues number, everybody stopped what they were doing and listened."

In 1965 Sundown quit music for the ministry. Twelve years later he cut the fine *Been Gone Too Long* and did a little performing with Phillip Walker, including a tour of Sweden, but then walked away from it again. There were no further comebacks. (*The Best*

Of The Excello Singles Excello; *Been Gone Too Long* Hightone)

joe hill LOUIS (1921–57)

As a one-man band, playing guitar, harmonica and a cut-down drum kit, Louis was one of Memphis' prime attractions in the 1940s and 1950s. He attracted the attention of Sun Records' Sam Phillips, who recorded him on several occasions, but he also made sides for Columbia, Modern and Checker, and had a show on the radio station WDIA. His raw, stomping music, epitomized by titles like 'A Jumpin' And A Shufflin'' and 'Boogie In The Park', left its mark on Dr Ross. (*The Be-Bop Boy* Bear Family)

LOUISIANA RED (1936–)

It seems odd to call Red an individualist, when so much of his energy has been devoted to raiding the legacies of Muddy Waters and Lightnin' Hopkins. Nonetheless it's true: his borrowings may be blatant but they serve a personal, if eccentric, vision. No mere copier would have been adventurous enough to try and fuse blues with the urban Greek music of the bouzouki player Stelios Vamvakaris, as he did on *From Blues To Rembetika* (Diastazi, 1994).

Mississippi-born but a wanderer since his childhood, Iverson Minter hit Chicago in his teens and recorded for Checker (1952) as Rocky Fuller. *The Lowdown Back Porch Blues* (Roulette, 1962) startled blues fans with its accomplished pastiches, varied guitar- and harmonica-playing and the straight-talking topical song 'Ride On Red, Ride On', but Red drifted in and out of music and did not make a firm impact on the scene until the late 1970s. A true internationalist, he has performed all over Europe, recording

Tennessee born, Joe Hill Louis learned from Memphis veterans like Will Shade.

"I'm a guitar king, singin' the blues everywhere I go," said Tommy McClennan on a 1941 recording, adding to himself, "Lord have mercy now!"

tommy McCLENNAN (1908–1962)

With his loose, the-hell-with-it approach, country through and through, McClennan might have seemed the last sort of bluesman to challenge city dudes like Tampa Red or Lonnie Johnson. Yet the compact singer-guitarist from Yazoo City, Mississippi, made an immediate impact in 1940 with his recordings of 'New "Shake 'Em On Down"', 'Bottle It Up And Go', 'Whiskey Head Woman' and 'New Highway No. 51'. It was raucous, foot-stomping juke-joint music, without much technical subtlety. "He had a different style of playing a guitar," Big Bill Broonzy remarked drily. "You just make the chords and change when you feel like changing." McClennan worked with the very similar-sounding Robert Petway, and can be heard shouting in the background on Petway's 1942 recording 'Boogie Woogie Woman'. After making 40 sides in a little over two years, including the first version of 'Cross Cut Saw Blues', later done by Albert King, McClennan faded into the Chicago background, though he was reportedly still playing occasional club dates in the 1950s. (*Travelin' Highway Man* Travelin' Man; *Tommy McClennan 1939–1942* Wolf)

charlie McCOY (1909–1950)

For most of the 1930s, as well as being a reliable and much employed studio guitarist, Charlie McCoy was the only mandolin player in Chicago with the flexibility required of a session musician, and his jazzy lines sparkled in many blues settings. His huge recording log begins with his sensitive guitar accompaniments to Tommy Johnson and Ishman Bracey in 1928, when he was still based in his home town of Jackson,

absorbing albums of his candid songs in England, Germany, Poland, Greece and very likely elsewhere. (*The Lowdown Back Porch Blues* Sequel; *Midnight Rambler* Charly; *Blues For Ida B* JSP)

willie MABON (1925–1985)

In sharp contrast to the brash, assertive music of Muddy Waters and Howlin' Wolf, Mabon offered the blues audience of the early 1950s a sly, confidential voice and an urbane piano. From Memphis, he came to Chicago in his teens, hoping to succeed as a jazz-club pianist. His 1953 debut single for Chess, 'I Don't Know', which he picked up from the older boogie-woogie pianist Cripple Clarence Lofton (1896–1957), was a runaway hit, chased to the top of the chart in the same year by 'I'm Mad', and nearly as far in 1954 by 'Poison Ivy'. After a lull he repeated the process more modestly in the early 1960s with 'Just Got Some' and 'I'm The Fixer'. In later years he found appreciative audiences in Europe and settled in Paris, where he died. His coolly humorous, slightly effeminate style greatly impressed the English R&B singer and keyboard player Georgie Fame. (*I Don't Know* Wolf Blues Jewels)

"Kansas Joe" McCoy, serious as a bible salesman in his 1920s photographs with Memphis Minnie, looked more cheerful in this 1934 publicity shot.

Mississippi. Even as a teenager he had a formidable reputation as a stringed instrumentalist. At the age of 20 he cut a series of sparkling mandolin showpieces, masked by the unrevealing group-name of the Mississippi Mud Steppers – probably an offshoot of the Mississippi Sheiks, with whom he also recorded. Soon afterwards he left for Chicago, where, when not recording, he sometimes played with his brother Joe and the singer-guitarist Johnny Temple in a string band that entertained the gangleader Al Capone with Italian polkas.

He made a couple of dozen sides in his own name, others under pseudonyms (The Mississippi Mudder, Georgia Pine Boy, Tampa Kid, Papa Charlie) and many more as a member of the Harlem Hamfats. His composition 'Too Long' was recorded several times by both black and white artists.

(*Charlie McCoy 1928–1932*, *The McCoy Brothers (Charlie & Joe McCoy) Vol 1 (1934–1936)*, *Vol 2 (1936–1944)* RST/Blues Documents)

Joe McCOY (1905–50)

The first stage of Joe McCoy's career was as the partner, in life and music, of Memphis Minnie (see Blues Legends). After their separation in the mid-1930s, McCoy kept up a busy schedule, singing with the Harlem

Hamfats, writing songs for them ('Oh! Red') and other artists, and from time to time recording in his own right, though not necessarily in his own name: like his brother Charlie he ducked for cover behind pseudonyms (Bill Wilber, Georgia Pine Boy, The Mississippi Mudder). He also recorded sermons under the sobriquet Hallelujah Joe, though it's not known whether he did so out of personal conviction or in order to re-enter the world of secular music with his composition 'Hallelujah Joe Ain't Preaching No More'. In the early 1940s he led a modernistic band, Big Joe and His Rhythm, with Charlie on mandolin and the unrelated Robert Lee McCoy (Robert Nighthawk) on harmonica. (*The McCoy Brothers (Charlie & Joe McCoy) Vol 1 (1934–1936), Vol 2 (1936–1944)* RST/Blues Documents)

jimmy McCRACKLIN (1921–)

Much of McCracklin's reputation lies in the small print of composer credits, after titles like 'Think', 'Just Got To Know', 'Tramp' and 'Every Night, Every Day', insinuating bluesy numbers with tenacious melodic hooks. It's easy to be unaware, since so little of his work is currently represented on CD, that he has a history as a recording artist that's half a century long.

McCracklin made his home in L.A. after World War II, had a short career as a boxer and began making records, contemplative piano-accompanied blues harking back to the 1930s style of Walter Davis. Over the next decade he was a kind of second-string Lowell Fulson, singing in a bone-dry voice while leading jump-blues combos from the piano. The strolling bass-and-drums riff and teenage lyrics of 'The Walk' (Checker) gave him a Top Ten pop hit in 1958, and although

"I can watch a guy work, listen to how he pronounce his words," says Jimmy McCracklin, "and I can tell just how to fit that guy with a song."

his other successes did not cross over like that, they did very respectably in the R&B charts, both for him and later for Fulson, Otis Redding and other singers. In the 1960s and 1970s, by then reckoned a soul rather than blues artist, he made fine albums for Imperial and the splendid *Yesterday Is Gone* (Stax, reissued as *High On The Blues*), but the next decade was quieter, and few expected his spirited return to the blues-soul

stage with *My Story* (1991). He continues to write for old friends like Fulson. (*High On The Blues* Stax; *My Story, A Taste Of The Blues* Bullseye Blues)

larry McCRAY (1960–)

With his debut album *Ambition* (Pointblank, 1990) McCray was touted as the blues' next move after Robert Cray – a difficult billing to

Larry McCray learned guitar from his sister. "She used to play real low-down and dirty."

live up to, and one that failed to impress old blues hands distrustful of high-gloss production values sprayed on to unmemorable material. At the time McCray was living in Detroit, where his family had moved from Arkansas when he was 12. His later albums for Pointblank and Atomic Theory have been patchy – the female vocal trio on the latter adds a flavour of diluted Manhattan Transfer that simply doesn't blend in – but at least they give plenty of space to his venomous guitar-playing, which can also be heard, perhaps to better effect, on James Cotton's *Living The Blues* (Verve, 1994) and Larry Garner's *Baton Rouge* (Verve, 1995). (*Delta Hurricane* Pointblank; *Meet Me At The Lake* Atomic Theory)

fred McDOWELL (1904–1972)

McDowell spent much of his life in farm work, but played occasionally around northern Mississippi and south-west Tennessee. Revealed to blues aficionados by Alan Lomax's 1959–60 field recordings, he was drawn on to the folk-festival circuit in 1963 and recorded LPs for Arhoolie, Testament and Milestone. He visited Europe with the AFBF in 1965 and solo in 1969. In the US he was a campus favourite but still played in his own community, accompanying singing groups in church.

Unlike many musicians McDowell made a reputation unassisted by revered vintage recordings. From local tradition and standard repertoire he synthesized a musical approach of considerable originality. Playing mostly with a steel slide, he piled impetuous decorations on top of hypnotic bass figures in personalized versions of 'Kokomo' and 'Louise' or his own 'Write Me A Few Lines'. When he used electric guitar he exchanged some delicacy of touch for an even more resounding beat. His style and charm attracted numerous white blues musicians, in particular Bonnie Raitt and Jo Ann and Dave Kelly. (MR; *I Do Not Play No Rock 'N' Roll* Capitol)

sticks McGHEE (1918–1961)

Brownie McGhee's less suave sibling, Sticks (or Stick) was a singer-guitarist who played with his brother in New York in the 1940s before enjoying a big hit (No. 2 on the R&B chart) with 'Drinkin' Wine, Spo-Dee-O-Dee' (Atlantic, 1949). Brownie played (and sang) on this record, and continued to work with him in the studio alongside other members of

the New York blues set, such as Sonny Terry and the pianists "Big Chief" Ellis and Harry "Van" Walls, but Sticks had no further success, despite moving to King and Savoy. His crisp guitar may be heard on some of Terry's 1947 Capitol sessions. (*New York Blues* Ace)

blind willie McTELL (1901–1959)

The blues offers no experience like the first encounter with McTell. With his high, clear voice, animated by laughter or sadness and cushioned by vibrant 12-string guitar playing, he seems somehow more present than many dead-and-gone blues figures. His

songs have been taken up by Taj Mahal and the Allman Brothers, while his name stands at the top of an extraordinary composition by Bob Dylan.

He grew up in Statesboro, Georgia – for which he named one of his finest blues – and after attending a couple of schools for the blind, made his living as an itinerant street musician. He had a knack of being around when field-recording units visited Atlanta, and between 1927 and 1935 recorded almost 50 issued sides for five labels. (Another dozen or so have been retrieved from the vaults and issued since his death.) His range encompassed slide-guitar blues ('Mama, 'Tain't Long Fo' Day'), boastful rag songs ('Southern Can Is Mine') and gospel songs like 'Ain't It Grand To Be A Christian', a duet with his wife Kate. In 1940 he gave a superb set of songs, blues-ballads, gospel numbers and reminiscences to John A. Lomax for the Library of Congress. His nose for opportunity no less keen in later life, he made further recordings for Atlantic and Regal around 1949 and a typically varied and fascinating last session for a local admirer in 1956. (MR; *Library Of Congress Recordings* RST/Blues Documents; *Last Session* Original Blues Classics)

MAGIC SAM (1937–1969)

"Magic Sam had a different guitar sound," said his producer Willie Dixon. "Most of the guys were playing the straight 12-bar blues thing, but the harmonies that he carried with the chords was a different thing altogether. This tune 'All Your Love', he expressed with such an inspirational feeling with his high voice. You could always tell him, even from his introduction to the music."

Sam was 20 when he cut 'All Your Love'. It is young man's blues, passionate and

Magic Sam (right) and Homesick James Williamson, with whom he worked in the 1950s.

romantic, turbulent and ambitious. He had things to say and, though he did not know it, not long to say them in. 'All Your Love' and the following year's 'Easy Baby', both on the Cobra label, never appeared on the charts yet they had a profound influence, far beyond Chicago's guitarists and singers. Together with the records of Otis Rush (also a Cobra artist) and Buddy Guy, they made a manifesto for a new kind of blues.

The Mississippi-born Sam Maghett had been in Chicago since his teens, taking in the music of Muddy Waters and B.B. King, working briefly with Homesick James Williamson. After the Cobra sides he recorded singles for Chief and a couple of other labels, but it was not until he cut *West Side Soul* and *Black Magic* in the late 1960s that he again found the right setting for his lean, hard, wind-chilled West Side blues. How he would have responded to the changing winds of later music we can only guess. (MR; *West Side Soul, Black Magic, Magic Sam Live, Give Me Time* Delmark)

MAGIC SLIM (1937–)

It's no accident that Morris Holt's professional name echoes another man's. He and Magic Sam were boyhood friends in Grenada, Mississippi, and they met again in Chicago in 1955. Deputizing one night for Sam's missing bass player, he was rewarded with the sobriquet Magic Slim. "You keep that name," Sam advised, "It's going to make you famous one day."

It took a while. At first Slim was not rated very highly by his peers. He returned to Mississippi to work and got his younger brother Nick interested in playing bass. By 1965 he was back in Chicago and in 1970 Nick joined him in his group, the Teardrops; four years later they added the guitarist Junior Pettis. Now people were talking approvingly about Slim's "straight no-nonsense blues", which was documented in the

late 1970s on albums for the French labels MCM and Black & Blue and on a few tracks in Alligator's *Living Chicago Blues* series. *Grand Slam* (Rooster Blues, 1982), Slim's best album, shows the Teardrops' dedication to the sound of the Muddy Waters band, but later sets for Wolf with John Primer, who joined at the end of 1982, also catch Slim's solid, unprogressive music well. In 1994 he moved to Lincoln, Nebraska, where the Zoo Bar had been booking him for years. *Scufflin'* (1996) presents the post-Primer line-up with guitarist-singer Jake Dawson. (*Raw Magic* Alligator; *Chicago Blues Session Vol 3* Wolf; *Scufflin'* Blind Pig)

john MAYALL (1933–)

Not all musical skills have to do with playing or singing. Assembling and maintaining a band, replenishing it when people leave, creating a musical and social climate in which musicians grow and help each other to grow – these abilities too are vital in any collaborative music. Mayall is not much of a singer (or guitarist, or pianist, or harmonica player), but over three decades he has well earned his reputation as a bandleader by hiring and encouraging some of the foremost names in modern blues, from Eric Clapton, Peter Green and Mick Taylor to Walter Trout and Coco Montoya.

In his youth in Macclesfield, Cheshire, he listened to his father's jazz records; soon he was forming his own collection of blues. He learned piano and guitar, got a band together and moved to London, on the advice of Alexis Korner, in 1963. He led several line-ups of the Bluesbreakers before hiring Clapton from the Yardbirds in 1965. The guitarist stayed a litle over a year before joining the bassist Jack Bruce (another ex-Bluesbreaker) to found Cream. He was succeeded by Green, who played on *Hard Road* (Decca, 1967), then by Taylor, who can be heard on the same year's *Crusade*, but by

1968 Mayall was tiring of his moderately authentic blues approach. He was tinkering with blues-jazz fusions and writing more of his own material, a stance he held throughout the 1970s, chiefly based in the United States and working with American musicians like the guitarist Harvey Mandel. In 1988 a new Bluesbreakers with guitarists Trout and Montoya produced *Chicago Line* (1988), and the refreshed energy of that album has been maintained on *Wake Up Call* (1993) and *Spinning Coin* (1995). (MR; *Blues From Laurel Canyon* Deram; *The Turning Point* BGO; *Wake Up Call, Spinning Coin, Blues For The Lost Days* Silvertone)

percy MAYFIELD (1920–1984)

The composer of 'Hit The Road, Jack' and other hits for Ray Charles, as well as the R&B standards 'Please Send Me Someone To Love' and 'River's Invitation', Mayfield was also a subtle singer in the laid-back West Coast manner. In the early 1950s he had some success with downbeat songs of love gone wrong like 'Two Years Of Torture', 'Strange Things Happening', 'Lost Love', 'The Big Question' and 'Memory Pain', the original behind John Lee Hooker's 'It Serves Me Right To Suffer'. Scarred by a road accident, he retired from public performing and worked for Charles, issuing an occasional communiqué to his admirers like *My Jug And I* (Tangerine). A trip to Europe in 1982 produced a delectable album of night-time blues, *Hit The Road Again* (Timeless), sensitively backed by the Phillip Walker band. (*Poet Of The Blues* Ace)

MEMPHIS JUG BAND

The original line-up of this prolific and fascinatingly fluid group, formed in 1926 by Will Shade (1898–1965), consisted of Will Weldon on guitar, Ben Ramey, kazoo, and Charlie Polk, jug; Shade himself played ser-

viceable guitar and attractive harmonica, and they all shared the singing. Shade had been spurred to action by the jugbands in Louisville, Kentucky, which had already been recording for a few years, and he quickly solicited the interest of Victor, which sent a recording team to Memphis in February 1927. The MJB were first at the microphone.

The personnel changed continuously over the band's nearly four years with Victor, drawing in the mandolin player Vol Stevens, tenor guitarist Charlie Burse, fiddler Milton Roby, singer Charlie Nickerson and several other musicians. Their repertoire expanded from the rather plain blues of their early sessions to embrace waltzes, rag songs and glee-club harmony numbers like 'Stealin' Stealin'', 'On The Road Again' (later performed by Canned Heat) and the poignant 16-bar blues 'K.C. Moan'.

Their last sides, for OKeh in 1934, featured hectic fiddling by Charlie Pierce and Jab Jones's piano in the hottest dance music they ever recorded. It was the final flourish of the jugband era on disc, but the MJB still had places to play: "picnics, elections, for people won a race, and parties of that kind. People who drink and have a good time – mostly the jugband plays for that", remembered a contemporary, adding, "When they don't get drunk, there's not much pep in them." Shade stayed as active as he could, and made a few last, shaky recordings with Burse and Gus Cannon not long before he died. (*Memphis Jug Band* Yazoo)

MEMPHIS SLIM (1915–1988)

In France Memphis Slim was an ambassador for the blues just as Sidney Bechet was for jazz. One of the first blues musicians to emigrate, he was followed by Curtis Jones, Eddie Boyd, Willie Mabon, Mickey Baker and others, though tactfully none of those who were pianists stayed around Paris long enough to discommode the Artist in Residence.

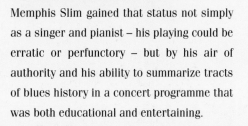

Memphis Slim gained that status not simply as a singer and pianist – his playing could be erratic or perfunctory – but by his air of authority and his ability to summarize tracts of blues history in a concert programme that was both educational and entertaining.

Born Peter Chatman in Memphis, at 22 he came to Chicago, worked with Big Bill Broonzy and made his first records. 'Beer Drinking Woman', a 1940 hit, found him soaked in the work of Roosevelt Sykes, an influence he was still working off during a busy and productive period from 1947 to 1954, when he recorded his philosophical song 'Mother Earth'. In the 1950s he also made the first entries in what became a vast log of albums, mostly solo blues recitals with an occasional boogie-woogie venture, though *At The Gate Of Horn* (Vee Jay, 1959) gave a rare impression of his club act with a punchy band. In autumn 1961 he settled in Paris. A key contact for the AFBF, he played

For a few years in the 1950s Amos Milburn was featured in touring "Rock 'n' Roll Caravans" and movie musicals such as *Basin Street Revue*.

on the 1962 and 1963 tours. Over the next couple of decades he travelled all over Europe and recorded, among his dozens of albums, urbane meetings with Buddy Guy, Mickey Baker and Roosevelt Sykes. (*The Complete Recordings 1940–1941* EPM/Blues Collection; *Rockin' The Blues* Charly; *Raining The Blues* Ace)

amos MILBURN (1926–1980)

Milburn is an important marker on the map of black music in the first decade after World War II. His high-energy numbers about getting high turned on the lights for a decade-long party, jointly celebrated with his acolytes Little Willie Littlefield, Floyd Dixon and Fats Domino.

After wartime army service he returned to play music in his home town of Houston, but the huge success of his hipster's romp 'Chicken Shack Boogie' in 1948 made him a black national hero; he was *Billboard's* Top R&B Artist in both 1949 and 1950. Among further hits were 'Bad Bad Whiskey' (1950) and 'One Scotch, One Bourbon, One Beer' (1953), a favourite of John Lee Hooker, but after the mid-1950s his recordings increasingly reflected the sound of his disciple Domino, while his day-to-day work became ever seedier. In 1972, incapacitated by a stroke, Milburn returned to Houston. His last recording was an album for Johnny Otis, who had to play the left-hand piano parts for his enfeebled old friend. (*Blues, Barrelhouse And Boogie Woogie 1946–1955* Capitol)

roy MILTON (1907–1983)

Drummer, singer and bandleader, Milton, like his contemporary Joe Liggins, poured his musical ideas into the mould fashioned by Louis Jordan, to produce the low-cost big sound of early post-war jump blues.

He spent his youth in Tulsa, Oklahoma, and in the early 1930s worked with bandleader Ernie Fields, before going west and forming his own band, the Solid Senders, in L.A. in 1938. Its core members included saxmen Buddy Floyd (tenor) and Jackie Kelso (alto) and the flashy boogie-woogie pianist Camille Howard, and it condensed the sound of a big band into a six- or seven-piece combo. Their recording 'R.M. Blues' for Juke Box (an antecedent of Specialty) topped the R&B chart for half of 1946, a start that would keep Milton in the R&B race until the mid-1950s, when he went into the same downhill skid as virtually every other R&B act and soon afterwards retired. Encouraged by Johnny Otis, he made a comeback in the 1970s and recorded albums for Kent, Otis's Blues Spectrum label and, in France, for Black & Blue. (*Roy Milton & His Solid Senders* Ace)

MISSISSIPPI SHEIKS

On records, the Sheiks were usually the fiddler Lonnie Chatmon (dates unknown) and singer-guitarist Walter Vincson (1901–1975), occasionally joined by Lonnie's brothers Sam and Bo (Carter). In public they may often have included further Chatmon family members, the mandolinist Charlie McCoy and possibly other players from the Jackson, Mississippi vicinity. The records are probably delusive evidence of their repertoire, too, being predominantly blues like their 1930 hits 'Stop And Listen Blues' (derived from Tommy Johnson's 'Big Road Blues') and 'Sitting On Top Of The World', whereas eyewitnesses remember Lonnie Chatmon as a fine hoedown and waltz fiddler.

The Sheiks and related groups under other names, such as the Mississippi Mud Steppers and Blacksnakes, recorded about a hundred sides in the first half of the 1930s, among them original compositions (probably by Vincson) like 'The World Is Going Wrong' and 'I've Got Blood In My Eyes For You' (1931) – both recorded since by Bob Dylan – or the topical 'Sales Tax' (1934). Lonnie Chatmon then disappears from blues history, but Vincson made further recordings, including some in the 1960s and 1970s under the Sheiks' name but with little of the old sound. (*Stop And Listen* Yazoo)

little brother MONTGOMERY (1906–1985)

Little Brother was a fascinating man: a pianist of enormous range and memory, equally ready to play with an electric blues barrd or a Dixieland jazz group; a singer with an immediately recognizable, rather affecting wobble; an oral historian as full of musical anecdotes as Jelly Roll Morton. As

Roy Milton at Marco's Café, Los Angeles, 1942, with Luke Jones (tenor sax), Betty Hall Jones (piano) and Forrest Powell (trumpet).

so often, records are clues to only part of the story.

He began playing in his boyhood in the logging-camp barrelhouses of his native Louisiana, Mississippi and Texas, reaching Chicago in his 20s and cutting the first version of his classic piece 'Vicksburg Blues' in 1930. A long session in New Orleans in 1936

produced fine blues and the sparkling rag instrumental 'Farish Street Jive'.

Over the next half-century Brother would record many more blues and play on numerous sessions by younger bluesmen such as Magic Sam and Otis Rush, but his diary was just as likely to list engagements with jazz bands, at piano bars or accompanying singers of show tunes. He visited Europe quite often in the 1960s and 1970s, cutting several of his 20-odd albums there. (*Little Brother Montgomery (1930–1936)* Document; *Tasty Blues* Original Blues Classics; *Blues Masters Vol 7* Storyville; *Goodbye Mister Blues* Delmark; *Bajes Copper Station* Blues Beacon)

whistling alex MOORE (1899–1989)

Moore was so odd a performer that some newcomers to blues have been uncertain whether to take him wholly seriously. By the time he became moderately well known on the international blues scene of the 1960s and 1970s, his always singular style had

burgeoned into florid eccentricity and he would reminisce tirelessly in a foggy half-shout about youthful high times back in his home town of Dallas, over skipping blues and boogie-woogie piano patterns with occasional bursts of shrill whistling. But he remembered and sang again the blues he had recorded in the 1920s and 1930s like 'West Texas Woman' and 'Blue Bloomer Blues', with their touching and sometimes arrestingly poetic lyrics. (*Whistlin' Alex Moore (1929–1951)* Document; *From North Dallas To The East Side* Arhoolie; *Wiggle Tail* Rounder)

Buddy Moss blows and Brownie McGhee picks at the 1969 Newport Folk Festival.

johnnie b. MOORE (1950–)

Moore's name first came to most blues-lovers' attention in the late 1970s when he was playing guitar in Koko Taylor's band, for instance on *The Earthshaker* (Alligator, 1978), though Chicagoans knew him already as a Magic Sam devotee. Born in Clarksdale, Mississippi, he came to Chicago in his teens and was encouraged by Letha Jones, widow of the pianist Little Johnny Jones. After years of scuffling on the club scene he made an impressive debut with *Hard Times* (B.L.U.E.S., 1987), but a decade on he was still one of Chicago's interesting secrets. (*Lonesome Blues* Wolf; *Live At Blue Chicago* Delmark)

buddy MOSS (1914–1984)

By his mid-teens the Georgia-born Moss was playing harmonica round Atlanta, and his first recordings were on that instrument with Barbecue Bob in a group called the Georgia Cotton Pickers (1930). Three years later he debuted on disc in his own name, now playing guitar in a style that occasionally – and sometimes, as in 'Daddy Don't Care' or 'Prowling Woman', broadly – hinted that he had been listening to Blind Blake. Though the record industry was struggling in the Depression, Moss cut over 40 sides in 1933–34, before Blind Boy Fuller, to whom he is sometimes likened, had even begun recording – which suggests that he had more

of a hand in forming Fuller's style than has been acknowledged. The fact that from 1935 onwards Moss's sound grew much closer to Fuller's, particularly on his 1941 sides with Brownie McGhee and Sonny Terry, probably indicates that Moss knew which way the wind of public taste was blowing, and obligingly turned with it.

His tracks were lost in the 1950s – it would turn out that he had been playing with his old buddy Curley Weaver – but he reappeared in the mid-1960s and performed in public sporadically over the next decade or so. He consented to make only one album, for Biograph in 1966. (*Buddy Moss Vols 1–3* Document)

matt "guitar" MURPHY (1929–)

While there may be some argument about how good a turn the movie *The Blues Brothers* did for the blues brothers, there is no doubt that it radically improved the prospects of Matt "Guitar" Murphy. It should not have had to: even in his early twenties he was recognized by his peers as a guitarist of unusual skill and imagination. But somehow his career never really got going.

He grew up in Memphis, absorbing guitar ideas from his aunt's record collection; he particularly liked the playing of the Moore brothers, Johnny with Charles Brown and Oscar with Nat King Cole. In the early 1950s he played with Howlin' Wolf and Junior Parker, though it was his brother Floyd, a capable guitarist himself, who played on Parker's Sun sides like 'Mystery Train'.

By 1952 Murphy was in Chicago, where he began a long association with Memphis Slim by playing, remarkably, on his dates for United and Vee Jay, including the exciting album *At The Gate Of Horn* (1959). He joined the 1963 AFBF and contributed to Sonny Boy Williamson II's Storyville albums. For the next 15 years or so he kept a low profile, till *The Blues Brothers* (1980)

offered him the chance to play himself, Aretha Franklin's husband and a heap of guitar. Work thereafter with the Blues Brothers Band turned him into one of the best-known blues guitarists in the United States. He played on albums for Antone's by Slim and James Cotton, and finally in 1990 made his own album debut, aided by Floyd, on *Way Down South*. (*Way Down South* Antone's; *The Blues Don't Bother Me!* Roesch)

charlie MUSSELWHITE (1944–)

If you insist on credentials, Musselwhite has them to spare. Originally from northern

"Hello, Belgium!" Matt Murphy in Europe in 1991. Freddie King once apologized to him for using his ideas in his famous instrumental 'Hideaway'.

Mississippi, he grew up in Memphis and learned harmonica and guitar from jugband doyen Will Shade. At 18 he moved to Chicago, where he hung out with senior bluesmen like Big Joe Williams and Johnny Young and refined his harmonica technique by listening to Little Walter, Walter Horton and Junior Wells. Having played on John Hammond's Vanguard album *Big City Blues* he made four albums of his own for the label in 1966–69, following them with two excel-

lent early-1970s sets for Arhoolie (reissued on *Memphis Charlie*). After a quiet spell he produced *Ace Of Harps* (1990), the first of several imaginatively produced Alligator albums. John Lee Hooker makes a guest appearance on *Signature* (1991), perhaps in exchange for Musselwhite's on *The Healer*, while *In My Time* (1993) features a variety of settings, including some blues and gospel songs with his own guitar. The blues writer Pete Welding, who provided the notes for that album as he had for Musselwhite's first, 27 years before, rightly concluded that "he's absorbed and transcended all of his influences . . . his music is now fully matured."

After Kenny Neal toured Africa in 1993, a Kenyan musician said, "We're all blues fans now!"

(*Stand Back! Here Comes Charley Musselwhite's South Side Band* Vanguard; *Memphis Charlie* Arhoolie; *Ace Of Harps* Alligator)

kenny NEAL (1957–)

Neal preserves the "swamp blues" sound of his native south Louisiana, as befits someone who learned from Slim Harpo, Buddy Guy and his father, the harmonica player Raful Neal (1936–). Adept on guitar and harmonica, he sings with murky, reptilian confidentiality. In 1991 he also proved to be a talented actor in the Broadway production of the folk musical *Mule Bone* (by Langston Hughes and Zora Neale Hurston), singing numbers written by Taj Mahal. (*Big News From Baton Rouge, Walking On Fire, Bayou Blood, Hoodoo Moon* Alligator)

robert NIGHTHAWK (1909–1967)

An influential background figure through three decades, Nighthawk was a strong but dour singer and a weighty, deliberate slide guitar player, like a slower-thinking Tampa Red. Born Robert Lee McCullum in Helena, Arkansas, he moved to St Louis in the mid-1930s and recorded for Bluebird as Robert Lee McCoy. He also accompanied Sonny Boy Williamson I and other artists, using both guitar and harmonica. In Chicago in the late 1940s and early 1950s, now using the name Robert Nighthawk (probably derived from his song 'Prowling Night-Hawk'), he had a little success with Tampa Red's 'Black Angel Blues' (Aristocrat) and other sides, but his constant shifting back and forth between Chicago and his Southern haunts made him a poor prospect for fame. As late as 1964 he could be found playing on Chicago's Maxwell Street. (*Robert Lee McCoy (1937–1940)* Wolf; *Live On Maxwell Street* Rounder)

THE NIGHTHAWKS

The Nighthawks were one of the most exciting blues bands of the 1970s and 1980s, working chiefly in the eastern United States. Created in 1972 by the guitarist Jimmy Thackery (1953–) and harmonica player Mark Wenner (1948–), with Jan Zukowski on bass and Pete Ragusa, drums, the band made its name in Washington, D.C., and was soon respected enough to accompany leading blues artists in person and on record. Chicago blues traditionalists at first, as demonstrated on *Open All Night* (Adelphi, 1976), the Nighthawks gradually found their own voice and material, as in *Jacks & Kings 'Full House'* (Adelphi, 1979), with guest appearances by Muddy Waters' sidemen Pinetop Perkins and Bob Margolin (1949–),

Omar Dykes calls his brand of music "deep South three-chord and tumble blues".

and in the 1983 anniversary set *Ten Years Live*. Thackery left in 1985 to head his own groups, most recently the Drivers, and record for Blind Pig. With various front-line personnel changes, the Nighthawks continued into the 1990s. (*Open All Night* Gene's; *Ten Years Live* Varrick)

st louis jimmy ODEN (1903–1977)

Oden is a rare bird: he specialized in writing blues, as much for other artists as for himself. Among his known songs – he may have sold others and lost his composer's credit – are 'Can't Stand Your Evil Ways', 'Bad Condition', 'Poor Boy Blues' and his big money number, 'Going Down Slow', versions of which run into dozens. He himself recorded it at least eight times. When singing he delivered his blues as a serious man's reflections on life as it is.

Born James B. Oden in Nashville, he moved in his teens to St Louis, where he hung out with Roosevelt Sykes, and in 1933 to Chicago. His recording career was fitful: after cutting some of his major songs for Bluebird in the 1940s he turned up on various Chicago labels including JOB, which he part-owned, but never met with much success. After a serious road accident in 1957 he devoted himself to writing and placed material with Muddy Waters, Howlin' Wolf and John Lee Hooker. In 1960 he made a pleasant album for Bluesville and sang on a Candid session with Robert Lockwood and Otis Spann. (*St Louis Jimmy Oden Vols 1–2* Document; *Goin' Down Slow* Original Blues Classics)

OMAR & THE HOWLERS

This Texas-based band started out reconstituting early rock 'n' roll with a 1950s blues feel (or, if you prefer, vice versa), leader

Kent "Omar" Dykes often sounding uncommonly like Howlin' Wolf. Their recent work leans towards a more conventional blues-rock idiom.

Born in McComb, Mississippi, Dykes began playing guitar in his teens. He formed the first Howlers in the 1970s and moved to Austin, Texas, where he has been based ever since. In the 1980s he cut albums for the local Amazing and Austin labels and for CBS, then signed with Antone's and issued *Monkey Land* (1990). Subsequent albums

The payroll of the Johnny Otis Orchestra has included notable jazzmen like tenor saxophonist Paul Quinichette and bassman Curtis Counce.

for the Dutch Provogue label have featured trios or larger line-ups, generally operating on the blues-rock frontier, though for *Blues Bag* (1991) Dykes deliberately backed himself into a blues corner to sing numbers by Hound Dog Taylor, Robert Johnson and Jimmy Reed. Omar & The Howlers have a devoted following in Europe, where they tour regularly; *Live At Paradiso* (1992) was recorded in performance in Amsterdam. (*I Told You So* Austin [US]/Dixiefrog [France]; *Blues Bag*, *Live At Paradiso*, *Courts Of Lulu* Provogue)

johnny OTIS (1921–)

Though his background is Greek-American (his real name is Veliotes), Johnny Otis has lived in the African-American community of Northern California since his childhood. A man of wide-ranging interests and skills, he is perhaps best known as the drummer-leader of an R&B revue, the Johnny Otis Show, for more than a quarter of a century, though his bandleading history stretches back to the mid-1940s.

In the early 1950s his jump-blues combo had several R&B hits like 'Double Crossing Blues'; later in the decade he made a small piece of rock 'n' roll history with the dance song 'Willie And The Hand Jive'. He also pro-

duced and wrote songs for Little Esther, Etta James and many other artists. *Cold Shot* (1968) featured his guitar-wielding son Shuggie (1953–), while *Live At Monterey* (1970) presented revue members like Roy Brown. Albums continued to appear at intervals in the 1970s, 1980s and 1990s, some on his own Blues Spectrum label, while he pursued parallel careers as a disc-jockey and author. (*The Original Johnny Otis Show* Savoy; *Johnny Otis Show* Alligator; *Spirit Of The Black Territory Bands* Arhoolie)

junior PARKER (1932–1971)

Parker deserves a high place in any poll of underrated blues artists. Early blues

authorities, judging by his 1950s recordings for Sun like 'Mystery Train' and 'Feelin' Good', decided that he was a downhome singer and harmonica player from the same musical roots as Little Walter or Junior Wells. Consequently his later work with big bands and soul-tilted material was seen as a regrettable falling-off, though to his own people he was a singer of comparable stature to B.B. King, Bobby Bland or Little Milton.

In the early 1950s Parker was part of the Memphis circle that embraced King and Bland. After his few remarkable singles for Sun, he signed, as Bland did, with Duke Records, and for the rest of the decade the two men headlined the touring show *Blues Consolidated*. Failing to match Bland's record sales, Parker conducted short-lived affairs with various record labels, producing sturdy albums such as *Like It Is* (1968) and *Blues Man* (1969) which meant nothing to the new blues audience. The all-blues set *You Don't Have To Be Black To Love The Blues*, for which he dug out his dusty harmonicas, might have made a different impression, had he not suddenly died. (*Mystery Train* Rounder; *Junior's Blues* MCA)

dave PEABODY (1948–)

For some years Peabody has specialized in bringing together songs and musicians he is enthusiastic about on albums that are many-handed celebrations of the blues in all its forms and homes. *Hands Across The Sea* (1993) found him collaborating with Chicago Bob Nelson, Big Boy Henry, Robert Lucas and the British band Big Joe Louis & His Blues Kings, while *Down In Carolina* (1996) involved Steve James, Cora Mae Bryant (the singing daughter of Curley Weaver) and the septuagenarian harmonica player Neal

Dave Peabody has soaked himself in the guitar music of the south-eastern states.

Not many octogenarian blues pianists are still in business, but Pinetop Perkins scorns retirement.

robust piano is fairly presented in *On Top* (1992), an easy-going recital of blues standards with his old Waters associate Jerry Portnoy on harmonica. (*Boogie Woogie King* Black & Blue; *On Top* Deluge [US]/Sky Ranch [France]; *Live Top* Deluge)

lucky PETERSON (1964–)

Peterson may be the only blues musician to have had national exposure in short pants. The son of a blues club owner in Buffalo, New York, he began playing drums and Hammond organ when he was three and, promoted by Willie Dixon, had a hit record at six. As a teenager he played with Little Milton. In 1984, while on tour in France with the Youngblood Blues Band, he made his first blues album, *Ridin'* (Isabel), confining himself to singing and playing keyboards, but after that he developed his guitar-playing, partly through studio work for King Snake Records in Florida. After albums for Alligator (*Lucky Strikes!* in 1989, *Triple Play* in 1990) he was signed by Polygram and made *I'm Ready* (1992), playing guitar, organ and electric piano on most of the tracks. The more adventurous *Beyond Cool* (1993) prefaced *Lifetime* (1995), where his gritty vocals seemed not altogether appropriate to the mostly original and not very blues-based material. While he has yet to find a wholly individual voice in his own projects, he is a reliable collaborator on other people's and has provided excellent keyboard- or guitar-playing for Kenny Neal and Rufus Thomas. (*Triple Play* Alligator; *I'm Ready* EmArcy; *Beyond Cool* Verve)

Pattman. He has also worked closely with Big Joe Duskin and Honeyboy Edwards. These collaborations are the outcome of three decades playing and promoting the blues: Peabody is not only a seasoned club and festival performer but a journalist and photographer. (*Dream Of Mississippi, Hands Across The Sea, Down In Carolina* Appaloosa)

pinetop PERKINS (1913–)

Pianist Joe Willie Perkins, from Belzoni, Mississippi, was one of the *King Biscuit Time* gang around Sonny Boy Williamson II in the 1940s, before he split for Memphis (where he recorded some unissued sides for Sun with Earl Hooker and others) and, in 1951, for Chicago, where he played with his old acquaintance Robert Nighthawk. For most of the next 20 years he worked by turns in Chicago and East St Louis, until he was offered the piano stool in the Muddy Waters band, Otis Spann having left to further his own career. He stayed with Waters from 1969 to 1980, playing on several of his albums and cutting his own debut set with his band colleagues for Black & Blue in 1976. He and some of the other sidemen left Waters to form the Legendary Blues Band, but after a few years, weary of the road, he decided to retire. Not very firmly, though: he has gone on playing and recording. His

kelly joe PHELPS (1960–)

Phelps' brooding singing and hypnotic slide-guitar improvizations, deployed on original songs, blues by Skip James and pieces from the repertoire of the guitar-playing evangelist Blind Willie Johnson, recall both the

techniques and the almost Buddhist concentration of the 1960s guitarists John Fahey and Leo Kottke. A native of Washington, Phelps played jazz in his teens and later taught guitar, banjo and mandolin in schools in the North-West, before being awakened to the blues in 1989 and discovering the work of Fred McDowell and Robert Pete Williams. The success of *Lead Me On* (1994) led to work across the United States and in Canada and Europe. In 1996 he signed with American Records. (*Lead Me On* Burnside)

PIANO RED (1911–1985)

For an archer with only a couple of arrows in his quiver, Piano Red left the field with a pretty good score. His hit 'Dr Feelgood' was a valuable business asset for over 20 years (as well as giving a name to a British R&B band), while its flipside, 'Mister Moonlight', inspired a cover version by the Beatles. Under his own name, Willie Lee Perryman, he was known as a singer and pianist in his native Atlanta, until 'Rockin' with Red'/'Red's Boogie' (1950) put him on the national map as Piano Red. 'The Wrong Yo Yo' (1951) was a minor R&B hit too, ensuring a prolific if repetitive output for the rest of the 1950s. Red's merry two-beat manner admirably suited the endearingly silly lyrics of 'Dr Feelgood' (1962). The success of this song suggested another name-change, and for some years he worked as Dr Feelgood and his band as the Interns. For most of his later life he was Pianist in Residence at a bar in the Underground Atlanta entertainment area, though he visited Europe several times in the 1970s. His brother Rufus (1892–1973), known as Speckled Red (both men were albinos), was also a well-known pianist in a rough-and-ready, more ragtime-influenced style. (*The Doctor's In!* Bear Family; *Atlanta Bounce* Arhoolie)

Kelly Joe Phelps provides his own rhythm section by slapping his guitar and stamping his foot.

lonnie PITCHFORD (1955–)

Pitchford is the only blues musician active in the 1990s to play the diddley bow, a home-made, one-stringed instrument that has traditionally been the starting-point for many black guitarists. He also plays standard guitar, both acoustic and electric, with and without a slide, on a wide range of blues and other material.

Growing up in Lexington, Mississippi, Pitchford played at juke-joints from the age of 19 or 20 and accompanied local gospel groups. After spells living in Chicago, Kansas City and Kalamazoo, Michigan, he returned to Mississippi, where he met the folklorist Worth Long and found an entrée to the festival circuit. He also met and learned from older musicians like Eugene Powell, Honeyboy Edwards, Jack Owens and Houston Stackhouse, and took instruction in the repertoire of Robert Johnson from Robert Junior Lockwood. He contributed to several anthologies of field and festival recordings before making his own debut album in 1994. (*All Round Man* Rooster Blues)

sammy PRICE (1908–1992)

As the house pianist for Decca Records' New York studio from the late 1930s to the early 1950s, the Texas-born Price played on innumerable recordings by Peetie Wheatstraw, Johnny Temple, Joe Turner, Cousin Joe, Ollie Shepard, the gospel singer Sister Rosetta Tharpe and many lesser figures. But he was no specialist: he could play boogie-woogie, jazz and standard popular songs, all correctly and with economical grace rather than coruscating invention.

Before reaching New York in 1938 Price had played with several south-western orchestras. Once established in the city, he

Cold Blooded Blues Man (Wolf, 1997) found John Primer playing both electric and unplugged.

formed a small band, his Texas Blusicians, for both public engagements and studio jobs. Thanks to visits with jazz bands in the 1940s he acquired some cachet in France, where he frequently toured and made many records over the next 30 years, both solo and accompanying jazzmen. In the 1960s and 1970s he was active in the New York musicians' union and as a Harlem agent for the Democratic Party, while keeping his hands in trim by playing in clubs and, in the 1980s, in the bar of Boston's Copley Plaza Hotel, an engagement commemorated by *Play It Again, Sam* (1984). (*Sam Price 1929–41* Classics; *Midnight Boogie* Black & Blue; *Play It Again, Sam* Whiskey, Women And . . .)

john PRIMER (1945–)

Primer learned his slow-burning guitar technique in South Side Chicago clubs like Theresa's, taking over the lead guitarist's role in the house band from John "Mad Dog" Watkins. One of his mentors there was the guitarist Sammy Lawhorn. He went on to play in Willie Dixon's Chicago Blues All Stars and the early-1980s Muddy Waters band, then put in 13 years' service with Magic Slim's Teardrops. Such training explains the old-fashioned solidity of the Mississippi-born Primer's two Wolf albums, *Poor Man Blues* and *Blues Behind Closed Doors*, and the more considered *The Real Deal* (1995), where his songwriting and weighty singing plainly reflect the lessons he learned from Dixon and Slim. (*The Real Deal* Code Blue)

PROFESSOR LONGHAIR (1918–1980)

The vivacious rhumba-rhythmed piano blues and choked singing typical of "Fess" were too weird to sell millions of records; he had to be content with siring musical offspring who were simple enough to manage that, like Fats Domino or Huey ('Rockin' Pneumonia') Smith. But he is also acknowl-edged as a father figure by subtler players like Allen Toussaint and Dr John.

Born Henry Byrd in Bogalusa, Louisiana, he made his living as a street hustler until he started to play piano seriously in his thirties. In the late 1940s and early 1950s he recorded his pet numbers 'Tipitina', 'Big Chief' and 'Go To The Mardi Gras', but the 1960s were unfriendly to him, and it took a dramatic appearance at the 1971 New Orleans Jazz & Heritage Festival to restore his standing. He played at the 1973 Newport and Montreux jazz festivals and recorded albums for several labels, including a set *Live On The Queen Mary* (1978) at a party given by Paul and Linda McCartney. His single visit to Britain, in 1978, is commemorated by *The London Concert* (JSP). Records capture part of Fess's uniqueness, but only memory or film preserve his stage act, his strange clothes, his uniqueness as a person. (*Crawfish Fiesta* Alligator)

snooky PRYOR (1921–)

Pryor plays blues harmonica in the classic style of the 1940s and 1950s and sings a sturdy blues. But unlike many musicians you might describe that way, he does so with the inimitable authority of the man who was there. His 1947–48 recordings with Johnny Young and the singer-guitarists Moody and Floyd Jones are among the earliest documents of the Southern downhome blues-band style in transition in Chicago.

He was born in Mississippi, made the Chicago trip in 1940 and did his stint of playing on Maxwell Street. While never likely to unseat Little or Big Walter, he was a proficient second-rank harp player with a distinctively plaintive tone, exhibited on his own infrequent recordings such as 'Cryin' Shame' (JOB, 1953) and 'Judgement Day' (Vee Jay, 1956), and in his accompaniments to Sunnyland Slim and other artists. He quit music for carpentry in the 1960s but was

Professor Longhair, the most distinctive of New Orleans' piano players.

persuaded to make a comeback and toured overseas for several years with Homesick James Williamson. (*Too Cool To Move*, *In This Mess Up To My Chest* Antone's)

joe PULLUM (dates unknown)

Pullum's high clear voice drifting over the peaks and valleys of 'Black Gal What Makes Your Head So Hard?' brought the shock of the new into mid-1930s blues. No one before, male or female, had sung the blues with such feline grace. What's more, Pullum's ethereal manner hardly prepared the listener for the song's scenario of insults, smoking pistols and suicide.

Pullum was a Houston club singer, then probably in his twenties or early thirties, who worked, on and probably off record, with a pianist: Rob Cooper on his first discs, Andy Boy on later ones. The meandering eight-bar tune of 'Black Gal' (1934) was so popular that it was covered by several other blues artists, among them Leroy Carr, Josh White and the Harlem Hamfats, and Pullum himself recorded three follow-ups among the 30 sides he cut in 1934–36. Fifteen years later in L.A. he revived it as the two-part 'My Woman', accompanied by Lloyd Glenn. He was an artful songwriter, composing wordy and intricate verses that his plaintive voice negotiated with great skill. Yet few even of his Texas contemporaries remembered him, and he remains one of the obscurest of the blues' one-time stars. (*Joe Pullum Vols 1 & 2* Document)

yank RACHELL (1910–1997)

Rachell was the first important blues mandolinist. His cascading runs were first heard in 1929 on the debut recordings of his Brownsville, Tennessee friend Sleepy John Estes, but his distinctive playing, on guitar as well as mandolin, also decorated many records in the 1930s and 1940s by Sonny Boy Williamson I and Walter Davis. On his own recordings like '38 Pistol Blues' he more often played guitar.

The association with Estes did not last, though the two men would be reunited 30-odd years later for festivals, overseas tours and albums. Rachell spent some years in St Louis before making his home in 1955 in Indianapolis, where he continued to play locally until his death. (*Yank Rachell Vols 1 & 2* Wolf; *Chicago Style* Delmark)

ma RAINEY (1886–1939)

By a quirk of recording history, though she was eight years older than Bessie Smith and an acknowledged model for the younger woman, Rainey didn't begin making records until almost a year later. However, since she recorded exclusively for the technically modest Paramount label, her discs, which span 1923–28, sound appropriately archaic. Unlike Smith and most of her other contemporaries she was dedicated to the blues form, which she tackled in a slow and deliberate style, and seldom touched any other material.

Rachel got her apprenticeship in the first two decades of the century, working in the tent shows and theatres of the South with her husband William as "Rainey & Rainey, The Assassinators Of The Blues". Her road band was headed for several years by Georgia Tom Dorsey, who played on some of her records with his partner Tampa Red. Other disc collaborators were Louis Armstrong ('See See Rider Blues'), cornetists Shirley Clay ('Blues Oh Blues') and Tommy Ladnier ('Bo-Weavil Blues'), Blind Blake and, on the 1925 session that produced 'Yonder Come The Blues', a contingent from Fletcher Henderson's orchestra including Bessie Smith's favourite partners Joe Smith (cornet) and Charlie Green (trombone). After making almost 100 sides Rainey retired to her home town of Columbus, Georgia. (*Ma Rainey's Black Bottom* Yazoo; *Ma Rainey Vols 1–4* King Jazz)

bonnie RAITT (1949–)

The anodyne rock of her 1990s albums scarcely hints how interesting an artist Raitt used to be, and could be again. She was bitten by the blues at 14, and at 18 was opening for visiting blues acts at clubs round Boston, where she had gone to college. Here she first met Fred McDowell, whose songs and slide-guitar playing lie in the bedrock of her music. At 22 she cut her first, eponymous album, containing blues by Robert and Tommy Johnson. On later sets like *Give It Up* and *Home Plate* she developed her forceful bottleneck technique and called in helpers like Paul Butterfield and Junior Wells. In *Takin' My Time* (1976) Raitt commemorated McDowell with a medley of his songs, which she continues to perform on stage. A stagnant period was ended by the Grammy-winning *Nick Of Time* (1989) and her seductive duet with John Lee Hooker, 'I'm In The

Mood', on his *The Healer*. Though there is little trace of the blues in her recent work, her standing in the blues world remains high, thanks in part to her work on behalf of neglected artists through the Rhythm & Blues Foundation. In 1997 she made a guest appearance on Joe Louis Walker's *Great Guitars*. (*Give It Up*, *Takin' My Time* Warner Brothers)

a. c. REED (1926–)

As you might guess from song titles like 'I Am Fed Up With This Music' and 'I'm In The Wrong Business!', A.C. Reed is no Pollyanna. "Shoulda been a boxer and made that movie *Rocky 3*", he observes grumpily. "'Shoulda been like Michael Jackson when I was the age of five – but I chose this saxophone, now I'm broke and I can't survive."

Born Aaron Corthen, he took his professional name from his friend Jimmy Reed. In 1942 he moved from Missouri to Chicago, where he learned from the tenor saxophonists J.T. Brown and Gene Ammons, did session work and cut some singles before landing a decade-long gig with Buddy Guy and Junior Wells. Son Seals and Albert Collins also hired him for roadwork and recordings. His own album log opened with *Take These Blues And Shove 'Em!* (Ice Cube, 1982), then a French-recorded set shared with his guitarist Maurice John Vaughn, *I Got Money* (Black & Blue, 1985). Better yet was the boisterous *I'm In The Wrong Business!* (1987), with cameo appearances by Stevie Ray Vaughan and Bonnie Raitt. Reed's puckered singing, reminiscent of his namesake's, suits his comically morose lyrics. (*I'm In The Wrong Business!* Alligator)

sonny RHODES (1940–)

One of the most quietly satisfying albums of the 1970s was Rhodes's *I Don't Want My Blues Colored Bright*. With its lean guitar figures and

unforced singing, it captured the essence of Junior Parker and Lowell Fulson. Like almost everything he has done, it was commissioned by a European label (Amiga in Sweden): though not unknown on the American circuit, he is more appreciated abroad.

Born Clarence Smith in Smithville, Texas, Rhodes migrated in his twenties to Oakland, California, where he cut some transitory singles in the 1960s, including the anthem-like 'All Night Long They Play The Blues'. In the 1970s he learned from his fellow Oakland musician L.C. Robinson how to handle the electric steel guitar, which he introduced on record in a couple of ill-contrived albums made in Europe in 1980, when he toured with a San Francisco Blues Festival troupe. A few years later, feeling stale, he quit Oakland for Canada and then New Jersey. He greeted the 1990s with *Disciple Of The Blues* (Ichiban, 1991). (*I Don't Want My Blues Colored Bright* Black Magic; *Just Blues* Evidence)

sherman ROBERTSON (1948–)

Thanks to his dynamic stage act, Robertson was tipped as a talent to watch in the early 1990s. Louisiana-born, he grew up in Houston, Texas, and began playing guitar professionally in his teens. He worked with Clifton Chenier and Rockin' Dopsie, contributing to Chenier's *Live At The* [1982] *San Francisco Blues Festival* (Arhoolie, 1985) and Dopsie's *Crowned Prince Of Zydeco* (Maison De Soul, 1986); the latter contains an early example of his singing. While with Dopsie he also made the cast list of Paul Simon's *Graceland*. Around the beginning of the 1990s he formed his own band, appeared at important events in the United States and Europe and in 1993 cut *I'm The Man* for the British label Indigo. His approach was confident, but doubts about the durability of his repertoire, most of which was supplied by other writers, were not allayed by the unconvincing material

gathered for *Here & Now* (1995), and his contract with Code Blue was not renewed. (*I'm The Man*, *Here & Now* Code Blue)

duke ROBILLARD (1948–)

A charter member of the Roomful Of Blues band, Robillard has grown into one of the leading guitarists of his generation, not only in blues – every school of blues – but also in swing-era jazz.

He grew up in Providence, Rhode Island, which he remembers as an excellent base for a musically curious kid: many of the blues and jazz figures he holds as models, such as T-Bone Walker and B.B. King, he first saw and heard there or in nearby Boston. Following a dozen years (1967–79) in ROB, he created his own band, later titled the Pleasure Kings. He did stints in the Legendary Blues Band (1980) and the Fabulous Thunderbirds (1990–92) while cutting albums for Rounder that veered from the confidential nightclub jazz of *Swing* (1986), with tenor saxophonist Scott Hamilton (another Providence boy) and his group, to the more blues-slanted *You Got Me* (1988) with Dr John and Jimmie Vaughan. In the most vivid exposé of his multiple abilities, *Duke's Blues* (1995), he piles up *hommages* to idols like Walker, Roy Milton and (perhaps surprising some listeners who didn't think he could play that way) to the more agitated styles of Guitar Slim and Albert Collins. Judging by this album, Robillard could replace the guitar player in almost any blues band at an hour's notice. (*Rockin' Blues*, *Swing* Rounder; *Temptation*, *Duke's Blues* Pointblank)

fenton ROBINSON (1935–)

Fenton Robinson is a singer and guitarist of outstanding grace, taste and feeling. Preferring a tempered statement to an exuberant gesture, he nevertheless communi-

Unlike most blues guitarists of his age, Robillard has formidable jazz chops.

cates emotion, in the words of a song he has sung, "directly from my heart to you". That the blues audience has continually failed to recognize his merits for more than 20 years is not just inexplicable but disquieting.

He left his home in Mississippi at 18 to move to Memphis, where he made his first record, 'Tennessee Woman', in 1957. Over the next two years he released some singles on Duke and played guitar on label-mate Larry Davis's 'Texas Flood'. He settled in Chicago in 1962, but another dozen years went by before his startling calling card *Somebody Loan Me A Dime*. This and its 1977 successor *I Hear Some Blues Downstairs* – both these brilliant title songs

are his compositions – clarified what earlier, less sensitively produced work had sometimes masked: that, in mixing elements of T-Bone Walker and B.B. King, Robinson had achieved a refined yet penetrating guitar attack and a singing style that expressed soul without lavish ornament. *Night Flight* (1984), though not the equal of its forerunners, evinced the same calm maturity. (*Somebody Loan Me A Dime*, *I Hear Some Blues Downstairs*, *Night Flight* Alligator)

L. C. ROBINSON (1918–1976)

L. C. Robinson played a stand-mounted, solid-body, electric steel guitar, the sort often heard in Western Swing bands, and indeed it was Leon McAuliffe of Bob Wills' Texas Playboys who inspired his fellow Texan to take it up. He generally worked with his harmonica-playing brother A.C.: in Texas in the 1930s and after World War II in the San Francisco Bay Area, where they recorded sparsely for small labels. L.C.'s first album break was winning a half share in *Oakland Blues* (World Pacific, 1968) with his acquaintances Dave Alexander (later Omar Sharriff), Lafayette Thomas and Jimmy McCracklin; but he sounded better rehearsed on *Ups And Downs* (Arhoolie, 1971), singing in his small but determined voice and playing steel, standard guitar or extremely blue fiddle, backed either by Alexander's trio or by the Muddy Waters band. Though never widely known, he was a popular Bay Area club act – the Oakland disc-jockey Jumpin' George Oxford nicknamed him "Good Rockin'" Robinson – and was much enjoyed by the Swedish audiences who saw him on his only visit to Europe, in 1975. (*Mojo In My Hand* Arhoolie)

"I'm the only man in the world that plays the accordion upside-down," Rockin' Dopsie used to claim. "It's all because daddy didn't taught me how to play. I just picked it up."

ROCKIN' DOPSIE (1932–1993)

Ironically, the recording of Rockin' Dopsie that most people know puts him accurately but unkindly in his place – "standing in the shadow of Clifton Chenier, King of the Bayou", as Paul Simon sang in 'That Was Your Mother' on *Graceland*, while Dopsie's accordion tilted and trembled, Chenier-like, in the background. For much of his life Dopsie (pronounced Doopsy) did play Crown Prince to Chenier's monarch. It was not unjust: Chenier was the better player and the more charismatic representative of black French Louisiana and its colonies in Texas and California. But Dopsie did zydeco music a good turn by popularizing its blues and two-steps abroad among people who might otherwise never have heard it.

"It tickles me," says Jimmy Rogers. "People are just now beginning to catch on to the blues. But at the time I was facing reality. And I didn't like it."

Born Alton Rubin in Lafayette, Louisiana, he learned the accordion by playing his father's – upside down, because he was left-handed. In his twenties he had a duo with Chester Zeno on rub-board. There were a few locally distributed singles, but his career break was playing in Europe in the late 1970s and 1980s and recording a series of popular albums for Sonet. His band, the Twisters, at one time included Zeno and the tenor saxophonist John Hart; a later line-up drew in Dopsie's sons David on rub-board and Alton Jr on drums. (*Saturday Night Zydeco* Maison De Soul)

jimmy ROGERS (1924–)

A back-room boy in the Chicago blues factory, Rogers was a key member of the Muddy Waters band of the 1950s. His unobtrusive skill as a guitarist also buttressed other bluesmen, while he made a series of exceptional records of his own. Yet the Mississippi-born Rogers, like Leroy Foster and Eddie Boyd, was in some ways less attuned to Muddy's music than to the restrained West Coast manner of, say, Charles Brown.

James A. Lane, as he was born (Rogers was his stepfather's name), started playing in his teens. In Chicago in the late 1940s he gigged with Sunnyland Slim, Memphis Minnie and Sonny Boy Williamson I before getting together with Little Walter and Muddy Waters, an association first documented on record in 1949. "I listened to Muddy, and I said, 'I know what he need', you know? It's like if you don't have enough salt in your food, it don't taste right. So you need a little more salt, and then it taste better." His 1950 debut single for Chess, 'That's All Right'/'Ludella', with eloquent harmonica by Little Walter and Big Crawford's bass, was quite Muddyish, but his melodic guitar lines created a more reflective ambience. Little Walter also played with him on 'Chicago Bound' and 'Sloppy Drunk' (both 1954), but Walter Horton blew the magisterial harmonica on 'Walking By Myself' (1956).

For most of the 1960s, unable to live off music, Rogers took outside jobs, until he formed a band in 1969 with the pianist Bob Riedy and guitarist Johnny Littlejohn. *Gold-Tailed Bird* (Shelter, 1973) marked this new career as a front-man. His 1990s band has his son Jimmy D. Lane on lead guitar. (*Sings The Blues* Sequel; *Bluebird* Analogue Productions)

roy ROGERS (1950–)

Constantly being buttonholed by jokers enquiring about Trigger is enough to give anyone the blues, but this Roy Rogers, if no movie cowboy, has kept a sunny smile (and worn a big hat) while developing his considerable talent as a slide guitarist, though he may be better known as the producer of John Lee Hooker's life-changing *The Healer*.

California-born, he gigged around San Francisco in the 1970s and joined Hooker's

road band in 1982. He left after four years to initiate a career of his own, which he pursued through five albums for Blind Pig before signing with Liberty. His collaboration with Hooker on *The Healer* was renewed for its successor *Mr Lucky*. Hooker has guested on Rogers' recordings, as has Charlie Musselwhite, for instance on *Rhythm & Groove* (1996). Though not a natural blues singer, Rogers has a brawny way with a lyric, and his command of slide styles is as extensive as anyone's. (*Slide Of Hand, Slide Zone* Liberty; *Rhythm & Groove* Pointblank)

ROOMFUL OF BLUES

The quintessential good-time bar band, Roomful Of Blues has also been the premier college for blues instrumentalists over three decades. The band was founded in 1967 in Rhode Island by the guitarist Duke Robillard and pianist Al Copley. After a decade of playing on the East Coast it made its eponymous debut album for Island, at that point a seven-piece with Robillard as singer, drummer John Rossi and a three-man sax section of Rich Lataille (alto), Greg Piccolo (tenor) and Doug James (baritone). (Twenty years on, Rossi, Lataille and James were still on board.) Robillard was succeeded in 1979 by Ronnie Earl, and Earl in 1988 by Chris Vachon, and more horns were added (Bob Enos on trumpet, Porky Cohen on trombone), but the band's jump-blues approach, modelled on 1940s–1950s units like Buddy Johnson's orchestra, has remained largely unchanged. The mid-1990s line-up included the singer and harmonica player Sugar Ray Norcia.

Other graduates of the ROB academy are the keyboard player Ron Levy, now a producer and session musician much in demand, and the singer Lou Ann Barton. In

The Roomful Of Blues horn section at the 1986 Amsterdam Blues Festival.

addition to their own genial albums, the band has worked on record with Eddie Vinson, Joe Turner and Earl King, and the horn section is frequently hired to add the beef. (*Hot Little Mama* Varrick [US]/Ace [UK]; *Dressed Up To Get Messed Up, Live At Lupo's Heartbreak Hotel* Varrick; *Turn It On! Turn It Up!* Bullseye Blues)

doctor ROSS (1925–1993)

The personable Ross was a one-man blues band, playing harmonica, guitar and a cut-down drum kit like his predecessor Joe Hill Louis. He was born Isaiah Ross in Tunica, Mississippi, and by his late teens, when he moved to Helena, Arkansas, was a devoted blues harmonica player. In 1951 he began to be heard on Mississippi and Arkansas radio stations, now nicknamed Doctor because of his interest in medical books, and over the

next three years he recorded in Memphis for Chess and Sun, creating exhilarating harmonica or guitar boogies made distinctive by his sidemen playing washboard (with a spoon and fork) and broom.

In 1954 he took a job with General Motors in Flint, Michigan, and played less. Some singles, among them his first true one-man band effort, 'Industrial Boogie', filtered into blues circles, leading to a Testament album and a 1965 AFBF booking. While in London he recorded what would be the first LP on Blue Horizon. Europe loved the Doc and gave him work and recording opportunities; he was never as popular at home, and in the 1980s his performing profile was barely visible. He last appeared in Britain at a 1991 festival. (*Boogie Disease* Arhoolie)

Dr Ross on one of his few European jaunts in the 1980s, at the Cologne Blues & Boogie Festival 1986.

otis RUSH (1934–)

Moody and unpredictable, Rush can give performances so riveting that you forget there are other ways to sing and play the blues. Unfortunately they are rare, but even at half throttle he is worth listening to.

He left Mississippi for Chicago in his teens and by 1955 was involved in the blues scene alongside Magic Sam and Buddy Guy. His records on Cobra (1956–58) like 'I Can't Quit You Baby', 'Checking On My Baby', 'All Your Love' and 'Double Trouble' are turbulent performances, and it seemed for long afterwards that he found it hard to equal their passion, though 'So Many Roads' (Chess, 1960) and 'Home Work' (Duke, 1962) came close. Contractual mishaps and personal problems fragmented his progress for the next dozen years, and it was not until the mid-1970s that he had albums out that fairly represented his talent, like *Right Place, Wrong Time* (Bullfrog) and *Cold Day In Hell* (Delmark). A 1975 Japanese tour was well received and generated an excellent live album, *So Many Roads* (Delmark). For much of the 1980s Rush was sidelined by depression or disenchantment, but admirers were rewarded in 1994 by a very sound album, *Ain't Enough Comin' In* (This Way Up). (MR)

jimmy RUSHING (1903–1972)

Rushing's singing had the tangy smoked flavour of good barbecue, and it glowed hotly in the campfire circle of the Count Basie orchestra, where he sang on and off for nearly 30 years. During his heyday with the band (1935–50) he dealt with every kind of material from 'London Bridge Is Falling Down' to 'Pennies From Heaven', but his refrains on blues sides like 'Good Morning Blues', 'The Blues I Like To Hear' and, in particular, 'Sent For You Yesterday' are famous. His pitch was accurate, his phrasing supple, and whatever the song, there was a quality in his voice that prompted a warm smile.

He was born in Oklahoma City, where he learned violin and piano. In the 1920s he sang in Kansas City with Walter Page's Blue Devils and Bennie Moten's orchestra, which became Basie's on the leader's death. In the 1950s and 1960s, known affectionately because of his solid build as "Mr Five-By-Five", he headed his own groups and sang at jazz events such as the 1957 Newport Jazz Festival, where he and Basie had a reunion. His mid-1950s Vanguard albums like *Going To Chicago*, made with small bands of Basie alumni usually including tenor saxophonist Buddy Tate, are classics of their kind. (Count Basie *The Original American Decca Recordings* GRP/MCA; Jimmy Rushing *His Complete Vanguard Recordings* Vanguard)

SAFFIRE

The band's full title is Saffire – The Uppity Blues Women, and their repertoire is loaded with amusing, sassy songs about the shortcomings of men, like 'Bitch With A Bad Attitude' or 'How Can I Say I Miss You?' ("when I can't get you to leave?") They also perform many songs from the archives of women's blues such as 'Do Your Duty', 'In My Girlish Days', 'You Got To Know How' and 'Tain't Nobody's Business'.

The trio of pianist Ann Rabson, guitarist Gaye Adegbalola and Earlene Lewis (bass) came together in 1984 and went full time in 1988. 'The Middle Aged Blues Boogie' from their eponymous debut album (Alligator, 1990) won a Handy award as the year's best composition. Lewis left in 1992 and was replaced by Andra Faye McIntosh, who plays mandolin, fiddle and other stringed instruments.

Opinions are mixed about Saffire. To some they are vivacious and amusing. Others, used to more macho blues styles, have decided that their acoustic playing and pleasant, nondescript singing are better suited to the cosy atmosphere of the folk club. (*Hot Flash, Old, New, Borrowed & Blue, Cleaning House* Alligator)

son SEALS (1942–)

Seals' rumbling, somewhat Muddy Watersish singing and blazing guitar make one of the most aggressive combinations in Chicago blues since the 1970s. His press kit spits words like "growling" and "searing". Born in Osceola, Arkansas, he grew up listening to the blues visitors at his father's juke-joint,

and when he started on guitar it was under his father's tuition. By 18 he was playing drums at the club, a role he went on to fill in Earl Hooker's band and then with Albert King. Since 1973 he has recorded eight albums for Alligator, aided by sidemen like his long-serving bassist Johnny B. Gayden and reedsman Red Groetzinger. His star was high in the blues sky in the late 1970s, when he made overseas tours; lower in the second half of the 1980s, when he broke away from Alligator. In the mid-1990s, with two decades of roadwork behind him, he decided to spend more time in Chicago, where he recorded *Live – Spontaneous Combustion* (1996) at Buddy Guy's Legends club. (*Midnight Son, Live & Burning, Living In The Danger Zone* Alligator)

omar SHARRIFF (1938–)

Experience playing in piano bars and with big bands, coupled with an instinctive musical curiosity, has made Sharriff a knowledgeable and versatile pianist, at home with standards and rock tunes as well as blues, though most of his recordings stress his blues side. His singing is West Coast Conversational.

Born in Shreveport, Louisiana, he grew up in Texas and was playing in public by his mid-teens, using his birthname of Dave Alexander. He later settled in California, working in Oakland from the late 1950s as a solo bar act or with L. C. Robinson and Jimmy McCracklin. He first recorded on an *Oakland Blues* collection (World Pacific, 1969), accompanying Robinson and Lafayette Thomas and himself backed by George Smith and Albert Collins, then made two albums for Arhoolie (1971–72). He continued to work regularly at clubs and festivals in the San Francisco Bay area, taking the name Omar Hakim Khayyam and then Omar Sharriff. After a spell of obscurity he began recording again in the early 1990s. (*The Raven* Arhoolie; *Baddass* Have Mercy)

eddie SHAW (1937–)

In his teens the Mississippi-born Shaw played his tenor sax with local blues artists like Little Milton and Willie Love. At 20 he joined Muddy Waters' band and moved to Chicago, where he gigged widely, more or less dividing the tenor territory with A.C. Reed. In 1972 he joined Howlin' Wolf, leading his band, the Wolf Gang, and writing half the songs on *The Back Door Wolf* (1973); after the singer's death in 1976 he took over the band and its West Side residency at the 1815 Club, renamed Eddie's Place. He led the Gang on *Living Chicago Blues Vol 1* (Alligator, 1979) and *Have Blues – Will Travel* (Simmons, 1980) and has made albums in different company for Isabel, Rooster Blues and Wolf.

Eddie Shaw playing the King Street Palace, Charleston, South Carolina, in 1993.

His son Eddie "Vaan" Shaw (1955–) grew up surrounded by blues people and soon became one too, joining the Wolf Gang and playing guitar on some of his father's records. A disciple of Wolf's protégé Hubert Sumlin, he has cut two albums of his own, *Morning Rain* and *The Trail Of Tears* (Wolf). (*Movin' And Groovin' Man* Evidence; *In The Land Of The Crossroads* Rooster Blues)

robert SHAW (1908–1985)

In the 1930s Texas was constantly criss-crossed by a group of pianist-singers who furnished weekend entertainment for the isolated communities of railroad builders and lumber-camp workers. Some of them, like Pinetop Burks and Son Becky, made records at the time, but many are known only from the reminiscences of survivors from that era, and there were few of those: the life of a barrelhouse pianist was hard and short.

Robert Shaw, who was born in what is now a suburb of Houston, played for some years with this set, roaming as far afield as Oklahoma and Kansas City, but eventually he chose the quieter life of a grocery store owner in Austin. He still played, though, and in 1963, at the prompting of the folklorist Mack McCormick, recorded an album of old barrelhouse favourites like 'The Ma Grinder', 'The Cows' and 'Whores Is Funky', some of them too pungent to have been recorded before without being bowdlerized. He was often invited to play at Texas events, and even made it to Europe in 1974. *The Ma Grinder*, which augments the 1963 album with later recordings, offers a uniquely clear view of a style and repertoire that almost escaped preservation. (*The Ma Grinder* Arhoolie)

kenny wayne SHEPHERD (1978–)

Shepherd won't forget 1995 in a hurry. The 17-year-old guitarist's debut album spent 20 weeks topping *Billboard's* blues chart and the magazine *Guitar World* voted him planetary No. 3 after B.B. King and Eric Clapton.

The Shreveport, Louisiana boy was turned towards the blues at the age of seven by hearing Stevie Ray Vaughan; later he listened to Howlin' Wolf, Albert Collins and Albert King, and he spent some time around Shreveport's venerable bluesman Jesse Thomas. Vaughan is clearly the moulding force on Shepherd's tense playing, but not the only one: 'Aberdeen' is an excitingly souped-up treatment of Booker White's slide-guitar piece. The live 'While We Cry', by contrast, shows that Shepherd can play cool and pretty, too. Most of the singing is handled by band-member Corey Sterling, Shepherd restricting himself to a drifting J.J. Caleish vocal on 'Riverside'. If the jury is necessarily still out on Shepherd's long-term prospects, the early verdict must be one of cautious but warm approval. (*Ledbetter Heights* Giant)

johnny SHINES (1915–1992)

Shines was that rare being, a blues artist who overcomes age and rustiness to make music that stands up beside the work of his youth. When he came back to the blues in 1965 he was 50, yet his voice had the leonine power of a dozen years before, when he made the records his reputation was based on.

He was born in what is now north Memphis and spent part of his boyhood living on Beale Street, where he was fascinated by the street musicians. "They lived in a world of their own. They sang like they were overcome with sadness, in a trance." He began playing guitar at 17 in Arkansas, where he met Howlin' Wolf, who impressed him greatly, and Robert Johnson. "He played a good guitar, the best I'd heard. I knew he was the man of the day." They travelled together for a year or two until the mercurial

Johnson disappeared. Shines never saw him again but remembered his songs, little imagining that they would one day be his most marketable possession.

In 1941 he settled in Chicago. A 1946 session for Columbia went unissued, a 1950 Chess single unheard, but the Johnson-like 'Ramblin'' (1952) and the exquisite duets with Walter Horton, 'Brutal Hearted Woman' and 'Evening Sun' (1953), staked his claim as a sublime singer. His ensuing disenchantment with the music business was suspended when he started playing again in the 1960s, but although he delighted audiences at home and abroad and made several fine albums, he came to feel undervalued, and when he went back south to live in Alabama he played less. For a while he collaborated with the most logical partner of his generation, Johnson's stepson Robert Lockwood, but a stroke in 1980 weakened his guitar-playing. He made a last album with Snooky Pryor and appeared in the TV documentary *The Search For Robert Johnson*. (MR; *Chicago/The Blues/Today! Vol 3* Vanguard; *Last Night's Dream* Columbia; *Johnny Shines* Hightone)

little mack SIMMONS (1933–)

A pleasant, ungripping singer and harmonica player, the Arkansas-born Simmons made a few obscure singles in the late 1950s and early 1960s as Little Mack (or Mac), then went into the ministry and was scarcely heard of for 30 years, except on an undistinguished 1975 album cut in Paris, *Blue Lights*. His return to blues-making with *High & Lonesome* (1995) was an early strike for St George, an independent label dedicated to turning the Chicago clock back. Simmons's spirited performance, supported by Studebaker John on guitar, certainly belied his age, and the album achieved an excellent reading on the Chicago Traditionalist authenticity meter. So did 1996's *Come Back*

To Me Baby, with sympathetic sidemen like John Primer, Willie Kent and guitarist Jake Dawson. (*High & Lonesome* St George; *Come Back To Me Baby: Chicago Blues Session Volume 38* Wolf)

SLIM HARPO (1924-1970)

Singer, guitarist and harmonica player Harpo was born James Moore in Baton Rouge, Louisiana, his home throughout his life. His big money song was 'I'm A King Bee' (Excello, 1957), a sexy little number set to a jogging, hypnotic riff that has endeared it to many artists, from the Rolling Stones to Sue Foley. With his whining, pleading vocal manner, somewhat like Jimmy Reed's but with better diction, Harpo could appeal more readily to white teenagers than, say, Howlin' Wolf – potential that was enhanced by the mildly exotic production effects on his records, like the woodblocks and maraccas on 'I Got Love If You Want It' or the bubbling 'Boogie Chillen' pattern under 'Shake Your Hips' (a riff brilliantly reworked by Taj Mahal 25 years later in 'Squat That Rabbit' on *Like Never Before*). 'King Bee' was followed into the R&B charts by 'Rainin' In My Heart' (1961) and the talking blues 'Baby, Scratch My Back' (1966): Harpo was far and away the most commercially successful of the south Louisiana bluesmen on Excello, and in the late 1960s could find work on the rock circuit. (*I'm A King Bee, Shake Your Hips* Ace)

byther SMITH (1932-)

In the early 1980s several blues singers stepped out of the shadows, or came up from nowhere, to reaffirm the tenets of 1950s-style Chicago bar blues: sweat rather than synthesizers, Wolf rather than wa-wa. One of them was the singer-guitarist Byther Smith, whose *Tell Me How You Like It* (Grits), a kind of mixed tribute to Howlin' Wolf and Otis Rush, swept across the blues scene like a

wind blowing back good old memories. The Mississippi-born Smith had been around Chicago for two decades, learning from Robert Junior Lockwood and Hubert Sumlin, playing with Rush and Junior Wells. The album brought him European opportunities, and his next album was on an English label, *Addressing The Nation With The Blues* (JSP, 1989). He has since cut for Bullseye Blues and Delmark, whose boss Bob Koester observes, "There's a mellowness there that is disappearing in all but B.B. King." (*Addressing The Nation With The Blues* JSP; *Housefire* Bullseye Blues; *Mississippi Kid* Delmark)

clara SMITH (1895-1935)

Clara Smith was extremely popular in the 1920s, when she was billed as "Queen of the Moaners", and she and Bessie Smith were the twin jewels in Columbia Records' blues crown. Yet her life is poorly documented, perhaps because she died so early, and her recordings have never attracted the attention of any but the most specialized reissue labels.

Reportedly from Spartanburg, South Carolina, she had the usual apprenticeship on the Southern theatre circuit before settling in New York in 1923, the year she began recording with 'Every Woman's Blues'. Over the next nine years she would make about 120 sides. She was on the whole less fortunate than Bessie in her accompanists, often having to endure the uncouth clarinet and alto of Ernest Elliott, humdrum piano by Fletcher Henderson or quaint combinations of stringed instruments, organs and kazoos, but she did earn a couple of dates in 1925 with Louis Armstrong ('Nobody Knows The Way I Feel Dis Mornin'', 'Shipwrecked Blues'), and later with the cornetists Joe Smith and Ed Allen. Her voice was less imposing than Bessie's but to some tastes prettier, and many of her songs were interesting. (*Clara Smith Vols 1–6* Document)

george "harmonica" SMITH (1924-1983)

A second-division Chicago-style harmonica player, Smith made the wise move of getting out of Chicago and spending much of his life on the West Coast, where blues harmonica had not previously flourished. Born in Helena, Arkansas, and brought up in Cairo, Illinois, he began playing in Chicago in 1951 and held the harmonica job in Muddy Waters' band in 1954, between the short-lived Henry Strong and James Cotton. (He would rejoin Waters in 1966.) He commuted between Chicago and California and finally settled in the late 1960s in L.A., where he played with the blues band Bacon Fat and tutored its harmonica player Rod Piazza (1947–), who went on to lead his Mighty Flyers and record for Black Top. In the 1970s Smith worked with Big Mama Thornton, appearing on her album *Jail* (1975), and with another harmonica student, William Clarke. His few albums (mostly not transferred to CD at the time of writing) reflect his admiration for Little Walter. (*Harmonica Ace* Ace)

trixie SMITH (1895-1943)

At 20 Trixie Smith left her home town of Atlanta for New York, where she sang in vaudeville and recorded for the Black Swan and Paramount labels (1922–26), introducing songs that would stay with her throughout her career like 'My Man Rocks Me', 'He May Be Your Man (But He Comes To See Me Sometimes)' and 'Freight Train Blues' ("I hate to hear that engine blow boo-hoo . . ."). She was usually accompanied by small groups from Fletcher Henderson's orchestra, and the coupling of 'The World's Jazz Crazy And So Am I'/'Railroad Blues' (1925), one of her better-selling discs, has solos by Louis Armstrong which rather overshadow her smallish voice. The cornetist Freddie Keppard and clarinettist Johnny Dodds played on 'Messin' Around' (1926).

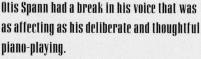

Otis Spann had a break in his voice that was as affecting as his deliberate and thoughtful piano-playing.

After a dozen years' retirement she recorded sturdy new versions of her hits with support by a particularly exotic-sounding Sidney Bechet. Her voice sounded weightier, and she took well to the relaxed swing tempo of the period. (*Trixie Smith Vols 1–2* Document)

otis SPANN (1930–1970)

Even if he had never emerged from the half-shadowy role of a sideman in the Muddy Waters band, Spann would be regarded as one of the finest of modern blues pianists. Fortunately he had time to enjoy a short but marvellously productive career of his own, engaging his listeners with stories of life down home in Mississippi, set to a mill-wheel rhythm of tumbling piano phrases. Deeply influenced by Big Maceo, he shared his hoarse, cloudy singing manner.

He joined Waters' band about 1952 and played on many of his most famous records, while also doing session work with other Chess artists like Howlin' Wolf and Bo Diddley. His own early recordings, including the sensitive *Otis Spann Is The Blues* (1960)

with Robert Junior Lockwood, were not widely circulated, and it was his trip to Europe with Waters on the 1963 AFBF that made him internationally known, followed by excellent albums for Storyville, Decca, Prestige, Testament and other labels. Although he never broke his link with Waters, Spann played piano for Buddy Guy, Johnny Young, Floyd Jones and other singers, always with great empathy and dedication. (*Otis Spann Is The Blues* Candid; *Blues Masters Vol 10* Storyville; *The Blues Of Otis Spann Plus!* See For Miles; *The Biggest Thing Since Colossus* Columbia)

dave SPECTER (1963–)

Only the most stiffnecked blues purist is unlikely to enjoy a gig or record by Specter: the Chicagoan's guitar-playing, motivated equally by T-Bone Walker and B.B. King, and his choice of material seat him firmly on the other side of the room from the experimentalists and blues-rockers. For an extended, uncluttered view of his music hear his performance at a 1994 German concert in a

quartet with the correspondingly idiomatic harmonica and soulful singing of Tad Robinson. Specter has also made several Delmark albums, two with the Mississippi-born singer Barkin' Bill Smith (1928–). (*Bluebird Blues* Delmark; *Live In Europe* Crosscut; *Left Turn On Blue* Delmark)

victoria SPIVEY (1906–1976)

You look to Bessie Smith for majesty, Alberta Hunter for vivacity; Spivey's small, acrid voice conveys different blues qualities, especially in her compositions like the slum lament 'T.B. Blues' or the darkly witty 'Moaning The Blues'. In her heyday she commanded the best musicians in the business, working on record with Louis Armstrong, Red Allen and Lonnie Johnson.

Texas-born, by her teens Spivey was playing the piano semi-professionally. In 1926 she went to St Louis to talk her way into a recording contract and straightaway made a stir with the slyly sexy 'Black Snake Blues'. Over the next decade she recorded many of her own songs, which dwelt on disease, crime and outré sexual images. Away from the studio she worked in revue. Her career declined in the 1940s and 1950s, but she was too positive to be content with retirement, and in the 1960s she reclaimed her spotlight, creating a Spivey record label to promote music by friends like Roosevelt Sykes and Big Joe Williams, and blueswomen from the past like Lucille Hegamin. She visited Europe with the 1963 AFBF and made many other festival appearances in her last years. (*Victoria Spivey Vols 1–4* Document; *Songs We Taught Your Mother* Original Blues Classics; *Grind It!: The Ann Arbor Blues Festival Volume 3* Sequel)

Victoria Spivey in 1932. Her sisters Addie ("Sweet Peas") and Elton ("Za-Zu") were singers too.

frank STOKES (1887–1955)

Stokes was a pioneer figure in the story of Memphis music, his intricate guitar duets with Dan Sane inspiring a line of picking partnerships. Born in Whitehaven, Tennessee (now a section of south Memphis), he grew up to hold a day job as a blacksmith while spending the weekends beating out the blues with Sane, a younger player from Hernando, Mississippi. Between 1927 and 1929 they recorded for Paramount as the Beale Street Sheiks and for Victor under Stokes' name, Sane sometimes being replaced by the fiddler Will Batts (1904–1956). In his deep, rumbling voice Stokes sang blues and rag songs like the locally popular 'Mr Crump Don't Like It' (about Memphis mayor "Boss" Crump and his campaign to clean up the city's low-life sections). Unusually for their time, the Stokes-Sane recordings were as much instrumental as vocal, the verses alternating with muscular guitar choruses. In 1933 Sane and Batts recorded, with the singer-guitarist Jack Kelly, as the South Memphis Jug Band. Stokes, though no longer of interest to record companies, continued to play into the 1940s, when he worked for a while with Booker White. (*Creator Of The Memphis Blues* Yazoo)

STUDEBAKER JOHN (1952–)

The shades of Hound Dog Taylor and J.B. Hutto haunt the stage when Studebaker John & The Hawks play their raw Chicago-style blues. The leader, John Grimaldi, is a native Chicagoan who decided when he was 16 to dedicate himself to playing blues harmonica, but after a few years, inspired by Taylor, began playing slide guitar too. The first Hawks gathered in 1971 to play the North Side Chicago clubs, but it was only with *Rocking The Blues* (1985) that their name spread far outside Chicago – ultimately to Europe, where they have toured and played at festivals and their albums are licensed by the Dutch label Double Trouble. Studebaker John writes his own material but masks the fact with worn-out titles like 'Last Night', 'Hey, Hey, Hey' or 'Talk To Me Baby'. In 1995 he played on Little Mack Simmons' *High & Lonesome* (St George). (*Outside Lookin' In*, *Too Tough*, *Tremoluxe* Blind Pig)

SUGAR BLUE (1955–)

Blue's travels with his harmonica have put him in unusual company. In Paris in the late 1970s he played on stage with Frank Zappa and in the studio with the Rolling Stones ('Some Girls', 'Miss You'). He had made the trip on the advice of Memphis Slim, but gigs were scarce and he played in the streets and métro stations, earning an article in the *New York Herald-Tribune*, probably written by the trombonist Mike Zwerin, who with other expatriate jazzmen backed him on *Cross Roads* (Free Bird, 1980). After making *From Chicago To Paris* (Blue Silver, 1982), Blue returned home, not to Harlem, where he was born (as James Whiting), but Chicago, where he spent a couple of years with Willie Dixon's Chicago Blues All Stars. He would rejoin Dixon in 1988 on *Hidden Charms*.

Meanwhile he had had a cameo part, playing with Brownie McGhee, in the 1987 movie *Angel Heart*. They had worked together before, on McGhee's *Blues Is Truth* (Blue Labor, 1976); the label had also hired him for sessions with Johnny Shines and Roosevelt Sykes, where he had met Louisiana Red, and the two had gone on to tour and record together in 1978.

After a long hiatus in his own recording log, Blue cut *Blue Blazes* (1994), demonstrating that technically he was one of the fastest, hottest harp men around. (*Blue Blazes* Ruf [Europe]/Alligator [US])

Sunnyland Slim, said Chicago's famous broadcaster and writer Studs Terkel, was "a living piece of our folk history, gallantly and eloquently carrying on in the old tradition."

SUNNYLAND SLIM (1907–1995)

Though you might not guess it from scanning the blues racks in the record stores, Slim was one of the great men of Chicago blues for half a century, both in his own right and as an accompanist. His singing and playing were as strong and hard-wearing as he was, the piano florid when it needed to be, restrained and collaborative in the service of another artist.

He was born Albert Luandrew in Vance, Mississippi; his professional name came from a song he composed about the Sunnyland train that ran between Memphis and St Louis. He knew Memphis in the 1930s, and first met there many of the men he would later work with in Chicago, where he settled in the early 1940s. He first recorded in 1947, at the turning-point in Chicago blues history: his sides for Victor as "Dr Clayton's Buddy" belonged to the old order, whereas those he did for Aristocrat with the young Muddy Waters heralded the new. Over the next decade he recorded for almost all the city's blues labels, introducing compositions like 'Brown Skin Woman', 'Devil Is A Busy Man' and 'It's You Baby', and played on countless sessions by J.B. Lenoir, Snooky Pryor, Floyd Jones, Robert Lockwood and others.

He grazed in the new pastures of the 1960s, making albums for Bluesville, Storyville (on tour with the 1964 AFBF), Blue Horizon and Delmark, among others, while in the 1970s he nurtured the career of the stentorian singer Big Time Sarah (1953–). In the last decade of his life, though relatively frail, he continued to record and play in public. His enormous gift to Chicago music was recognized by a City of Chicago Medal Of Merit and a National Heritage Fellowship from the National Endowment for the Arts. (*Chicago Blues Session* Southland; *Slim's Shout* Original Blues Classics; *Blues Masters Vol 8* Storyville; *Midnight Jump* Columbia; *House Rent Party* Delmark)

roosevelt SYKES (1906–1983)

Though he was adaptable enough to walk into a piano bar and play jazz and standards all night, Sykes spent half a century as one of the most visible – and audible – performers in the blues. Draw a diagram of blues piano history and he will sit in the centre like a genial spider, the lines of his influence radiating in all directions. His robust singing, too, was a model for Memphis Slim, Sunnyland Slim and numerous other blues-singing keyboardmen.

He grew up in Arkansas, learned to play as a child and absorbed lessons in blues while travelling with the pianist Lee Green. In the late 1920s he settled in St Louis and in 1929 made his first record for OKeh, '44 Blues'/'Boot That Thing', an immediate

Roosevelt Sykes, a pacemaker of blues piano.

hit. He recorded for several other labels under pseudonyms before joining Decca, for whom he made about 70 sides in 1934–40, many of them good sellers, some destined to become standards, like 'Night Time Is The Right Time', 'Mistake In Life', 'Driving Wheel' and 'Soft And Mellow'. From 1936 he was billed as The Honey Dripper. He moved between St Louis and Chicago, but by the early 1940s had settled in Chicago. As well as his own, he played on records by Walter Davis, St Louis Jimmy Oden and other singers.

By the mid-1950s he was off the recording scene and making a living as resident pianist in one club or another in New Orleans. For years he spent much of his time at resorts along the Gulf Coast, from Houma,

Louisiana, to Biloxi, Mississippi, playing in saloons for tourists, though he took breaks to cut albums in New York and London in the early 1960s, was on the 1965 AFBF and made several other visits to Europe. (*Roosevelt Sykes Vols 1–10* Document; *Hard Drivin' Blues, Goldmine* Delmark)

TAJ MAHAL (1942–)

Taj Mahal has made innovative music for 30 years, constantly refreshing himself with draughts from the original wellsprings of the blues. On top of that, he has become a prime, though not always acknowledged, model for younger black musicians of the 1990s who have gone exploring in the backwoods of early blues.

He was born Henry St Claire Fredericks in New York and raised in Springfield, Massachusetts, taking up guitar in his teens. In his early twenties he played in clubs round Boston, then moved to L.A. and formed the Rising Sons with Ry Cooder.

Though the group's Columbia album was shelved, Taj made several iconoclastic recordings for the company like *The Natch'l Blues* and *Giant Step/De Old Folks At Home*. In the 1970s he investigated Caribbean idioms like reggae and steelband music (*Music Para Tu*, 1976; *Live And Direct*, 1979), while also writing and playing music for the movie *Sounder*.

Taj Mahal's 1988 children's album *Shake Sugaree* won two US awards.

In the 1940s Tampa Red swapped his trademark gold guitar for an electric model.

On his 1990s recordings *Like Never Before*, *Dancing The Blues* and *Phantom Blues* he began to call up blues and R&B memories of his youth, rearranging numbers like 'Mockingbird' and 'Lonely Avenue' with ingenuity and gusto. His instrumental versatility, now encompassing guitar, banjo, keyboards and harmonica, found a showcase in the music he wrote and played for the Lincoln Center Theater production *Mule Bone*. In a 1995 encounter with N. Ravikiran and V.M. Bhatt, *Mumtaz Mahal* (Waterlily Acoustics), the trio applied African-American and Indian stringed instrument methods to Robert Johnson's 'Come On In My Kitchen' and the R&B classic 'Stand By Me' – just the sort of inquisitive, capricious idea that makes Taj's music so bracing. (*The Natch'l Blues* Columbia [US]/Edsel [UK]; *Like Never Before*, *Dancing The Blues* Private; *An Evening Of Acoustic Music* Traditional & Moderne)

TAMPA RED (c1903–1981)

Gifted with a warm voice, a totally original slide-guitar sound and a talent for thoughtful composition, Tampa Red was a comprehensively equipped blues artist. Nice guy, too, according to Big Joe Williams – "no argument, he didn't believe in nothin' like that. He tried to keep the peace all the time." Joe was in a position to know: Tampa once prevented him from beating up Big Bill Broonzy. He was less accommodating about his music: "whatever he wanted done", said Blind John Davis, "it had to be done just like he did it, or else you didn't work with Tampa."

He was born Hudson Woodbridge in Smithville, Georgia, but his parents died when he was young and he was raised by a grandmother Whittaker, whose name he took for official purposes. She lived in

Tampa, Florida; he was light-skinned; hence Tampa Red. By the mid-1920s he was working in Chicago with Georgia Tom Dorsey. Sales of their 1928 duet 'It's Tight Like That' (Vocalion) were incredible – it may have been the best-selling blues of its era – and set Tampa off on a recording career that generated more than 300 sides over 25 years, beside his accompaniments to Ma Rainey, Frankie Jaxon and many other artists. He interspersed the popular hokum numbers with slow blues, slide-guitar instrumentals (practically unique in their day) and jugband novelties.

The partnership with Dorsey broke up in 1932, and for the rest of the decade he alternated between blues in a trio setting with a

pianist (sometimes himself – he played competently in the manner of Leroy Carr) and novelty hot numbers with his Chicago Five. In the 1940s he had a rewarding collaboration with Big Maceo. He weathered every climate change in blues until the early 1950s, working with younger musicians like Walter Horton and the pianist Johnny Jones. The careful imitations of his smooth slide-playing by Robert Nighthawk or Earl Hooker, and the constant revivals of his songs 'Love Me With A Feeling', 'It Hurts Me Too', 'Black Angel Blues', 'Don't You Lie To Me' and 'Let Me Play With Your Poodle', confirmed his status as a major creative figure.

The death of his wife Frances in 1954 knocked the stuffing out of him, and except

for a brief comeback in 1959–60, when he recorded a pair of Bluesville albums, he was in retirement for the rest of his life. (*It Hurts Me Too* Indigo; *Bottleneck Guitar* Yazoo; *The Bluebird Recordings 1934–1936* RCA/Bluebird)

eddie TAYLOR (1923–1985)

Hard to know if Eddie Taylor was born to be a backing musician or just slipped into the habit of it. On record, at least, he had enough personality to carry a performance – his mid-1950s Vee Jay sides 'Bad Boy' and 'Big Town Playboy' are gems – yet he spent years putting rhythmic muscle into the messy music of Jimmy Reed, a player not remotely his equal.

In Mississippi as a young man Taylor moved among musicians like Howlin' Wolf and Honeyboy Edwards. Like them, he headed for Chicago, where he renewed his boyhood acquaintance with Reed and spent the 1950s playing guitar and bass guitar with him. By the mid-1960s the partnership was over and Taylor worked with other bluesmen (John Lee Hooker, Roosevelt Sykes) or as a leader. His albums for Testament, Big Bear and Blind Pig are journeyman performances but *I Feel So Bad* (Advent, 1972) set him alongside George Smith and Phillip Walker, an inspired combination. (*Bad Boy* Charly; *I Feel So Bad* Hightone)

hound dog TAYLOR (1917–1975)

Hound Dog Taylor's huge toothy smile seemed an invitation to good-time blues, and it was no fraud. A singer of wild abandon, playing a slide guitar with the tone of a chainsaw, he created an atmosphere of noisy bonhomie that drew many listeners to Florence's Lounge on Chicago's South Side in the 1960s and 1970s. One of the visitors, an assistant at Bob Koester's Jazz Record Mart named Bruce Iglauer, thought Taylor ought

to be recorded. Koester didn't want him on his Delmark label, so Iglauer created his own company, Alligator Records, to put out *Hound Dog Taylor & The House Rockers* (1971). It was a good move for both parties.

Theodore Roosevelt Taylor arrived in Chicago from Mississippi in the early 1940s, and became a full-time musician in 1957. His guitar-playing owed a lot to Elmore James (though Taylor chose to phrase it the

Koko Taylor, Chicago's queen of the blues, belting out a number at the New Orleans Jazz & Heritage Festival.

other way round), but his attack was much more jagged and propulsive, almost the approach of a heavy metal axeman. His favourite format was a trio with rhythm guitar (Brewer Phillips) and drums (Ted Harvey), a line-up replicated more or less exactly by George Thorogood & The Destroyers, Studebaker John & The Hawks, Omar & The Howlers, and numerous other bands. (*Hound Dog Taylor & The House Rockers, Natural Boogie, Beware Of The Dog* Alligator)

koko TAYLOR (1935–)

Koko Taylor sings the blues. You can bank on it. She will probably never sing anything else. No women and few men on the scene can match her straight-from-the-heart performances, her unswerving belief that the blues says it all.

Until she was 18 she lived in Memphis, but when she married she moved to Chicago, where she worked as a house cleaner by day and sang in the clubs at night. She cut her own song 'Like Heaven To Me' for the USA label in 1963, and in the following year linked up with Willie Dixon, who had told her, "You got the right voice to sing the blues – that growl you got will put you over." Her second Checker single, Dixon's song 'Wang Dang Doodle', was one of the notable discs of 1966 and helped her get on the 1967 AFBF. She worked regularly in the clubs with Mighty Joe Young, cut a couple of albums and visited Europe in 1972–73, but she still needed her day job in domestic service. In the mid-1970s she signed with Alligator, a partnership that has produced a handful of hearty albums and established her without peer among female singers. She specializes in songs celebrating women's strength, like 'Mother Nature', 'Queen Bee' and 'I'm A Woman'. There's a brief but telling sequence of her singing in a New Orleans club in David Lynch's 1990 movie *Wild At Heart*. (*I Got What It Takes, The Earthshaker, Force Of Nature* Alligator)

melvin TAYLOR (1959–)

Though born in Mississippi, Melvin Taylor has spent almost all his life in Chicago,

where he began playing guitar in public in his teens. He had mostly learned from records by B.B. and Albert King and Jimi Hendrix, though later he would cock an ear to jazz pickers like George Benson and Kenny Burrell. At 22 he joined the Legendary Blues Band when they first toured Europe, and made enough impact for the French Isabel label to record him the following year in Chicago (*Blues On The Run*). In 1984 he made *Plays The Blues For You* for the same company with Lucky Peterson. For the next decade or so he was the resident bluesman at Rosa's Lounge on Chicago's West Side and appeared at several of the city's blues festivals, but except for a track on *The New Bluebloods* (Alligator) he was barely heard on record. In 1995 he broke the silence with a fiery trio album, *Melvin Taylor & The Slack Band*, with numbers ranging from the Larry

Melvin Taylor is among the more promising of Chicago's thirty-something bluesmen.

Davis/Stevie Ray Vaughan song 'Texas Flood' to Hendrix's 'Voodoo Chile' among his originals. Though his singing is relaxed, even sometimes conversational, his guitar improvisations have much of Hendrix's tightly curled strength. (*Blues On The Run, Melvin Taylor & The Slack Band* Evidence)

johnny TEMPLE (1906–1968)

An acquaintance and near-contemporary of Skip James, Temple made his mark in the later 1930s as a very different kind of artist, delivering sedate blues in the "what's a reasonable man to do?" vein of Lonnie Johnson, generally accompanied by the Harlem Hamfats or a similar line-up. That he

henry THOMAS (dates unknown)

Leadbelly's apart, no recordings are more revealing about black recreational music in the late nineteenth century than the couple of dozen reels, rags, minstrel songs and blues left by "Ragtime Texas". Almost nothing is known about his life: he is reported to have been born in 1874, which is consistent with the repertoire he knew. His springy guitar-playing, probably inspired by banjo-picking styles, implies that he was used to catering for dancers. Practically uniquely among Southern musicians of his time, he also played the quill, or panpipes, which lent his music a fairy lilt. (MR)

jesse THOMAS (1911–1995)

Jesse Thomas was one of the blues' more original thinkers. His clipped, dry-toned guitar-playing, which sounded rather meagre on 'Blue Goose Blues' (Victor, 1929), gained greatly from amplification, and his 1940s–1950s recordings, mostly made in L.A., are fascinatingly varied responses to tradition and innovation. One song may follow the unpredictable contours of his brother's slide-guitar blues. (Willard "Ramblin'" Thomas [1902–c1945] recorded some notable pieces in the late 1920s.) Another throbs to a bass pulse like Lil' Son Jackson's; another has the swagger of T-Bone Walker. 'Long Time' is pure Lowell Fulson. But stylistic versatility is only half the story, because Thomas also wrote artfully in several manners, pausing now and then to dredge up an old memory. In 1953, for instance, on a Specialty single, he coupled a minor-key blues in the current West Coast idiom, 'When You Say I Love You', with a re-examination of the

enjoyed a fairly long career on record was largely due to the lasting appeal of 'Louise Louise Blues' (1936), which set Southern downhome language against the disengaged piano-guitar accompaniment developed by the period's studio musicians from the model of Leroy Carr and Scrapper Blackwell.

Temple grew up round Jackson, Mississippi, where he probably began his

association with Joe and Charlie McCoy, continued in Chicago. His connection with the producer Mayo Williams earned him recording opportunities as late as 1949, but although he gamely hung on in the Chicago milieu until the 1960s (and even recorded for Chess), his style had long been overtaken by younger men. (*Johnny Temple Vols 1–3* Document)

dinah WASHINGTON (1924–1963)

After Bessie Smith and Billie Holiday, Washington was the next great singer to apply blues techniques and feeling to the entire range of popular song. Her acrid, unsentimental style was an essential model for successors like Aretha Franklin.

Born Ruth Lee Jones in Tuscaloosa, Alabama, she grew up in Chicago, where she won a talent contest when she was 15. She was spotted singing in her local church by Sallie Martin, an associate of the gospel songwriter and promoter Thomas A. Dorsey, and hired to tour with her. "But shoot", Martin remembered, "she'd catch the eye of some man and she'd be out the church before the minister finished off the doxology." In the early 1940s she adopted her stage name while working with Lionel Hampton and made 'Evil Gal Blues' (Keynote, 1943) with a small group from his band. Quitting Hampton in 1945 she recorded for Apollo with the tenor saxophonist Lucky Thompson, then signed a contract that proved to be lifelong with Mercury. Blues, often saucy in their sentiments, like 'Long John Blues' or 'T.V. Is The Thing This Year', or the topical and clever 'Record Ban Blues', gave way to standard pop songs, and small-group jazz accompaniments to lush orchestrations; but she made fine recordings with jazz colleagues like the trumpeter Clifford Brown, did a Bessie Smith songbook album and had chart hits like 'What A Diff'rence A Day Made' and 'Baby, Get Lost', before succumbing to an accidental but fatal cocktail of alcohol and medication. (*First Issue: The Dinah Washington Story* Mercury; *Mellow Mama* Delmark; *The Queen Of The Blues* Charly; *Jazz Masters 19* Verve)

johnny "guitar" WATSON (1935–1996)

Watson was one of the Houston, Texas, gang who latched on to the T-Bone Walker sound in the 1950s, though by his mid-teens he had left for L.A. Even at that age he played with daring (hear the instrumental 'Space Guitar' from 1954), and by the time he was 20 he had "Guitar" pinned on to his name, earning it with his hit recording of 'Those Lonely, Lonely Nights' (1955) and 'Cuttin' In' (1962). Despite his talent (he also played piano) and cool-dude presence, he failed to become a major name, though British R&B fans who caught his act in 1965, when he was on tour with the rock 'n' roll singer Larry Williams, thought him equal to Chuck Berry, Bo Diddley or Buddy Guy. But in the mid-1970s he remade himself with

As well as "Guitar", Johnny Watson sometimes used the sobriquet "Gangster Of Love" from an early hit.

great success as a soul man playing funk and disco music ('A Real Mother For Ya', 'I Don't Want To Be A Lone Ranger'). Art directors took to photographing him in sharp threads surrounded by soignée, subservient women. After a low period in the 1980s he made the Grammy-nominated *Bow Wow* (1994) and returned to the international touring circuit: he died on stage in a Japanese blues club. (*Hot Just Like TNT* Ace)

curley WEAVER (1906–1962)

Weaver joined the Atlanta, Georgia, blues circle in the mid-1920s, where he hob-nobbed with Barbecue Bob, Buddy Moss and Blind Willie McTell. On his first record, 'No No Blues' (Columbia, 1928), his slide-playing was memorably punctuated by double hammer-strokes on the bottom string. The record was quite popular and he repeated or varied it several times, partnered on one occasion by the superb harmonica player Eddie Mapp. In 1930 he recorded infectious small-group music with Moss and Barbecue Bob as the Georgia Cotton Pickers, and in 1933 with Moss and the singer-guitarist Fred McMullen as the Georgia Browns. He also collaborated with McTell on a number of sides, an association that lasted at least until the end of the 1940s, when they record-ed for Regal. Weaver subsequently recorded a few solos for Sittin' In With. Both men responded to musical changes in the blues in the 1930s by remaking their styles: Weaver exchanged his lively slide-guitar playing for a graver approach more like Moss's. (*Georgia Blues (1928–1933), Curley Weaver (1933–1935)* Document)

katie WEBSTER (1939–)

Until the 1980s this boisterous singer and pianist was known only to record-collectors, as an obscure but prolific studio musician behind Louisiana artists on the Excello and Goldband labels, such as Lightnin' Slim and Lonesome Sundown. She also played piano with Otis Redding in the 1960s, and after his

Katie Webster. "Her speciality", wrote critic Dave Gelly in 1985, "is a monologue about men – their conceit, ingratitude and general crumminess."

death went into temporary retirement. But in the early 1980s she was repeatedly booked for European tours and recorded albums for the German label Ornament. To balance these solo efforts she cut *You Know That's Right* (Arhoolie, 1985) with the band Hot Links and the album that established her in

the United States, *The Swamp Boogie Queen* (1988), with guest spots by Bonnie Raitt and Robert Cray. With great good humour she served a mixed menu of blues and R&B, epitomized by her song 'Zydeco Shoes And California Blues', until she was compelled by a stroke to hang up the one and play no more

of the other. (*The Swamp Boogie Queen, Two-Fisted Mama!, No Foolin'!* Alligator)

casey bill WELDON (1909–)

One Will Weldon was a founder member of the Memphis Jug Band, but on musical evidence there is scarcely any reason to identify him with the singer and electric steel guitarist Casey Bill Weldon, who made 60-odd records in the 1930s, among them "point" numbers like 'Somebody Changed The Lock On My Door', the topical 'W.P.A. Blues' and 'Flood Water Blues', and up-tempo dance tunes like 'Round And Round' and 'You Shouldn't Do That'. Casey Bill had a faintly pugnacious singing manner, not unlike that of Peetie Wheatstraw, whom he sometimes accompanied on disc. As a steel guitarist he pursued some of the same sound effects as white players like Leon McAuliffe with Bob Wills' Texas Playboys. His combo sides, like those with the Hokum Boys or Washboard Rhythm Kings, might be called black Western Swing. Big Bill Broonzy remembered him as being from Pine Bluff, Arkansas, which may explain why some of his songs ('Lock On My Door', 'We Gonna Move To The Outskirts Of Town') were re-used by the Arkansas-born Louis Jordan. He stopped recording abruptly in 1938 and may have gone to live in California, but surprisingly little is known for sure about him. (*The Hawaiian Guitar Wizard 1935–1938* EPM/Blues Collection)

junior WELLS (1934–)

No one fills the gap left by the early death of Little Walter, but Wells is the best-known and most charismatic of his surviving contemporaries, thanks in part to his long and – sometimes – fruitful partnership with Buddy Guy. He arrived in Chicago from Memphis at 12, and before he was 20 was filling Walter's place in the Muddy Waters band. His first recordings in his own name, for States in 1953–54, were vigorous, youthful exercises in the manner of Sonny Boy Williamson I ('Cut That Out', 'Hoodoo Man'), but later (1957–62) sides on Chief and Profile like 'Little By Little' and 'Messin' With The Kid' fashioned him as a lively pop-blues singer not unlike Billy Boy Arnold.

his gruff delivery and even borrow his titles: there was a Peetie's Boy, a Devil's Daddy-in-Law, a Peetie Wheatstraw's Buddy.

The name Peetie Wheatstraw itself may belong to black folklore. The bluesman who appropriated it was born William Bunch in Ripley, Tennessee, and probably raised in Cotton Plant, Arkansas, though before he was 30 he was living in East St Louis, Illinois, on the other side of the Mississippi from St Louis, Missouri. Other St Louis musicians remember him as a guitarist as much as a pianist, and his few recordings with guitar show him to have been capable and distinctive, but he settled on the piano as his main instrument. His listeners probably didn't care either way: it was the humour and urban savvy that they valued in songs like 'Working On The Project' or 'Third Street's Going Down', and the instrumental interludes were generally dominated by the guitar of Kokomo Arnold or Charley Jordan. His later sides, accompanied by session musicians, are less appealing. (*Peetie Wheatstraw Vols 1–7* Document)

booker WHITE (1909–1977)

The riveting songs Booker White put on record in 1937–40 (see Milestone Recordings) were at once an end and a beginning. He would never again give so much of himself with such concentration: his later work tended to be diffuse. Yet that later work might never have been heard if some blues-lovers, inspired by the old records, had not written a letter on a whim to a town he had once mentioned in a song – Aberdeen, Mississippi. By then (1963) he was in Memphis, but he could be found, and was.

White's youth in Mississippi was a patchwork of farm labour, pro baseball and playing blues at parties. He was much impressed

Meanwhile he worked regularly at the Chicago clubs Pepper's Lounge and Theresa's, often with Guy, who played on his debut album *Hoodoo Man Blues* (1966) and the Vanguard sets *It's My Life, Baby!* (1966) and *Coming At You* (1968). The duo went to Europe with the 1966 AFBF and have gone back many times since, sometimes as support to the Rolling Stones; they have also toured Africa, Australia and Japan. Although Wells' albums *South Side Blues Jam* (1971), with Guy, and *On Tap* (1975) proved he had not lost his aptitude for Chicago band blues, his 1980s and 1990s discs have been as inconsistent as his in-person appearances, but *Come On In This House* (1996) is an intriguing set of classic blues songs with a rotating cast of slide guitarists, among them Alvin Youngblood Hart, Corey Harris and Sonny Landreth. (*Hoodoo Man Blues, South Side Blues Jam, On Tap* Delmark; *Come On In This House* Telarc)

peetie WHEATSTRAW (1902–1941)

Boastful and streetwise, Wheatstraw was a rap artist disguised as a blues singer. Posing as "The Devil's Son-in-Law", he chanted Satanic verses about his power over women, punctuating his lines with a strangulated "ooh, well, well" that prompted one of his hearers to remark, "Good God, why doesn't that man yodel and be done with it?" Between 1930 and 1941 he made over 160 recordings, accompanied another dozen or so artists and influenced many more to copy by Charlie Patton, whose gruff delivery he shared, but on guitar he preferred the rush and clatter of a slide, which he demonstrated on his first record, 'The Panama Limited' (Victor, 1930). After his 1940 sides he settled in Memphis, where he played for a while with Frank Stokes but was soon in virtual retirement.

His re-emergence, trumpeted by an encouragingly sturdy album on Takoma, led to many engagements (such as the 1966 Newport Folk Festival and a trip to Europe with the 1967 AFBF) and albums for labels both at home and abroad. Unbounded by the playing time of a 78 rpm disc, he would spin long narratives, packed with anecdotes and private references, over guitar patterns that lacked the rippling fluidity of his younger playing. But while it could be difficult music, it was always, inexorably, music that only he could have made. (MR; *Sky Songs* Arhoolie; *Big Daddy* Biograph; *1963 Isn't 1962* Gene's [US]/Edsel [UK])

georgia WHITE (1903–c1980)

A hard-edged but not unmusical singer, Georgia White seems to have been the most prolific blueswoman of the 1930s. Her output of 90 issued recordings between 1935 and 1941 exceeds that of her rivals Lil and Merline Johnson and even Memphis Minnie during those years. Her own piano accompaniments on slow and medium-paced blues are tidy and unobtrusive, but if the buoyant playing on 'The Blues Ain't Nothin' But . . . ???' (1938) is hers, she was an accomplished stomper too. The song has been widely circulated, though in her own day she was best known for 'You Done Lost Your Good Thing Now' (1935). One of her most vivid songs was 'Walkin' The Street', a rewrite of the prostitute's lament that Jelly

Georgia White. "She was very easy to get along with," said Big Bill Broonzy. "Real friendly."

Roll Morton called 'Mamie Desdume's Blues'. She seems to have been closely associated with the pianist and tunesmith Richard M. Jones, who played piano on many of her records and wrote some of her material; she also recorded his already popular numbers 'Trouble In Mind' and 'Jazzin' Babies Blues'.

Born in Georgia, she reached Chicago in the 1920s and sang with the clarinettist Jimmie Noone's band at the Apex Club. In later years she led her own all-women orchestra. She was last heard of in Chicago in the late 1950s. (*Trouble In Mind 1935–1941* EPM/Blues Collection)

josh WHITE (1915-1969)

Josh White made an unusual journey in his career. In the 1930s he was a blues singer and guitarist making records for the "race" market, in the 1940s a member of New York's political folk-singing clique, and in the 1950s a sleek cabaret artist.

As a young man he worked as the eyes of sightless street singers like Blind Willie Johnson and Joe Taggart, recording with the latter. In New York in the early 1930s he was a jobbing record artist on ARC, deploying his high, clear voice on both sacred songs (released under his own name) and blues (as Pinewood Tom). His lissom guitar was also heard on some late sides by Leroy Carr. By the end of the decade, however, he was more likely to be sharing a stage with Paul Robeson or Leadbelly, and in the 1940s he almost deserted the blues for gospel music, worksongs and political message pieces like 'Southern Exposure' and 'Strange Fruit', a repertoire later swelled with traditional ballads and whiskery popular songs.

White was popular in Britain, where he was one of the very few black singers to be heard on radio, and visited there at least five times in the 1950s and 1960s, recording on several occasions, but neither these tours nor his numerous albums for Elektra and

Mercury made much impression on the new blues audience of the 1960s. His son Josh Jr and daughters Beverly and Judy followed him into the business. (*Blues Singer 1932–1936* Columbia; *Josh White Vol 4 (1940–1941)* Document)

robert WILKINS (1896-1987)

The most striking feature of Wilkins' early recordings is how elegantly, if unconventionally, melodic they are, in both singing and guitar-playing. This is as true when they follow commonplace blues progressions ('Get Away Blues') as when they are quirkier in shape, like 'I'll Go With Her', 'Fallin' Down Blues' or the lovely 'That's No Way To Get Along'. By contrast there is little you could call melody in the one-chord tune 'Rollin' Stone', which sounds like something carved from the earliest geological layer of the blues.

Wilkins was from Hernando, Mississippi, the home of important blues guitarists such as Garfield Akers and Joe Calicott, as well as the less gifted but more famous Jim Jackson. Some of his guitar patterns recall Akers, while others resemble ideas of Frank Stokes, whom he knew in Memphis in the 1910s and 1920s. Alarmed by fighting at a party where he was playing, he deserted secular music in the 1930s and took up the twin careers of herbalist and minister in the Church Of God In Christ.

Almost 30 years later he was persuaded to record again. Though he would not sing blues, he refashioned 'That's No Way To Get Along' as a Biblical narrative, 'The Prodigal Son', on his album *Memphis Gospel Singer* (Piedmont, 1964), where it was heard by the Rolling Stones, who recorded it on *Beggar's Banquet* (1968). Wilkins' rich, flowing guitar interpretations of sacred songs had much in common with his blues playing. (*The Original Rolling Stone* Yazoo; *Remember Me* Gene's [US]/Edsel [UK])

big joe WILLIAMS (1903-1982)

Williams was the archetypal footloose bluesman, forever on the road, from St Louis to Chicago to New York to L.A., with regular turns south to his birthplace in Crawford, Mississippi, where he finally retired. He met everyone, remembered everyone. "To know this man", wrote the blues guitarist Mike Bloomfield, "was to know the story of black America."

By the time he left home in his teens he had picked up some music from relatives and neighbours. He played with minstrel troupes and jugbands and travelled with Little Brother Montgomery, the harmonica player "Bullet" Williams and Honeyboy Edwards, who remembers how he "used to play a lot of guitar in Spanish [open G tuning], put that clamp [capo] on there, and it sound mostly betwixt a guitar and a mandolin." By the mid-1930s he was based (as much as he ever was) in St Louis, where he had married the singer Bessie Mae Smith. On disc he created classic duets with Sonny Boy Williamson I such as 'Baby Please Don't Go' and 'Highway 49' (1941), but the partnership was broken when Williamson was killed in 1948 and by the 1950s Williams was almost forgotten.

Like Blind Willie McTell, however, he could smell opportunities, and he ran across Bob Koester just as the St Louis record store owner was planning a collectors' record label, Delmark. *Piney Woods Blues* (1961) and subsequent albums for Delmark and Arhoolie introduced Williams' wild and wayward music and his personally customized nine-string guitar to the new blues audience, which came to see him at folk clubs across the nation, from the Ash Grove in L.A. by way of Chicago's Blind Pig and Fickle Pickle to

Big Joe Williams, disc star. "When I went back down south, boy, they'd put me up on top of a house to hear me play."

Gerde's Folk City in New York, where he played with the young Bob Dylan on harmonica, an encounter commemorated in recordings for Victoria Spivey's label. He logged further albums for Folkways, Bluesville, Testament and Storyville, and pointed his travelling shoes towards Europe, though by the 1970s he carried a walking-stick as well, in which he cut a notch for every gig he played. He is fondly remembered by thousands of blues-lovers who had glimpsed his world through his songs. (MR; *Joe Williams (1935–1941)* Blues Document; *Blues On Highway 49* Delmark; *Back To The Country* Testament; *Blues Masters Vol 2* Storyville)

robert pete WILLIAMS (1914–1980)

If ever an artist listened to a different drummer it was Robert Pete Williams. His blues are like nobody else's – impromptu soliloquies over rambling guitar lines, free in their rhythm, disorderly in their harmony. Like Booker White he was preoccupied with his time in prison, with more reason since he had to endure many years of it, and in the hated penitentiary of Angola, Louisiana.

He was born near Baton Rouge, and spent virtually his whole life within Louisiana. He began playing in his twenties but never made any records until a couple of folklorists visited Angola in

Robert Pete Williams. "It's a sounding in the air, and that sounding works up to be a blues."

the early 1960s to collect prisoners' songs and taped his 'Prisoner's Talking Blues' and 'Pardon Renied [*i.e.* Denied] Again'. These and other songs on albums for Folk-Lyric (reissued on CD by Arhoolie) and Bluesville helped to secure his parole in 1959, and when he was finally allowed out of Louisiana in 1964 he was immediately engaged for the Newport Folk Festival. He played at many other festivals and visited Europe twice, impressing his hearers with his ability to compose on the spot. Perhaps he felt that he could most truly speak his mind by giving himself the challenge of spontaneous invention. (*Robert Pete Williams Vols 1 & 2* Arhoolie; *Free Again* Original Blues Classics; *Blues Masters Vol 1* Storyville)

"homesick" james WILLIAMSON (1914–)

A cousin of Elmore James, Homesick was also his bass-guitarist sidekick for several years and played on many of his later recordings. Not long before Elmore's death he recorded a version of 'Crossroads' (USA) with his own idiosyncratic slide guitar, and for a time after that he took the role of Elmore's legatee, as on *Blues On The Southside* (Prestige) or his tracks on Vanguard's *Chicago/The Blues/Today! Vol 2*.

His early life is somewhat mysterious. He no doubt met many other bluesmen while hoboing in the 1930s, as he asserts, but his claim that he recorded then does not seem valid. He was probably in Chicago by the late 1930s or 1940s, when he played with the pianist Jimmy Walker. His early-1950s singles on Chance included 'Homesick', from which he presumably took his name. He visited Europe with the 1970 AFBF and frequently afterwards, often with the harmonica player Snooky Pryor, with whom he made several albums. (*Blues On The Southside* Original Blues Classics; *Sad And Lonesome* [with Snooky Pryor] Wolf)

sonny boy WILLIAMSON I (1914–1948)

John Lee "Sonny Boy" Williamson's impact on blues was prompt and profound. Making his name with his second release, 'Good Morning, School Girl', in 1937, he poured out songs over the next few years, captivating record-buyers and impressing fellow musicians with his inventive compositions, chewed-over singing and the quick-change artistry of his harmonica-playing.

In his youth he was acquainted with fellow-Tennesseans Sleepy John Estes and Yank Rachell, and when he established himself as a Bluebird recording artist in Chicago in the late 1930s he often worked with Rachell as well as Big Joe Williams, Walter Davis, Robert Nighthawk and Big Bill Broonzy. In 10 years (1937–47) he made over 100 sides, among them such enduring pieces of the blues harmonica repertoire as 'Better Cut That Out', 'Early In The Morning'

Sonny Boy Williamson II (see next page) – a blues maverick disguised as a city gent.

(both later recorded by Junior Wells), 'I Been Dealing With The Devil' and 'My Black Name Blues'. He also worked productively on record accompanying Big Joe Williams, notably on their 1940s sides for Bluebird and Columbia like 'King Biscuit Stomp'. His music was eagerly studied by Little Walter, Billy Boy Arnold, Snooky Pryor and many other young harmonica players, and he would certainly have been a figure of substance in Chicago in the 1950s, had he not been ice-picked to death by a mugger while on his way home from a job. (*The Bluebird Recordings 1937–1938* RCA/Bluebird; *Sugar Mama* Indigo)

sonny boy WILLIAMSON II (1899–1965)

He used to say that he was the first Sonny Boy Williamson – sometimes that he was the only one, though anybody with half an ear could tell that his bleating harmonica and sly, half-spoken vocals were a different approach altogether from his forerunner's. His contemporaries knew him as Alex "Rice" Miller from Glendora, Mississippi. In the 1930s he played with Robert Johnson, Elmore James and Howlin' Wolf. In the 1940s he became widely known for his *King Biscuit Time* broadcasts on the KFFA radio station in Helena, Arkansas and his road-work with the King Biscuit Entertainers, a shifting aggregation of musicians that included Robert Junior Lockwood, the pianist Willie Love (1906–1953) and the drummer James "Peck" Curtis (1912–1970). He made his first recordings for Trumpet (1951–54), among them the original versions of 'Eyesight To The Blind' and 'Nine Below Zero'. In Detroit he worked with the singer-guitarist Baby Boy Warren (1919–1977), while in Chicago he opened an eight-year association with Checker Records with 'Don't Start Me Talkin'' (1955). His album *Down And Out Blues* (Chess, 1959) was a set book for British R&B bands in the

1960s, as was his 1963 single 'Help Me' with its organ figure out of Booker T. & The M.G.s' 'Green Onions'.

In Europe, which Williamson first visited with the 1963 AFBF, he was appreciated for his Mephisthophelean goatee, two-tone suits and meandering reminiscences, which he developed into a new free-form blues genre on two Storyville albums with Matt Murphy and Memphis Slim. He also recorded in Britain with the Yardbirds (including Eric Clapton), the Animals and the organist Brian Auger (*Don't Send Me No Flowers*, 1965). Long after his death, KFFA continued to broadcast his old taped shows. (*King Biscuit Time* Arhoolie; *The Essential* MCA/Chess; *Blues Masters Vol 12* Storyville; *Live In England* Charly)

ralph WILLIS (dates unknown)

Willis's background is obscure, but references in his lyrics support Brownie McGhee's impression that he came from Alabama. Like McGhee, or Alec Seward from Virginia or Gabriel Brown from Florida, he emigrated from the South to New York before or during World War II, recording in the 1940s on independent labels like Signature, Savoy and Jubilee, sometimes accompanied by McGhee and Sonny Terry. His output was surprisingly large (over 40 issued sides) for an artist who, unlike McGhee, was rustic in delivery and timing and evidently disinclined to modify his style. Still, the records have a pleasantly casual air, rather like the contemporary Harlem skiffle of Dan Burley or the McGhee brothers. Though he was aware of predecessors such as Blind Lemon Jefferson or the Virginian Luke Jordan, whose 'Church Bells' he rang again, the studio ambience of Willis's later sessions sometimes lent his guitar-playing the more up-to-date booming sound of a Lightnin' Hopkins. In the end, though, it was probably his records' growing resemblance to McGhee and Terry's joint output

that rendered him commercially superfluous. (*Ralph Willis Vols 1 & 2* Document)

hop WILSON (1921–1975)

Like his fellow steel guitarist Robert Nighthawk, Hop Wilson let the low, brooding tone of his instrument drift into his singing, making songs like 'Feel So Glad' and 'Merry Christmas Darling' more sombre than their titles, and spreading throughout much of his work an air of unhappiness and disillusion. In truth his career was hardly a successful one. A native Texan, Harding Wilson first played harmonica (his nickname may originally have been "Harp"). In the 1950s and early 1960s he worked in Houston, often with the drummer "King Ivory Lee" Semiens, and recorded for Goldband and Ivory, but by the late 1960s he had lost interest in making records and played, between bouts of respiratory illness, mainly in Houston's blues clubs. (*Steel Guitar Flash Plus* Ace; *Houston Ghetto Blues* Bullseye Blues)

smokey WILSON (1935–)

Since 1970 Smokey Wilson has lived in Watts, L.A., where for many years he ran the Pioneer Club, booked local and visiting blues names and led the house band. Anyone expecting him to echo the glossy music of T-Bone Walker is in for a shock, though: Howlin' Wolf is the declared model for his hoarse shouting, while his down-to-earth guitar lines unwind out of a past in Mississippi, where he was born and played as a young man with Frank Frost, Big Jack Johnson and Roosevelt "Booba'" Barnes. "I bring the cottonfield with me", he says, "and I got the juke-joint inside."

He made a couple of albums in the 1970s for Big Town, and the more considered *88th Street Blues* (Murray Brothers, 1983) with Rod Piazza producing and playing harmonica. A dozen years later he reappeared

on Bullseye Blues. (*88th Street Blues* Blind Pig; *Smoke 'N' Fire, The Real Deal, The Man From Mars* Bullseye Blues)

u.p. WILSON (1935–)

Like his Texas contemporary Johnny Copeland in Houston, U. P. Wilson spent many years content with a local reputation – in his case as the hot guitar player and blues singer around Dallas-Fort Worth. Copeland had to go elsewhere to find his break; Wilson never left, but thanks to his own persistence, word-of-mouth reports and interest from European blues enthusiasts, he stepped out into a wider blues world in the 1980s, and by the mid-1990s was known internationally.

Wilson puts on a show, playing one-handed while drinking, smoking or greeting fans, but behind the tricks and the over-heated language of his billing ('Texas Tornado', 'Atomic Guitar' . . .) is an artist with a talent for more than just getting good old boys to boogie down, as he proved on *Boogie Boy!* (1994). Its successor, *This Is U.P. Wilson* (JSP, 1995), was flawed by his peculiar decision to sing in falsetto, but on

U.P. Wilson. *"It's tough here in Texas. Everywhere you look there's guitar players."*

Whirlwind (1996) he rediscovered the mixture of Texas shuffles and low-down blues that suits his considerable guitar skills and resonant voice. (*Boogie Boy! The Texas Guitar Tornado Returns!*, *Whirlwind* JSP)

johnny WINTER (1944–)

In some ways Winter's early career prefigured Stevie Ray Vaughan's a decade later. He too was a Texan, from the Gulf Coast city of Beaumont, and he played electric guitar blues with a fire stoked during years of clubland scuffling.

He was playing in public by 14. At 19 he tried his luck in Chicago, unrewardingly, and returned to Texas, where he did a great deal of recording for small labels, both in his own name and accompanying local blues artists. In 1968, through a combination of luckily timed publicity and a showcase gig in New York, he attracted a lot of attention and signed a lucrative contract with Columbia. His eponymous debut did well, but its successors mixed blues and rock material, increasingly favouring the latter, and much of his 1970s output has not weathered well. He did, however, play both producer and

sideman with great expertise on four albums by Muddy Waters for Blue Sky, and his collaboration with Sonny Terry, *Whoopin'* (Alligator, 1983), was among the best work either man had done for years. Winter himself then signed with Alligator to produce satisfying and very popular albums like *Guitar Slinger* (1984). In the 1990s he recorded for Pointblank. Now that all the hysteria attending his early work has faded,

Johnny Winter. "There's nobody that really plays *original*. You can't. You can find some of everybody's licks in almost everybody's playing."

it can be seen that his raw talent has matured well. (*Johnny Winter* Columbia; *The Progressive Blues Experiment* ITM; *Nothin' But The Blues* Blue Sky [US]/BGO [UK]; *Guitar Slinger* Alligator; *Let Me In* Pointblank)

jimmy WITHERSPOON (1923–)

"Spoon" belongs to that shadowy world where the identities of blues singers and jazz singers collide. Unlike his fellow denizen Joe Turner, he approaches the blues verse not as rhythmic vocalese but as a story to be acted out, using what in his prime was a naturally handsome voice.

When he was 21 he replaced Walter Brown in Jay McShann's band: "Tain't Nobody's Business' (1949) spent seven months in the R&B chart. Later he worked as a solo and with bands led by the De Paris brothers, Jesse Stone and McShann again, refreshing his fading career in 1959 with his triumphant appearance at the Monterey Jazz Festival. In the 1960s he worked with jazzmen Ben Webster, Buck Clayton and Count Basie and cut a series of interestingly diversified albums for Prestige, while in the following decade he experimented, not very profitably, with rock material and musicians (Joe Walsh, Eric Burdon). Thereafter he made his living chiefly as a club singer, maintaining a prolific recording log until his voice began to give out in the late 1980s. (MR; *Blowin' In From Kansas City* Ace; *Evenin' Blues* Original Blues Classics)

jimmy YANCEY (1898–1951)

Yancey, like Thelonious Monk, seems at first to be an awkward, even primitive pianist, but the attentive listener will find

After a run of hits in his twenties Jimmy Witherspoon made an unexpected return to the charts in 1975 with 'Love Is A Five Letter Word'.

johnny YOUNG (1918–1974)

Unglamorous, not an exciting singer nor, according to some of his colleagues, easy to get on with, Johnny Young was never likely to become a blues star, but he was an outstanding example of that equally valuable figure, the versatile sideman. Born in Vicksburg, Mississippi, he carried his guitar and mandolin through Chicago's blues history for 35 years, yet had recorded only obscurely or behind other artists (Floyd Jones, Snooky Pryor) before receiving a small measure of disc fame in the 1960s and 1970s, first as a reliable backing musician on projects like *Modern Chicago Blues* (Testament, MR), then on his own albums for Testament and Blue Horizon. Even in a Chicago blues-band setting, as on his Arhoolie albums with Walter Horton, he implied his own links with the past – he had been acquainted, for instance, with the Mississippi Sheiks – without making overt or nostalgic connections. (*Johnny Young And Friends* Testament)

mighty joe YOUNG (1927–)

Don't be misled by his tiny personal discography: Mighty Joe Young has been one of the busiest sidemen in Chicago since the late 1950s. He arrived there in 1956, from Louisiana by way of Milwaukee, and his guitar-playing soon took on the West Side colouring of Magic Sam and Otis Rush. Not surprisingly, he was in Rush's band for several years in the 1960s, and played on Sam's Delmark albums *West Side Soul* and *Black Magic*. He filled other dates for Delmark – Jimmy Dawkins' debut album, Rush's *Cold*

beneath the apparently artless surface a keen musical intelligence working inventively within the boundaries of the blues form to create music with great emotional resonance. He popularized a left-hand figure which became known as the 'Yancey bass' and was later used in Pee Wee Crayton's 'Blues After Hours', Guitar Slim's 'The Things That I Used To Do' and many other songs.

Yancey first began to play the piano in his teens, instructed by his brother Alonzo. For most of his life he worked as a groundkeeper for the Chicago White Sox baseball team, but in the late 1930s and early 1940s he was borne up on the swell of interest in boogie-woogie (though he himself was an untypical boogie player) and recorded tunes such as 'State Street Special' and 'Tell 'Em About Me'. In addition to his work in the studio, he left several informal recordings. He also accompanied his singing wife Estella, known as "Mama" (1896–1986), on 'Make Me A Pallet On The Floor' and other numbers, as well as occasionally singing himself, in a tremulous voice reminiscent of the elderly Jelly Roll Morton. (*Jimmy Yancey Vols 1–3* Document; *Eternal Blues* Blues Encore)

Day In Hell – and had his own first album on that label, *Blues With A Touch Of Soul*. He was also regularly booked for record dates by Willie Dixon, and between times worked under Billy Boy Arnold, Jimmy Rogers and other leaders. Young's own albums, though few, are reasonably good: his singing is plainer than, say, Rush's and his guitar-playing is more vigorous than brilliant; but he tends to run on a little too long, and his own material is not particularly distinctive. (*Bluesy Josephine* Black & Blue; *Live At The Wise Fools Pub* Aim)

zora YOUNG (1948–)

A blues-belter in the Koko Taylor mould, the Mississippi-born Young, a cousin of Howlin' Wolf, started out in soul music, modelling herself on Aretha Franklin and Gladys Knight, before being converted to the blues by Junior Wells. Teamed with Bonnie Lee and Big Time Sarah in 'Blues With The Girls', she toured Europe in 1982 and recorded an album in Paris. She later played the role of Bessie Smith in the show *The Heart Of The Blues*. In 1991 she cut *Travelin' Light* with the Canadian guitarist Colin Linden. (*Travelin' Light* Deluge)

Johnny Young, last of the first-generation blues mandolinists.

Milestone Recordings

Louis Jordan in the studio for Aladdin Records, New York, around January 1954. In a three-day stint he recorded more than 20 songs.

The only known photograph of Blind Blake.

BLIND BLAKE
Ragtime Guitar's Foremost Fingerpicker
Yazoo

As with several other Twenties artists, you get the wrong idea about Blind Blake's work if you go by the number of times "Blues" appears in the titles. 'Skeedle Loo Doo Blues' and 'Too Tight Blues No. 2', for example, are rag songs, the kind of material he excelled at. A pleasant if rather glum singer, he was at his happiest and best when cartwheeling through the changes in pieces like 'Southern Rag', 'Blind Arthur's Breakdown' or 'Seaboard Stomp', with their intricate picking patterns, unusual melodic strains, and shifts and suspensions of the beat to accommodate dancers' manoeuvres. Still, the fluency and easy swing of blues performances such as 'Police Dog Blues' or 'You Gonna Quit Me Blues' are as impressive today as they were 70 years ago, when they

Mamie Smith and her Jazz Hounds, with Willie "The Lion" Smith on piano.

influenced a generation of south-eastern guitarists like Josh White, Blind Boy Fuller and Buddy Moss. This judicious 23-track selection includes, as well as all the songs already mentioned, Blake's exuberant duet with pianist Charlie Spand, 'Hastings Street'.

....

BLUES WOMEN
Fattenin' Frogs For Snakes: The Essential Recordings Of The Blues Ladies
Indigo

You might look for a long time and unsuccessfully for a better collection of women singers from the Twenties to the Forties. On the bill, just to mention the first-rank names, are Bessie Smith (with three tracks), Ma Rainey, Ida Cox, Sippie Wallace, Clara Smith, Victoria Spivey ('Black Snake Blues'), Chippie Hill ('Trouble In Mind'), Alberta Hunter and Dinah Washington. The tough-voiced Alabamian singer Lucille Bogan and the more ingratiating Georgia White have a couple of songs each. So does Lil Green, one of them 'Why Don't You Do Right', the sultry minor-key blues later exploited by Peggy Lee and Jessica Rabbit. There are also examples of those tireless workwomen of the Thirties blues recording business, Lil and Merline Johnson. It's hard to see how more ground could have been covered in 24 tracks. Louis Armstrong accompanies Hunter, Hill and Rainey on 'See See Rider Blues'.

Ladies Sing The Blues
ASV Living Era

A further two dozen performances, with some repetition in the cast list (Rainey, Cox, Wallace, Spivey, Bessie and Clara Smith) but no duplicated material at all. While the Indigo compilation acknowledges Thirties figures like Memphis Minnie and the Johnsons, this CD stays longer with the theatre singers of the previous decade, such as Mamie Smith, Laura Smith and the raunchy Ada Brown from Kansas City. Its nod to the Thirties beckons instead the jazz singer Mildred Bailey ('Down Hearted Blues') and, for two of her few but delectable blues recordings, Billie Holiday. Sippie Wallace's 'I'm A Mighty Tight Woman' and Victoria Spivey's 'Moaning The Blues' are performances of superbly self-confident sexual boasting. Among the secondary pieces, though in this company that's hardly a slur, are Lizzie Miles's 'My Man O' War', a composition stuffed with rococo suggestiveness, and Rosetta Howard engaging Joe McCoy in sexy banter in 'Let Your Linen Hang Low'. Distinguished jazzmen litter the scene like the bodies at the end of *Hamlet*.

BOOGIE-WOOGIE
Various Artists:
Volume 1 – Piano Soloists
Jasmine

The best way to make your acquaintance with piano boogie-woogie is to listen to a lot of hands. Its rhythmic energy apart, the most engaging thing about this music is how different its practitioners can sound from each other, despite sharing the almost statutory 12-bar blues form. Here the exhilarating Albert Ammons, there the sober, hesitant Jimmy Yancey. In one corner Speckled Red and Cripple Clarence Lofton exuberantly banging out 'The Dirty Dozens' and 'Streamline Train', in another Meade Lux Lewis demonstrating his virtuoso's fingering

in 'Honky Tonk Train Blues'. Boogie-woogie's reputation for mechanical facility was earned by its lesser players; the masters each had their own approach.

From the names and tunes already dropped, the reader who knows a little about boogie-woogie will recognize a promising selection. Add Montana Taylor, Romeo Nelson and Cow Cow Davenport all playing their most famous pieces, a pair of uncharacteristically slow but attractive blues by Pete Johnson, and the record that supposedly started the boogie ball rolling, Pine Top Smith's 'Pinetop's Boogie Woogie'. The recordings date from 1928–43, but there is nothing quaintly archival: this was boogie-woogie's golden age, and many of these performances have never been surpassed.

Various Artists: Barrelhouse Boogie
Bluebird

This more narrowly focused compilation, spanning 1936–41, gives us the Big Three of boogie-woogie – Albert Ammons, Pete Johnson and Meade Lux Lewis – and Jimmy Yancey, the original cat who walks alone. Lewis plays another version of 'Honky Tonk Train Blues' and a limpid 'Whistlin' Blues', and the rest of the CD is split between Ammons and Johnson, playing together on two pianos, and Yancey. The duets are famous, and rightly so: given a naturally busy music and a pair of technically superb players, it would have been all too easy for the lines to become entangled and the texture clogged, but Ammons and Johnson show each other the courtesy of self-restraint without depriving the music of its vitality. Yancey, by contrast, seldom plays very fast: 'Yancey Stomp' is the only tune to venture beyond a brisk medium tempo. His way was to set percussive right-hand patterns against variants of a clipped bass figure that became his trademark, always in the format of a slow or medium blues. The mood is unhurried, even peaceful, but taut

with feeling, particularly in the vocal numbers 'Crying In My Sleep' and 'Death Letter Blues', where his mournful singing recalls Jelly Roll Morton. Like the preceding CD, this collection admits its listeners to a gathering of musicians whose typical work is excellent and their best incomparable.

PAUL BUTTERFIELD BLUES BAND
The Paul Butterfield Blues Band, East-West
Elektra

The PBBB's eponymous debut album was released in 1966. The difference between its grasp of the Chicago blues idiom and, say, the John Mayall band's, as revealed on *Blues Breakers* the same year, was stunning. While Eric Clapton might match Mike Bloomfield, the American group's lead guitarist, in raw talent, Paul Butterfield's harmonica-playing was not streets but city blocks ahead of Mayall's, and the rest of the PBBB dealt their rhythmic cards with the terse competence of professional gamblers.

With its unfussy approach and a repertoire drawn from Little Walter, Muddy Waters and Elmore James, the music on that debut album had "Chicago" running through it like lettering in a stick of rock. On *East-West*, however, the PBBB seemed to be caught in the process of moving house. While Robert Johnson's 'Walkin' Blues' was executed as a kind of Chicago blues march, long passages in 'Work Song' and the whole of the 13-minute title track smell less of Chicago's South Side than of San Francisco's Haight-Ashbury: not so much funky as hippy. It was a blues band's riposte to the Grateful Dead or Jefferson Airplane: free improvisation teetering on the edge of a freak-out, music simultaneously evoking Buddy Guy and Buddha. On a parallel course with Clapton and his peers in Britain, the PBBB was setting the controls for the heart of the

sun, heading towards a fusion where the discipline of the blues would melt in the reckless, leaping fires of rock. It was a journey in which some would be burned and others not return, but you can still catch the exhilaration of the countdown.

....

CANNON'S JUG STOMPERS
The Complete Works 1927–1930
Yazoo

Of all the jugbands, in Memphis, Louisville or anywhere else, that decorated the Twenties with their lilting harmonicas and robustly blown jugs, none was as elegant in a dance tune or as affecting in a blues as Cannon's Jug Stompers. Though the leader Gus Cannon's bright banjo-picking and jug-puffing were indispensable, and his medicine-show buddy Hosea Woods' pungent contributions on banjo, guitar, kazoo or voice were valuable additives, the group's outstanding musician was the harmonica player Noah Lewis. Whether playing a rag tune like 'Pig Ankle Strut' or 'Bugle Call Rag' or a sombre slow blues like 'Going To Germany', Lewis always maintained a melodic line and a subtly beautiful tone –

just the ingredients that many later jugband players have sacrificed to a frantic Keystone Kops jollity. 'Ripley Blues' is a lesson in how to play a commonplace slow blues tune with grace and feeling.

The album's title needs corrective surgery: these 24 tracks are not quite the band's complete works, and the date-span is 1928–1930. Nevertheless, this should be the first jugband album in any collection, followed quickly by the Memphis Jug Band set on the same label.

....

CHICAGO BLUES
Various Artists: Chess Blues
MCA/Chess (4 CDs)

The history of the Chess label between 1947 and 1967, the subject of this exemplary four-CD boxed set, is not the whole story of Chicago blues in that period. It misses Magic Sam and Jimmy Reed, to mention just two important chapters. But no other label even approaches the range and depth of a catalogue headed by Muddy Waters, Howlin' Wolf, Sonny Boy Williamson II and Little Walter, and embracing figures as different in age and approach as Memphis Minnie and

Willie Mabon, or Robert Nighthawk and Little Milton. All of these are represented in this 101-song collection, sometimes with classics like Waters' 'Rollin' Stone', Walter's 'Juke' or Williamson's 'Don't Start Me To Talkin'', sometimes with rarities or unissued recordings.

A Chess record may have been the goal of Southern blues artists Chicago bound, but the catalogue was not bound by the city limits: there is music here by Detroit's John Lee Hooker and St Louis's Albert King, Jimmy Witherspoon, Lowell Fulson and Floyd Dixon. The story ends with Koko and Hound Dog, the two Taylors who would help to design the next Chicago Look.

Various Artists:
Modern Chicago Blues
Testament

The title was as eccentric in 1965, when this album was first issued, as it seems today. The producer, Pete Welding, claimed that it represented "the music made in the small clubs and street markets of Chicago", but it has almost no point of contact with the club blues of young men like Buddy Guy, Magic Sam or Otis Rush. What these small groups of guitars, harmonica and piano – but, crucially, almost never drums – evoke most vividly is the blues of the late Forties and early Fifties that appeared on obscure small labels and is now high on the price list of collector's items. Some of the participants had in fact been involved in that earlier milieu, like Robert Nighthawk, Walter Horton and Johnny Young. Others, equally old, had always been throwbacks, like the guitar-playing street singers John Lee Granderson and Maxwell Street Jimmy. Young is the pivotal musician here, singing or playing guitar or mandolin on 11 of the 21 cuts.

Gus Cannon (left) and his Jug Stompers Ashley Thompson (guitar) and Noah Lewis (harmonica).

Maxwell Street Jimmy Davis on his home turf, September 1976.

With its combination of slightly archaic material – songs drawn from earlier figures like Leroy Carr, Memphis Minnie and Walter Davis – and reflective, intimate performances, the original album never made much of a stir, but its reissue on CD (with five additional tracks) vindicates what its admirers had long maintained. It shows a different face of Chicago blues from any other mirrored on record, and does so in music of great charm and honesty.

ALBERT COLLINS
Ice Pickin'
Alligator

This is an excellent album, as strong as anything Collins recorded, and at the time it did him a great deal of good, but its significance doesn't stop there. Released in 1978, it was one of the first modern blues albums with high production values. Previously the average active blues artist (as opposed to the

veteran hauled out of retirement) could expect to be recorded in one of two ways: in the United States by a label like Delmark, with a gritty realism that didn't cost very much, or in France, probably by Black & Blue, in a hasty and usually unimaginative replica of its club act – which also came cheap. Alligator took another tack, encouraging Collins's previously suppressed singing, assembling strong material like Freddie King's 'When The Welfare Turns Its Back On You' and T-Bone Walker's 'Cold, Cold Feeling' to stiffen the artist's own repertoire of steely instrumentals and genial talking-and-picking dialogues like 'Conversation With Collins'. Alligator also rehearsed the proceedings before rolling the tapes – by no means standard practice then. This strategy of treating an album as something more elaborate than a simple transfer of a live show underlay the label's productions from the beginning, but *Ice Pickin'* was a landmark. Not only was it a particularly thoughtful and well-made contribution to Collins's career, but it did much to reactivate and extend it.

THE ROBERT CRAY BAND
Bad Influence
Hightone (US)/Mercury (UK)

This album was the making of Cray. You might say the remaking, since he had earlier cut a record (*Who's Been Talkin'* on Tomato) with a strong but conventional blues flavour. *Bad Influence* and its successor *False Accusations*, however, represent not the road-to-Damascus conversion of a bluesman quietly going about his business but the self-discovery of an artist whose connections and allegiances are untypical and diverse. You see this straightaway in the opening track, 'Phone Booth'. Though structurally a blues, one of the few songs on the record that are, its loping rhythm and looping verse shapes lend it an unusual colour. Cray's guitar solo epitomizes his rubber-band sound, half taut, half slack, now stinging, now boinging like an old squash ball – a curious compound of Albert Collins and Mark Knopfler. His material, mostly written by combinations of the band and its producers Bruce Bromberg (writing as D. Amy) and Dennis Walker, replaces the direct confrontations of the blues with more cautious emotional encounters, though in 'I Got Loaded' and 'So Many Women, So Little Time' Cray has a last chance to do a little macho strutting. By the next album his preoccupations would have changed from gin and screwing around to Chardonnay and commitment.

FATS DOMINO
'They Call Me The Fat Man . . .':
The Legendary Imperial Recordings
EMI/Imperial (4CDs)

Domino's blend of bonhomie and bouncing boogie-woogie offered teenagers in the Fifties an attractive hors d'oeuvre that prepared them for the red meat of Wynonie Harris or Muddy Waters. The genial rocking rhythm of 'Ain't It A Shame' or 'I'm In Love

Again' and the Creole tang of 'Jambalaya' and 'Blueberry Hill' were flavourings that made familiar ingredients taste mildly exotic. And such small portions! Not the least part of producer Dave Bartholomew's skill was knowing when to stop. It's a rare Domino number that goes on for much more than two minutes. Merely as a study course in record production, this 100-song module is packed with information. (There is an even richer source, the complete Imperial recordings spread over eight Bear Family CDs, but that is the postgraduate course.)

Finishing the menu with 'Nothing New (The Same Old Thing)' – "you got me singin' the blues again" – is a good joke, since Domino has spent so much time beforehand dipping into every other dish on the table, from country ('You Win Again') to pop ('When My Dreamboat Comes Home') to Dixieland jazz ('Margie'). A feast, decoratively served.

DOWNHOME BLUES
Various Artists: Big Bad Blues (25 Sun Blues Classics)
Charly

Like some painstaking analytical drawing in a Victorian horticultural manual, this collection exposes the Southern roots of the music that bloomed in Chicago. The garden is Memphis, the hothouse the Sun studios, the time the early Fifties. It is a little before Sun develops its most successful hybrid, rock 'n' roll, and producer Sam Phillips is still experimenting with local stock such as singers Rufus Thomas and Jackie Brenston or the one-man-band Joe Hill Louis. Now and then he catches the mood of the market, as with Thomas's 'Bear Cat' or Billy "The Kid" Emerson's rocking chant 'Red Hot', but he sometimes hands an open mike to an oddball like D.A. Hunt,

whose 'Greyhound Blues' doesn't so much nod to Lightnin' Hopkins as salaam. Thanks to radio and records, musicians in and around Memphis were deluged with ideas from every direction, and for each downhome harmonica-guitar act (James Cotton and Pat Hare, Sammy Lewis and Willie Johnson) there was some sax-headed combo like Tot Randolph's or Billy Love's jumping the blues. Some of this is work in progress – you would barely recognize Little Milton or Lost John Hunter from these juvenilia – but you can smell the ferment of experiment, and occasionally you stumble upon a minor milestone like Junior Parker's Mystery Train'.

The "swamp blues" sound produced by Jay Miller in his Crowley, Louisiana, studio during the Sixties for the Nashville label Excello, in collaboration with southern Louisiana artists like Lightnin' Slim, Lonesome Sundown and Slim Harpo, appealed not only in the South-West – where Excello records sold to black buyers at a time when Chicago artists were finding that market more difficult – but also overseas, thanks to the British compilations *Authentic R&B* and *The Real R&B*. Like the Sun sound, which they sometimes echoed, Miller's productions had a strong character that could be more noticeable than the artist or the song – which was all to the good, since some of the artists, like the flagrant Jimmy Reed imitator Jimmy Anderson, looked as if they might not have much staying power. Not that Anderson's 'Naggin'' isn't a catchy piece, with its lopsided rhythm guitar riff and squealing harmonica. Miller and his studio hands were skilled at providing commonplace blues with novel and infectious rhythmic or melodic hooks, as on Lazy Lester's 'I'm A Lover Not A Fighter' or Slim Harpo's 'I'm A King Bee', probably the best known of all Excello recordings, thanks to versions by The Rolling Stones and other bands. This CD, which reissues the *Authentic R&B*

For years Junior Parker deserted downhome harmonica blues for uptown blues-soul music.

LP with a handful of additions, is the best available trip down this intriguing regional sideroad. Also on board are Silas Hogan, Whispering Smith, Tabby Thomas, Arthur Gunter and Shy Guy Douglas.

SLEEPY JOHN ESTES
I Ain't Gonna
Be Worried No More
Yazoo

Almost all of Estes' important recordings are assembled here. About a third of them are from his 1929–30 sessions with mandolinist Yank Rachell and pianist Jab Jones, the remainder from his Thirties and Forties work with the superb harmonica player Hammie Nixon. The early sides are sometimes a little stiff, but at their best they have an appealing swagger, as in 'Milk Cow Blues', where Rachell's mandolin trickles playfully over the sober thump of piano and guitar.

On the later sides, where only harmonica and guitars are involved, Nixon shadows Estes' hesitant rhythms with almost telepathic expertise. 'Someday Baby Blues', 'Drop Down Mama' and 'Down South Blues' are among the subtlest duets in the blues. Estes' gift for reportage is illustrated by tracks like 'Street Car Blues', about the electrification of Memphis public transport, 'Floating Bridge', about his own near-death experience in a flood, or the powerfully sung 'Working Man Blues', packed with agricultural detail about tractors, trucks and fertilizer.

BLIND BOY FULLER
Get Your Yas Yas Out
Indigo

Fuller's affable singing and the warm ring of his National steel-bodied guitar, deployed on blues with a jaunty swing and jovial lyrics, are among the most winning blues combina-

For all his fame in the 1930s, there is only one known photograph of Blind Boy Fuller.

tions. This excellent collection acknowledges almost all his hits, from 'I'm A Rattlesnakin' Daddy' (1935) to 'Step It Up And Go' and 'Little Woman You're So Sweet' (1940). Though he seldom deserted the 12-bar blues format, Fuller individualized his performances with novel lyrics, small but ingenious variations in his guitar parts and the assistance of accompanying musicians. Sonny Terry adds his harmonica to 'Bye Bye Blues', Fuller's version of the standard 'Crow Jane'/'Red River Blues' theme, and other songs, while the washboard player George Washington, alternately known as Bull City Red and Oh Red, clatters happily on 'Jitterbug Rag'. Fuller was particularly adept on rag songs, and among other vivacious examples are 'Piccolo Rag' (with his trademark device of a downstroke across the strings above the bridge) and 'Rag, Mama,

Rag', the inspiration for The Band's song of the same name.

LARRY GARNER
Double Dues
JSP

Even if *Double Dues*, made in 1991, should come to be regarded as half-formed early work, it will always have the cachet of being the album that introduced most listeners to Larry Garner. He is unquestionably a songwriter of unusual powers, but where are they leading him? Is he expanding the content and form of the blues, or working outside the idiom but closely parallel to it? And is there, at this late stage, any point in distinguishing the two pursuits?

Some of his most impressive pieces, like 'Scared Of You', 'No Free Rides' and 'Past 23', are not blues in any conventional sense. Though they use rhythm patterns and other musical devices that suggest blues, their language and narrative techniques are new-minted: you won't catch Garner waking up

Larry Garner came out of the South Louisiana club scene in the 1980s.

this morning or going down a big road by himself. The standard blues melody of 'Broke Bluesman' is the backdrop for a novel commentary on the occupation of blues singer, while the swaying John Lee Hooker rhythm of 'Shut It Down' underpins a father's straight talk about life to his schoolboy son. There is ingenuity at work in the arrangements, too. Terry Dockery's harmonica-playing is particularly fresh. A couple of pieces drift and would have profited from a more definite conclusion, but this is an error of inexperience or hurry. The superior production of Garner's later Verve albums has not yet elicited a consistently higher quality of work, but there are few artists whose progress will be more interesting to follow.

JOHN LEE HOOKER
The Legendary Modern Recordings
Ace

Not just a milestone but a cornerstone of any collection, this album gathers two dozen of Hooker's recordings from the late Forties and early Fifties: not the aurally challenging small-label rarities (compelling though many of them are) but the mostly quite well recorded sides on Modern. Among these are his first and often best versions of his personal standards 'Boogie Chillen', 'Sally Mae', 'Hobo Blues', 'Crawling Kingsnake' and 'I'm In The Mood', but lesser-known pieces like 'Wednesday Evening' or 'Turn Over A New Leaf' have the same strong flavour of blues darkly chanted to the hammered rhythm of guitar and foot.

Very occasionally Hooker reworks a standard blues melody or is inspired by something he has heard from another blues singer: 'Women In My Life', for instance, is set to the tune of 'Brownsville Blues', while 'Queen Bee' is traced over the faded blueprint of Memphis Minnie's 'Bumble Bee'. But all in all this is as concentrated a dose of

original thinking as you will discover anywhere in the blues.

The Healer
Chameleon (US)/Silvertone (UK)

Forty years on, give or take a year or two, Hooker proved that the principles of his earliest music still worked, both for him and for the hundreds of thousands of people who made *The Healer* the best-selling blues album ever. 'Sally Mae' and 'Baby Lee' sound almost exactly like their originals, so far as Hooker's singing and playing are concerned, but the contributions of his admiring friends – George Thorogood's steely slide, Robert Cray's economical prodding – are more than simple decorations: they discreetly modernize Hooker's music without weakening or diffusing its brooding pulse. Canned Heat and Los Lobos raise the octane of 'Cuttin' Out' and 'Think Twice Before You Go', while Bonnie Raitt's erotic responses in 'I'm In The Mood' actually make more of the song, give it a body heat that couldn't have been generated in 1951. As to whether the free-form solo tracks 'My Dream' and 'No Substitute' maintain the mood or lose it, probably no jury will ever agree, and there are some who feel that *The Healer* would have been better without 'The Healer'. But this is still a remarkable album.

LIGHTNIN' HOPKINS
The Gold Star Sessions Volumes 1 & 2
Arhoolie

Hopkins' early (1947–53) recordings are remarkably consistent in quality, but these two CDs combine exceptional performances, key items of his repertoire and enchanting oddities. The velvety texture of his voice in 'Thunder And Lightning Blues' or 'Death Bells' only emphasizes the funereal subject matter; similarly, the chiming interlining of voice and guitar raises the emotional tem-

perature of 'Somebody Got To Go', 'Grosebeck Blues' and 'Lonesome Home'. The actual sound of Hopkins's guitar varied from session to session according to microphone placement or amplification. These small textural differences, together with Hopkins's own subtle variations on his stock phrases, help to distinguish blues otherwise similar in key, tune or tempo.

Among the curiosities are 'Big Mama Jump', a boogie-woogie guitar duet with his brother Joel; 'Lightning Boogie', with a friend buck-dancing along in the studio; the ghostly steel guitar effects in the background of 'Traveler's Blues' and 'Jail House Blues'; and Lightnin''s eccentric ventures at the keyboard of a Hammond organ.

HOWLIN' WOLF
The Genuine Article: The Best Of Howlin' Wolf
MCA/Chess

Only a fanatic would jib at the title. If not the absolute to-die-for best of Howlin' Wolf, this is an admirable 25-track selection from the top end of his work, beginning with 1951's 'Moanin' At Midnight' and 'How Many More Years', cut in Memphis, and concluding almost two decades later in London with Wolf teaching Eric Clapton how to play 'The Red Rooster'. The years between find him in Chicago, slowly growing out of the downhome sound of 'Smokestack Lightnin'' until he reaches the apex of his recording career in the early Sixties with the huge flamboyance of 'Wang Dang Doodle', 'Back Door Man' and 'Spoonful'. Yet while the studio walls were still shaking from this battery of sound he could suddenly go quiet and paint a pastoral watercolour like the original version of 'The Red Rooster', or sweep the canvas with bands of purple and black as he elegizes the dying of the light in 'Goin' Down Slow'.

You don't want to give Wolf a whole lot of words to remember, Willie Dixon once said,

and sure enough, he was sometimes handed a lyric of triple-decker silliness like '300 Pounds Of Joy' ("Hoy, hoy, I'm the boy"), which he would deliver with unimpaired gusto. But some words he remembered all his life, and one of the last things you hear is his recollection of a Tommy Johnson blues from his youth, 'Ain't Goin' Down That Dirt Road', sung quietly to his own guitar accompaniment. It is not the old Wolf, more the Old Wolf, but you know at once that you are still listening to a leader of the pack.

MISSISSIPPI JOHN HURT
1928 Sessions
Yazoo

The 13 enchanting pieces that John Hurt recorded at two sessions in 1928 open a gate into the secret garden of black folksong. Though seven of them had "Blues" in their title, it was only to gain them a hearing in the blues-beguiled market of the day. 'Stack O'Lee Blues', 'Candy Man Blues' and 'Spike Driver Blues' were rags or ballads, perhaps from a time before the blues, and Hurt's wheedling way with them, singing and playing them as if they were lullabies to quieten restless children, belonged to a performing tradition far removed from the assertive blues voice and muscular guitar of fellow Mississippians like Charlie Patton.

Even in an out-and-out blues like 'Got The Blues, Can't Be Satisfied', with its fleeting resemblances in the guitar-playing to Memphis artists like Robert Wilkins or Frank Stokes, Hurt's unemphatic, on-the-beat singing reveals him as a house-party songster rather than a street-corner blues singer. His later recordings are no less appealing, but these performances have a little more clarity and edge.

ELMORE JAMES
The Classic Early Recordings
Ace (3 CDs)

Elmore James is one of the twin bridges – the other is Muddy Waters – that link the Thirties Mississippi blues of Robert Johnson with the bar-band music of post-war Chicago. The three CDs in this attractive boxed set span 1951–56, beginning with his first reworking of Johnson's 'Dust My Broom' for the Trumpet label and winding through his recordings for Flair, Meteor and Checker, mostly with his regular colleagues J.T. Brown (tenor) and Little Johnny Jones (piano).

James was an unabashed recycler of his own pet phrases, but even listeners attuned to that will probably keep the remote control close, so as to skip a little when confronted by six consecutive takes, five full-length, of 'Strange Kinda Feeling'. No button-pressing whatever is necessary in the roaring sequence of 1953 tracks 'I Believe', 'I Held My Baby Last Night', 'Baby What's Wrong' and 'Sinful Woman' (the last a draft blueprint of Otis Rush's sound four years later), or in other stretches of James's

impassioned singing and rapid-fire slide guitar.

King Of The Slide Guitar
Capricorn (2 CDs)

James's last recordings, made for the producer Bobby Robinson in New York in 1959–62/3, these songs stamped themselves on the consciousness of blues musicians coming up in the Sixties like Eric Clapton, Duane Allman and Fleetwood Mac's Jeremy Spencer. The brute force of James's singing and playing in 'The Sky Is Crying', 'Something Inside Of Me' or 'Bleeding Heart' still leaves the listener reeling, exhausted by the display of emotion. James continues to live off his own and the blues' past, dusting his broom in various disguises and redrafting songs by Leroy Carr ('Mean Mistreatin' Mama') and Tampa Red ('It Hurts Me Too', 'Anna Lee').

The first of the two CDs in this set (another nice-looking box) has the more presentable performances. Much of the later material was never finished off and survives unmixed and unedited, giving us the chance to hear some studio backchat and James's reminiscence of hunting with . . . tractors?

SKIP JAMES
Complete Early Recordings
Yazoo

With his ghostly crooning and spectacularly wilful guitar and piano-playing, Skip James may be for newcomers one of the most challenging figures in the blues. It is worth

confronting his music, even in the worn copies that are all that survive of some of his recordings, since it reveals so much of its maker, an introspective, isolated man for whom singing and playing blues seems, at times, less a professional routine than a psychological necessity. Yet while the Depression era lament 'Hard Time Killin' Floor', 'Hard Luck Child' or the famous 'Devil Got My Woman' are heavy with loneliness, the piano stomps 'If You Haven't Any Hay Get On Down The Road' and 'How Long "Buck"' (a blithe reconstruction of Leroy Carr's 'How Long – How Long Blues') and his reworking of the pop song 'I'm So Glad' as a virtuoso guitar showpiece are exhilarating exercises in pure sound.

Skip James, bluesman and preacher. "It must have been the devil changed my baby's mind."

BLIND LEMON JEFFERSON
King Of The Country Blues
Yazoo

Compare this with other Jefferson CDs and at once you see the value of a discriminating producer. A thoughtless selection of material, especially if it drew at all extensively from the later recordings, could make Jefferson seem tiresomely repetitive. These 23 songs, though they have some moments of personal cliché or uninspired songmaking, not only take a firm hold on the listener's imagination but show clearly how exceptional, how mould-breaking Jefferson's music was. For example, the first track, 'That Crawlin' Baby Blues', begins with the pathetic image of a crying baby but grows through jokes, aphorisms and blues common-places into a layered meditation on infidelity.

Subsequent blues, including such celebrated pieces as 'Match Box Blues', 'One Dime Blues', 'Easy Rider Blues' and 'Prison Cell Blues', are carefully interleaved with rag songs and tunes ('Beggin' Back', 'Hot Dogs') and sacred songs like 'See That My Grave Is Kept Clean'. Jefferson's original conception of the rhythmic relationship of voice and guitar never ceases to surprise and delight. With his recordings it is particularly necessary to have the clearest transfers from the best originals, and Yazoo, as usual, offers just that.

ROBERT JOHNSON
The Complete Recordings
Columbia (2 CDs)

This double CD has sold better than all the other collections of early blues put together. Why?

For one thing, the array of expert witnesses testifying to Johnson's pre-eminence among blues artists is unparalleled. Keith Richards calls him "the greatest folk blues guitar player that ever lived". For Eric Clapton he is "the greatest singer, the greatest writer." To the folklorist Mack McCormick, who followed his trail for 20 years, Johnson is "a visionary artist with a terrible kind of information about his time and place and personal experience". They are not paying respectful visits to a museum exhibit. If Johnson lives in his songs, he has been vigorously alive in the widest arena of popular music for the last 30 years – when the Rolling Stones perform 'Love In Vain', the Red Hot Chili Peppers do 'They're Red Hot', or countless other artists restage his one-act dramas of seduction, betrayal, flight and exaltation.

All those plays are here. (Twenty-nine of them, and a dozen alternative versions.) This is the First Folio of Johnson's work, and it seems unlikely that it will ever need to be re-edited. There are other blues records that are as artistically and emotionally satisfying, but none that has inflamed the imagination of so many people, so many different ways.

LOUIS JORDAN
Let The Good Times Roll
Bear Family (8 CDs and 1 LP)

A massive monument to the Arkansas demo-crat of R&B, this luxurious boxed set of eight CDs and an LP enshrines Jordan's entire Decca output from 1938 to 1954, a 200-piece jigsaw of gaiety, wit, social comment and scrupulously organized small-band music. Jordan and his sidemen and songwriters made a match of Southern blues and the novelty pop number, not only uniting the audiences of (say) Big Bill Broonzy and Fats Waller but offering them a music that was more sharply observed, more streetwise and more up-to-date than either of those models.

Jordan's specialities 'Ain't Nobody Here But Us Chickens', 'Saturday Night Fish Fry' and 'Boogie Woogie Blue Plate', interspersed with swing numbers like 'Pompton Turnpike', blues standards, mock calypsos and other exotica, make up an endlessly entertaining programme of lively music with an enviable ability not to sound dated. Coupled with the excellent and copiously illustrated booklet, they form a detailed history of a remarkable artist and the musical world he helped to change.

ALBERT KING
Live Wire/Blues Power
Stax

Some blues artists have to be heard *out* of the studio. Albert King made good records, but he bloomed in the less controlled sur-

roundings of a live set. Not that it sharpened the music. He was a good public speaker, as you might say, strong and clear, but he relied on pet phrases and in the course of an eight-minute piece he might well repeat himself. But that's the nature of stage performance, and King was certainly not the only blues artist to use repetition deliberately – for emphasis, to build tension, perhaps even to create the state of trance that a preacher induces with his reiterated cadences. It cheats time: the listener accepts it without noticing the minutes sliding by.

On a record it's different. If you insist on conciseness, go to King's earlier singles. *Live Wire/Blues Power*, recorded at the Fillmore Auditorium in San Francisco over two nights in June 1968, documents with merciless fidelity the King most people knew. Robert Palmer, describing another show, wrote that he "dug into the beat and heaved at it from underneath like one of the bulldozers he once drove", and this is what you hear in the instrumentals 'Night Stomp' and 'Look Out' and the extended guitar solos of 'Blues Power' and 'Blues At Sunrise'. It's relentless music, per-haps sometimes too insistent for comfort, but it's exactly the way King sounded.

Thanks to this album's reputation, over 20 years later Stax reopened the tape boxes and issued another 100 minutes of material on two CDs, *Wednesday Night In San Francisco* and *Thursday Night In San Francisco*.

B.B. KING
Singin' The Blues/
The Blues
Ace

This CD couples King's first two albums, which were selected from singles spanning 1951–58. *Singin' The Blues* was practically a greatest-hits-to-date compilation, including six of his most successful numbers. Today it and its successor are fascinating and valu-able as a guided tour of King's workshop. The

first track, 'Please Love Me', opens with a guitar burst out of the Elmore James manual, while 'You Upset Me Baby' has the flavour of T-Bone Walker, perhaps filtered through "Gatemouth" Brown. King sings 'Bad Luck' with some of the episcopal dignity of Lonnie Johnson and the ballad 'You Know I Love You' with the silkiness of Al Hibbler or Billy Eckstine. There are touches of Roy Brown ('Past Day', 'Ten Long Years'), of Lowell Fulson, of Louis Jordan. You would know without being told that King is constantly drenching himself in other people's music, and much of it soaks in.

He would go on to do more than he shows in these early recordings, but inevitably he could not revive what comes across here so sharply defined, the energy and ambition of a young man on the make.

Live At The Regal
MCA (US)/BGO (UK)

King professes surprise that this album should be so highly regarded. He's done hundreds of shows, he says, as good or better. Let's agree, then, that it wasn't especially important that the night of 21 November 1964 at the Regal Theatre in Chicago should be immortalized – so long as the other, better, nights were too. But they weren't, so we are left with this, a unique audio-verité document of King working to a (one supposes) predominantly black audience, supported by a six-piece band and bolstered by a set-list of hits from 'Everyday I Have The Blues' to 'It's My Own Fault' and 'You Upset Me Baby'. The performances are admirable, but it is the whole performance that is so impressive, King's artful progress from song to song, his rapport with his audience as they explode in delight at his sure-fire line "I gave you seven children, now you want to give them back". Even if it wasn't his greatest gig, most listeners will probably wish they had been there – and be glad that a recording engineer was.

MANCE LIPSCOMB
Texas Songster
Arhoolie

Lipscomb's repertoire, like Leadbelly's, extended into every area of Southern folk music: ballads like 'Ella Speed', rag songs like ''Bout A Spoonful' or 'Mama Don't Allow', blues ballads ('Freddie'), dance tunes ('Rag In G'), gospel songs ('Motherless Children') and, naturally, blues. Half of these 22 tracks were recorded at his home in Navasota, Texas, in 1960, and comprised his first album. The rest were taped before a club audience in Berkeley four years later. By then Lipscomb had discovered his new audiences' familiarity with blues, and the 1964 programme is perceptibly more blues-based, which would make Lipscomb seem a less interesting artist than he is if it were not juxtaposed with the earlier and more diverse material. The composite Lipscomb is a versatile performer with a gentle, dignified personality that comes across vividly, especially in the little stories he tells by way of prefaces to some of his songs. His guitar-playing, as you would expect of a man with decades of experience as a dance musician, is always anchored to a steady bass-string beat.

LITTLE WALTER
The Essential Little Walter
MCA/Chess (2 CDs)

What it says: all the key recordings on a double CD, from Walter's first record in 1952, the merry instrumental 'Juke' and its lovely slow-blues flipside 'Can't Hold Out Much Longer', with rippling duet guitars by Muddy Waters and Jimmy Rogers, to 1963's 'Southern Feeling'. En route you pass the big, wall-to-wall-echoing instrumentals like 'Sad Hours', 'Quarter To Twelve', 'Lights Out' – the last played with the chromatic harmonica, as is 'Fast Large One' – and 'Roller Coaster', which has the instantly identifiable chiming guitar of Bo Diddley. Between these come penny-plain but very satisfactory read-

Mance Lipscomb left a moving autobiography,
I Say Me For A Parable.

formerly known from a few tantalizing tracks on anthologies of field recordings, was alive, playing just as well and brimming with music. The impact of his warm, friendly voice and vigorous slide-guitar playing in songs like 'Write Me A Few Lines' and 'Kokomo Blues' stunned record-lovers and musicians alike. Thirty-odd years on, McDowell's amiability and the straightforwardness of his music come through undiminished. He also had a sure, sober way with gospel songs, illustrated by 'When I Lay My Burden Down', sung by his wife Annie Mae, and 'You Gotta Move', which was reshaped by the Rolling Stones on their *Sticky Fingers* album. Among the tracks added for the CD issue are a couple of blues sung by McDowell's teacher Eli Green, an older man who had known Charlie Patton.

- - - - - - - - - - - - - - - - - - -

BLIND WILLIE McTELL
Statesboro Blues
Indigo

One of McTell's songs, included here, was titled 'Hillbilly Willie's Blues', and in some ways he does sound whiter than most of his contemporaries. The even rhythm of his singing and its tidy relationship to the guitar

Fred McDowell used to tell his listeners: "I do not play no rock 'n' roll, y'all."

- - - - - - - - - - - - - - - - - - -

ings of 'Mean Old World', 'Blues With A Feeling', 'Key To The Highway' and of course 'My Babe'. The earlier sides, with Louis and Dave Myers and Robert Lockwood on guitars, are almost flawless small-band music in what, comparing it with the sound of the Muddy Waters band, you might call a chamber blues idiom. On the later sessions there are fewer instrumentals and less of Walter's harmonica altogether, while the material and arrangements sometimes seem to push him towards gestures that do not come naturally to him, like the Willie Dixon song 'As Long As I Have You' or the humorous 'Dead Presidents' (*i.e.* currency notes).

Not always, though: listen to 'Blue And Lonesome', a sly pastiche of the early Otis Rush sound, with queasy tremolo effects on rhythm guitar, a prickling lead, reportedly by Luther Tucker, and another colourful chromatic passage.

- - - - - - - - - - - - - - - - - - -

FRED McDOWELL
You Gotta Move
Arhoolie

Blues converts of the Sixties will recognize most of this CD as the album *Mississippi Delta Blues*, which burst on the blues world in 1965 bearing the news that McDowell,

- - - - - - - - - - - - - - - - - - -

Blind Willie McTell – "doing that rag, that Georgia rag".

accompaniment on 'Three Women Blues' and 'Love Changing Blues' are closer to Jimmie Rodgers than to Charlie Patton. The free-form narratives 'Travelin' Blues' and the extraordinary 'Atlanta Strut', where he does guitar impressions of mandolin, bass, cornet and trombone (a trick also played by Blind Blake in his 'Seaboard Stomp'), are from the racially shared tradition of humorous monologues that produced the talking blues. But the wistfulness McTell brings to 'Mama 'Tain't Long Fo' Day' and his seductive presentation of 'Mama Let Me Scoop For You' are effects only he could have brought off. There are several compilations of his Twenties and Thirties work, each good in its way; this one best combines length, variety and the songs every newcomer should hear.

MAGIC SAM
West Side Soul
Charly

Magic Sam's singles between 1957 and 1960 are an even more prominent landmark on the terrain of Chicago blues than Otis Rush's contemporary work (much of it for the same label and with similar musicians). Like Rush's, they are disconcertingly variable (Louis Jordan's 'Blue Light Boogie' suits Sam about as well as it would Pavarotti) and repetitious: 'All Night Long' and 'Love Me This Way' are weaker versions of 'All Your Love', 'Easy Baby' a decelerated 'Everything Gonna Be Alright'. You could throw half the album away and be no worse off. Even listening to what's left, you are torn between admiration for Sam's enthralling potential and despair at how it is wasted on ill-prepared recordings. He would be treated better on his Delmark albums *West Side Soul* (the originator of the title) and *Black Magic*, yet there's something extra here in the best of his singles like 'All Your Love' and 'Love Me With A Feeling', a raw glee in chucking out the wardrobe of old-fashioned Chicago blues and

refilling it with sharp new outfits. In 'Call Me If You Need Me' you can practically hear the clash of the coat-hangers. Nominally this was a record by the middle-aged cardsharp and occasional blues singer Shakey Jake Harris, but it turned out to be a bravura display of the new guitar style that would send many of Harris's generation packing.

JOHN MAYALL
Blues Breakers
Deram

A milestone on the journey of the British blues bandwagon, this 1966 album was also a direction sign into the future. It proved conclusively that Eric Clapton digested the lessons of his models more swiftly, and developed them more idiomatically, than any of his British contemporaries. Listen to his cocky facility in the instrumentals 'Hideaway' and 'Steppin' Out', the clanging introduction to Otis Rush's 'All Your Love' or the coruscating solo in 'Have You Heard'. In contrast, his handling of 'Ramblin' On My Mind' seems a little tentative, and for Robert Johnson's pride in his rootlessness he substitutes a more conventional blues attitude of weary resignation. Still, the very hesitancy of the performance, the way it hints at how hard it was for someone like Clapton – 21 years old, from an unexciting town in southeast England – even to approach someone like Johnson, is not only touching but obliquely revealing about the psychology of British blues. For this it is well worth enduring Mayall's strangulated singing or the narcotic drum solo in 'What'd I Say'.

MISSISSIPPI BLUES
Mississippi Masters: Early American Blues Classics 1927–35
Yazoo

Collections of first-generation blues artists are often promoted in extravagant language,

Joe Calicott survived to record a couple of albums in the 1960s.

but this disc's claim that its contents "rank among the all-time classic performances in blues history" would be hard to talk down. The propulsive guitar rhythm underlying Garfield Akers' two-part 'Cottonfield Blues' or William Harris's 'Bullfrog Blues' and 'Hot Time Blues' (the least twee version of 'Mama Don't Allow' you will ever hear), the booming bass-string slides in Blind Joe Reynolds' 'Outside Woman Blues', the doleful minor-key melody of Geeshie Wiley's 'Last Kind Words' – details like these enhance the eerie potency of performances that belong to a time and context beyond our imagination. Even when the song is anchored to a recognizable landmark, it may be by a long and twisted chain. The singer and slide-guitarist King Solomon Hill, in 'Whoopee Blues', delivers Lonnie Johnson's line "you'll be makin' whoopee with the Devil in Hell tomorrow night" with such curdling intensity that it is no longer a moral warning but a curse. Yet perhaps only a few counties away Joe Calicott was singing his lilting 'Fare Thee Well Blues' and Mattie Delaney issuing a matter-of-fact flood report in 'Tallahatchie River Blues'. These 20 performances are like flashes of lightning revealing a terrain not so much unknown as unknowable.

Masters Of The Delta Blues: The Friends Of Charlie Patton
Yazoo

What will not be immediately apparent from this CD's errant running-order is that it contains all the early recordings of Son House, Willie Brown, Kid Bailey and Patton's partner Bertha Lee, several of Tommy Johnson's, and valuable pieces by Booker White, Ishmon Bracey and the pianist Louise Johnson. If any of these names should be unfamiliar, it will also need saying that the title's "masters" is no overstatement. Recordings like Brown's 'Future Blues', Bailey's 'Rowdy Blues' and Tommy Johnson's 'Maggie Campbell Blues' have been exalted by hardcore blues-lovers for the best part of 40 years as miraculously happy unions of blues singing and guitar-playing. A later addition to the canon, because it was undiscovered until the early Nineties, is the unissued test-pressing of House's 'Walking Blues', a fore-runner of Robert Johnson's. While this is fascinating, House's totally absorbed performances of his two-part blues 'My Black Mama', 'Dry Spell Blues' and 'Preachin' The Blues' are among the most gripping experiences the blues has to offer.

MUDDY WATERS
The Complete Plantation Recordings
MCA/Chess

This collection of blues and gospel songs, recorded in rural Mississippi in 1941 and 1942 by Alan Lomax for the archives of the Library of Congress, would be remarkable

whoever the artists were. It catches both the sunset of the black string-band tradition and the first glimmerings of a blues form that before the end of the decade would burst into radiance. By chance Lomax's path had led him to the man who would dominate the Chicago blues scene of the Fifties and Sixties.

Muddy Waters was 26 when he sang 'Country Blues' and 'I Be's Troubled' into Lomax's disc recorder. The earnestness and youthful drive of his music recall Robert Johnson, whom he had heard but not met, but his chief and first-hand inspiration was Son House, as he describes in one of the interviews Lomax recorded, conversations almost as fascinating as the music. No questions were asked of Son Simms, the older man who played second guitar with Muddy on some of his songs and then took up a fiddle to lead Muddy and two other older men through some string-band blues. Lomax could hardly have been expected to know it, but this was the Henry Sims who had played with Charlie Patton. So the distant thunder of former blues giants rumbles in the background as Muddy unwittingly rehearses the future.

The Chess Box
MCA/Chess (3 CDs)

This wonderful anthology resumes the story of Muddy's music near the beginning of the first Chicago chapter, with his 1947 recording of 'Gypsy Woman'. For most of the first disc – this is a three-CD (72-track) boxed set – he is still playing as a soloist even when he has colleagues around him, the thunder of voice and slide guitar brooking no interruption, though Little Walter's harmonica presses close on 'Louisiana Blues' or 'Long Distance Call'. But the final track, 'Hoochie Coochie Man', is like a banner headline announcing the arrival of the definitive Chicago blues band, and in the second disc, spanning 1954–59, Muddy and his collabo-

rators, notably Little Walter, Otis Spann and Jimmy Rogers, develop their ideas in the disciplined riot of 'I'm Ready', 'Manish Boy' and 'Got My Mojo Working'. The final disc (1960–72) is inevitably more diversified, as Muddy and his producers look for new ways to present his music. Specimen tracks from the *Newport, Folk Singer, Brass And The Blues* and *Fathers And Sons* albums are interleaved with quirky late singles like 'You Shook Me', 'The Same Thing' and 'You Can't Lose What You Ain't Never Had'. By the end few of his old buddies have kept up with him, but Muddy is still exhibiting the vigour and appetite of a young man.

CHARLIE PATTON
Founder Of The Delta Blues
1929–1934
Yazoo

Compared with the clear, fast-flowing stream of Robert Johnson's music, Patton's may seem at first to be as muddy and sluggish as the Mississippi itself, and not just because his recordings are older and technically cruder. But to journey through them perseveringly is one of the great adventures in the blues, and the reader who has not yet made the trip is to be envied. A landscape opens of fields, bayous and dirt roads, ponies and roosters – and behind it, like a shadow, a less tangible terrain of adventure and survival. In the real riverside world of alternating drought and floods there are sometimes dry wells and sometimes "high water everywhere", but for Patton and his listeners the blues are continually falling, "like showers of rain".

He tells his stories in a voice as thick as silt, his guitar treading an intricate, absorbed dance. Sometimes he holds conversations with himself, commenting on his songs, speaking his lines before he sings them, as if tasting them. In 'A Spoonful Blues' and 'Down The Dirt Road Blues' the

"dialogue" is almost a ventriloquist's act. Patton was evidently a playful and exhibitionist performer – Stephen Calt's notes speak of his "unique sense of drama and comedy" – but we are free to wonder whether a line like "every day, seems like murder here" is humorous exaggeration or a twitch of the curtain, momentarily revealing the daily reality Patton's juke-joint listeners came to forget.

Jimmy Reed was sitting pretty in 1956, with five discs on the R&B chart.

JIMMY REED
Bright Lights, Big City
Charly

Subtitled "(His Greatest Hits)", as well it might be – of all Reed's charting singles, only 'Take Out Some Insurance' is missing. It could just as easily have been worded "(The Best Of Jimmy Reed)", because the touches that made 'Honest I Do' or 'Big Boss Man' sell also distinguished them from the generic mass of Reed's recorded material.

On 'Honest I Do' it was the pretty filigree by jazz guitarist Remo Biondi, on 'Big Boss Man' the descending opening figure played on harmonica and guitar, on 'Bright Lights, Big City' and others the half-asleep slow-rock rhythm, on 'Shame, Shame, Shame' the recurring two-bar rhythmic figure on several guitars . . . not strokes of genius, but clever enough to make Reed one of the most recognized (he was already one of the most recognizable) bluesmen of the Fifties and Sixties.

Beside the music of contemporaries like Muddy Waters or Otis Rush, this is lightweight stuff, sometimes flippant or emotionally shallow, but the blues would be a dull place if there were no room for the happy, zonked-out simplicity that Reed brought off so well.

RHYTHM & BLUES
Various Artists:
The King R&B Box Set
King (4 CDs)

No one record label can provide all the material for a comprehensive survey of R&B, but King Records' shelves are longer and better stocked than most. The music in this four-CD boxed set, spanning 1945–66, can be divided into a few generic clusters. The largest is the group of big (or big-sounding) bands with exuberant vocalists like Wynonie Harris, Bull Moose Jackson, Roy Brown and Eddie Vinson, exemplified by Brown's 'Hard Luck Blues' and Harris's 'Bloodshot Eyes'. After that the emphasis shifts to vocal groups such as the Five Royales, the Midnighters and Billy Ward & His Dominoes, the brilliant young soul singer Little Willie John ('Fever') and the small-group R&B of Bill Doggett ('Honky Tonk'). James Brown's 'Papa's Got A Brand New Bag' offers a peep into the future. Outside these stylistic encampments are nomadic

singing style that had grown out of, but not all that far away from, the cottonfield holler, together with a guitar palette loaded with the colours of darkness and rage. 'I Can't Quit You Baby' and 'Checking On My Baby' brim with suspicion and reproach, only just holding in the boiling emotions the singer has stirred up in himself. 'Double Trouble', though more detached, is no less angry – "It's hard to keep a job, laid off and having double trouble" – but Rush reaches for hope with the aspirational motto "you can make it if you try".

You would hardly expect a young artist trying to make it under the eye of a producer like Willie Dixon to lay all his bets on songs of turbulent passion and social comment, and Rush diligently tried to make something of Dixon's pop-ballad composition 'Violent Love' and the dance numbers 'Jump Sister Bessie' and 'Sit Down Baby'. In their way they are not unsuccessful, but amidst the dramas of 'Groaning The Blues', 'Love That

Otis Rush: 40 years on from his Cobra recordings, still coiled to strike.

Bull Moose Jackson gave King Records its first R&B chart hit.

figures like the elderly but still game Lonnie Johnson ('Tomorrow Night'), the abrasive alto saxophonist Earl Bostic ('Flamingo'), Little Willie Littlefield, Professor Longhair, Jack Dupree and Freddie King, the only significant Chicago artist King raided from the Chess ranch. At the end of an 85-stop roller-coaster ride through two decades, the listener is invited to eavesdrop on tapes of company president Syd Nathan's sales meetings.

OTIS RUSH
Double Trouble
Charly

These 16 sides were made as singles for the Chicago label Cobra in 1956–58. Rush brought to these, his first recordings, a

Woman' and the songs already mentioned they are like intermissions for ice-cream.

JOHNNY SHINES
Standing At The Crossroads
Testament

To stand alone with an acoustic guitar is to take a terribly exposed position. To do so with the ghost of a great artist at your shoulder is either bravery or madness. Johnny Shines sings Robert Johnson's songs not only with the authority of a man who learned them from the lips and fingers of their maker but with the self-assurance of a musician who knows he has his own unborrowed credentials.

This is not a Johnson recital: only the title track and 'Kind-Hearted Woman' are his. Yet almost everything Shines sings and plays is a kind of reminiscence of his time in Johnson's company, of lessons taught and learned, experiences shared. The words are mostly Shines's own, except for a 'How Long' derived from Leroy Carr, and the measured, dignified pace is his too. It is a tribute album not to Johnson's songs but to his spirit. It is also beautifully sung. Shines had one of the noblest voices ever devoted to blues singing. When he was a young man, he would recall, "I could holler pretty good. Oh, I could scream like a panther." Half a lifetime later – the album was made in 1970, when he was 55 – he could still raise the hair on your neck.

BESSIE SMITH
The Complete Recordings
Columbia (10 CDs)

"I've got a sad story today," sings Bessie Smith as she begins 'The Gin House Blues'. Or again, in 'Dyin' By The Hour': "It's an old story – every time it's a doggone man." To the women who bought her records in millions, Bessie's blues were the true-life sto-

ries that the romance magazines only pretended to offer. More, they were dispatches from the front-line of women's daily battle to find work, bring up families, deal with the men in their lives and have a little fun. It was like hearing a rallying cry when Bessie declared "I'm a young woman, and ain't done runnin' round," or boasted "There'll be a hot time in the old town tonight." Other blueswomen delivered similar messages, but few in her massively purposeful tone or with her air of knowing what she was talking about.

Of the 160 songs she recorded between 1923 and 1933, more than half have "Blues" in their title (and many more might have), but they are not a parade of matching melodies: 12-bar tunes are interspersed with 32-bar "vaudeville blues" and other forms. In any case, Bessie had an unequalled art of minutely varying her delivery, and her producer supplied a regularly changing cast of accompanists.

These five double CDs contain all the studio recordings and the 15-minute soundtrack of her film *St Louis Blues*. It's a magnificent collection, one you could spend a lifetime exploring. The final disc is devoted to interviews with her niece Ruby Smith, whose stories of life on the road with Bessie are so frank that the CD box carries the warning "Parental Advisory: Explicit Lyrics".

HENRY THOMAS
Texas Worried Blues
Yazoo

This CD is indispensable to anyone curious about the music that preceded the blues. It gathers the 23 songs that Henry Thomas, "Ragtime Texas", recorded at his few sessions in the late Twenties, when he was a man well into middle age. He was fortunate to document so much of his repertoire, but, as Stephen Calt observes in his long and informative notes, "The question remains: what does his music document?" The typical

repertoire of an itinerant musician, perhaps, but frozen at what point in time? How far, by the end of the Twenties, was his music an invitation to nostalgia? And whose nostalgia – black listeners' or white? He doesn't sing many blues, which might imply that his receptivity, or his audiences', had shut down by the time blues became fashionable, yet 'Texas Easy Street Blues' and 'Texas Worried Blues' are very proficiently played.

Aside from prompting historical speculation, Thomas's music is extremely likeable, with its bouncy guitar beat and its bursts of elfin piping on the quill (*i.e.* panpipes), and the tunes of 'Don't Ease Me In' and 'Fishing Blues' are impossible to get out of your mind.

JOE TURNER
The Boss Of The Blues
Atlantic

"Jazz would be an empty house without the blues," wrote the jazz critic Whitney Balliett, beginning his sleevenote for the original issue of this album in 1956. A discriminating blues collection, you might add, would have a glaring empty place without *The Boss Of The Blues*.

Almost continuously available for over 40 years, this is a certifiable classic of blues-singing in a Kansas City jazz setting – and if that sounds a narrow definition, think of all the singers whose roots lie there, in spirit if not in fact, from Turner, Jimmy Rushing and Walter Brown to Eddie Vinson and Wynonie Harris.

Crucial to the success of the project was the presence of Turner's piano buddy since the Thirties, Pete Johnson, and several alumni of the Count Basie band, which knew a thing or two about blues: Joe Newman (trumpet), Frank Wess (tenor), Freddie Green (guitar) and Walter Page (bass). Altoist Pete Brown had played on many blues dates, too. The programme consists of seven blues Turner could have sung in his sleep

like 'Cherry Red', 'Roll 'Em Pete' and 'Low Down Dog' and three amiable old pop songs. It must have felt as comfortable as an old shoe. Turner gives each song an expert going-over, as if he were teaching a blues-singing masterclass.

STEVIE RAY VAUGHAN
Texas Flood
Epic

This was Vaughan's first album, in 1983. Although he went on to make more ambitious, and more personal, music in the years that remained to him, there is something very engaging about his youthful keenness, and that of his band Double Trouble, on *Texas Flood*, and it remains an excellent introduction to the hardcore blues side of his music. While 'Tell Me' and 'Mary Had A Little Lamb' haven't quite shaken off the shapes of their models (Howlin' Wolf and Buddy Guy respectively), the ominous slow blues 'Dirty Pool' creates an Otis Rush mood out of original material, and the aerobic guitar exercises 'Rude Mood' and 'Testify' are plainly the work of an athlete with his own style. So, in a very different way, is the wind-beneath-my-wings ambience of 'Lenny', a sort of offspring of Fleetwood Mac's 'Albatross' but cleverer than its parent. Perhaps nothing so well expresses Vaughan's tempestuous creativity as the downpour of notes in the title song. One can imagine other guitarists hearing that for the first time and shivering as if, in the old saying, someone had walked over their grave.

JOE LOUIS WALKER
Blue Soul
Hightone

Walker's first couple of albums, though impressive, suggested that he was one of those blues artists – it isn't true of all – whose recordings would be improved by more musicians and more varied settings. So it proved with 1989's *Blue Soul*. Warmed by some extra logs on the budgetary fire, Walker expanded and produced one of the finest blues albums of modern times.

Actually, few of the nine songs (eight written or co-written by him) are blues in a strict sense, but Walker is so steeped in the history of the music and so widely versed in its tech-niques that he can't help coating everything in a blues glaze. Pleasing as that may be to the more conservative among his listeners, it shouldn't be allowed to obscure his craft as a song-writer. Few blues musicians, even young ones,

Joe Turner, a big blues wind blowing hot and strong out of the Midwest.

Joe Louis Walker, a pivotal figure in the blues of the 1990s.

really confront the challenge of writing in the language of the present and using its cultural references. Walker is different. "I swore I was gonna stay single – when I leave out and come back is up to me," he sings in 'Personal Baby', "But I gotta take a real good look at that *Playboy* philosophy." The album ends, after the magnificent high-tension blues 'City Of Angels', on a solo piece with slide guitar, 'I'll Get To Heaven On My Own', a kind of agnostic's gospel song deeply in the spirit of Blind Willie Johnson.

T-BONE WALKER
The Complete Capitol/
Black & White Recordings
Capitol (3 CDs)

There is a lot of music on this three-CD set – 75 tracks, about a third of them alternative takes – but it is all good and all important. In these recordings, almost all cut in 1946–47,

Booker White used to say that he reached up and plucked his songs out of the sky.

Walker published a revolutionary manifesto about blues guitar-playing that duly converted dozens of musicians. Any three or four tracks picked at random will exhibit his innovations: the effortless transition from chord-playing to time-defying single-string runs, his cat-like prancing on fast numbers (which reminds you that he first made his name as a dancer), his almost Hawaiian string-bending and sliding. Technically it was blues guitar-playing at an entirely new level, yet Walker never makes a big show of his expertise: the loudest and brashest he gets is at about the volume of a brisk conversation. So too with his singing, which was nearly as influential. He confides, he insinuates, he may raise his voice a little in gentlemanly reproof, but he never shouts.

The mannerly style perfectly suits the dry wit and street-smart vocabulary of songs like 'Bobby Sox Baby', 'Inspiration Blues', 'Description Blues' and the classic 'Call It

Stormy Monday', which are further enhanced by disciplined ensemble playing and crisp solos from Teddy Buckner (trumpet) and Bumps Myers (tenor). An exemplary set, well annotated and attractively packaged.

BOOKER WHITE
The Complete Bukka White
Columbia

These recordings, made at two sessions in 1937 and 1940, are as persistently autobiographical as any body of work in the blues. White lays bare his preoccupations with death, sickness and jail, brilliantly implying his own obsessiveness by doggedly using the same rhyme in verse after verse, as in 'Black Train Blues' and 'Strange Place Blues', or by repetitive guitar figures like the descending bass in 'Good Gin Blues' or his masterpiece 'Fixin' To Die Blues'. 'When Can I Change My Clothes' and 'Parchman Farm Blues' are

Jimmy Witherspoon swings happily in jazz or blues company.

bitter reminiscences of the indignities of prison life. But the music is not unrelievedly grim: 'Aberdeen Mississippi Blues' and 'Pinebluff, Arkansas' are boasts about his encounters with women, 'Good Gin Blues' is a merry tribute to a bootlegger friend and 'Shake 'Em On Down' a full-throated sexual invitation. About half the songs are played in open tuning with a slide, most colour-fully in the train-imitating piece 'Special Streamline' and the bustling 'Bukka's Jitterbug Swing'.

About the name: these first recordings, reissued in their entirety here, were released under the name Bukka White, not to be pro-nounced "Bucker" but as a novel spelling of Booker. He preferred his name to be spelled properly, and there is no reason to deny him that courtesy.

BIG JOE WILLIAMS
Shake Your Boogie
Arhoolie

Though it lacks the variety of Big Joe's earlier recordings, on which he had collaborators like Sonny Boy Williamson I and Henry Townsend, this solo album from the Sixties is a satisfying, intimate and affecting piece of work. According to the producer, Chris Strachwitz, the 1960 session which furnished the first dozen tracks found Big Joe in a dis-turbed frame of mind, which may be reflected in the intensity he brings even to jokey themes like 'Yo Yo Blues' or 'Vitamin A Blues', as well as to the autobiographical 'Mean Step Father' and the tribute song to President Roosevelt – a type of subject he returned to nine years later in 'The Death Of Dr Martin Luther King'. Among the other 1969 recor-dings, some of which are with the harmonica player Charlie Musselwhite, is an introspec-

tive 'Thinking Of What They Did To Me' and a gospel song, 'King Jesus', to balance the earlier session's 'I Want My Crown', fervently sung by Joe's wife Mary. The 1960 performances catch the strange sonorities of Joe's nine-string guitar, while on the later session he essayed a few numbers with a slide.

JIMMY WITHERSPOON
Jimmy Witherspoon Meets
The Jazz Giants
Charly

This is the finest album of jazz-blues singing you are ever likely to hear. The accompany-ing musicians are at least as distinguished, and the settings as sympathetic, as those of Joe Turner's famous album *The Boss Of The Blues*, but Spoon is a more versatile singer and has never sounded better than in these surroundings.

Two occasions are involved: the autumn 1959 Jazz Festival at Monterey, California,

and an engagement at the Renaissance Club in L.A. two months later. At Monterey Spoon walked on to a stage almost laughably full of great jazz musicians, among them Woody Herman, Earl Hines, Coleman Hawkins, the trumpeter Roy Eldridge and Ben Webster, who plays an arrestingly lovely tenor solo in 'Ain't Nobody's Business'. Spoon hadn't been doing well lately, and Monterey was a big chance. He grabbed it with both hands and an almost audible grin of triumph, romping through 'Good Rockin' Tonight' and 'Big Fine Girl' before singing his heart out on 'Ain't Nobody's Business'.

For the Renaissance gig he was backed by Gerry Mulligan's quartet and Webster again. Mulligan plays with great feeling on 'How Long', just one of a remarkable set of blues standards like 'Outskirts Of Town', 'St Louis Blues' and 'See See Rider'. Spoon's voice, as someone once described it, "is as smooth and rounded as an ocean-washed pebble".

BLUES FESTIVALS

UNITED STATES

February
Boston Blues Festival, Boston, MA
Lowcountry Blues Bash, Charleston, SC

March
Detroit Indoor Blues Festival, Detroit, MI
River City Blues Festival, Marietta, OH

April
Springing The Blues, Jacksonville, FL
New Orleans Jazz & Heritage Festival

May
Beale Street Blues Festival, Memphis, TN

Arkansas River Blues Festival, Little Rock, AR
Kerrville Folk Festival, Kerrville, TX

June
Chicago Blues Festival
Monterey Bay Blues Festival, Monterey, CA
Smithsonian Festival of American Folklife, Washington, D.C.
Arden Blues Festival, Washington, PA

July
Augusta Blues Week, Elkins, WV
Mississippi Valley Blues Festival, Davenport, IA

The Belgium Rhythm & Blues Festival at Peer is a popular annual celebration of the blues.

THIS IS A SELECTION FROM THE SCORES OF BLUES FESTIVALS STAGED WORLDWIDE EACH YEAR, CONFINED BY SPACE TO EVENTS IN THE UNITED STATES AND EUROPE. FESTIVAL DATES MAY VARY FROM YEAR TO YEAR (AND SOME OVERLAP FROM ONE MONTH TO THE NEXT), AND THE READER PLANNING A VISIT IS ADVISED TO OBTAIN PRECISE INFORMATION. THE BEST SOURCES ARE THE MAGAZINES LISTED ON PAGE 221, LOCAL PRESS AND TOURIST OFFICES.

Waterfront Blues Festival, Portland, OR
Marin County Blues Festival, San Rafael, CA
Memphis Music & Heritage Festival
Pittsburgh Blues Festival, Pittsburgh, PA
Kansas City Blues & Jazz Festival, Kansas City, MO
New York State Budweiser Blues Festival, Syracuse, NY
Pocono Blues Festival, Poconos, PA
Kalamazoo Blues Festival, Kalamazoo, MI
Utah Blues & Jazz Festival, Snowbird, UT

August
Sunflower River Blues & Gospel Festival, Clarksdale, MS
Bayfront Blues Festival, Duluth, MN
House Of Blues Festival, Santa Barbara, CA
Blues Fest, Jonesboro, AR
Sonoma County Blues Festival, Santa Rosa, CA
Long Beach Blues Festival, Long Beach, CA

September
St Louis Blues & Heritage Festival, MO
Dusk Til Dawn Blues Festival, Muskogee/ Rentiesville, OK
D.C. Blues Festival, Washington, D.C.
Ann Arbor Blues & Jazz Festival, Ann Arbor, MI
Riverfront Blues Festival, Fort Smith, AR
Boulder Blues Festival, Boulder, CO
Mississippi Delta Blues & Heritage Festival, Greenville, MS
San Francisco Blues Festival
Bull Durham Blues Festival, Durham, NC
Blues 2000 and Beyond, Kiamesha Lake, NY

October
Blind Willie Blues Festival, Thomson, GA
Sarasota Blues Festival, Sarasota, FL
King Biscuit Blues Festival, Helena, AR
Garvin Gate Blues Festival, Louisville, KY
Baton Rouge Blues Festival, Baton Rouge, LA
Tucson Blues Festival, Tucson, AZ
Fresno Blues Festival, Fresno, CA
Blue Ridge Folklife Festival, Ferrum, VA
Ojai Bowlful of Blues, Ojai, CA

November
Riverwalk Blues Festival, Fort Lauderdale, FL

EUROPE

February
Brussels Blues Festival

March
Amsterdam Blues Festival

April
Burnley Blues Festival, Burnley, Lancashire
Feel The Blues Festival, Utrecht, Netherlands

May
London Blues Festival
Boogie Town Festival, Louvain-la-Neuve, Belgium
Ecaussinnes Spring Blues Festival, La Louvière, Belgium
Bluesfest Leverkusen, Germany
Moulin Blues Ospel, Weert, Netherlands

June
Dundee Jazz & Blues Festival, Dundee, Scotland
Ascona Festa, Ascona, Switzerland

July
Belgium R&B Festival, Peer
North Sea Jazz Festival, The Hague, Netherlands
Montreux Jazz Festival, Montreux, Switzerland
Stockholm Jazz & Blues Festival, Sweden

August
Great British Rhythm & Blues Festival, Colne, Lancashire
Edinburgh International Blues Festival, Edinburgh, Scotland
Notodden Blues Festival, Notodden, Norway

November
Vredenburg Blues Estafette, Utrecht, Netherlands

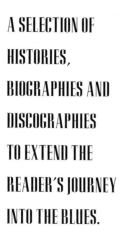

BLUES BOOKS

A SELECTION OF HISTORIES, BIOGRAPHIES AND DISCOGRAPHIES TO EXTEND THE READER'S JOURNEY INTO THE BLUES.

Big Bill Broonzy and Yannick Bruynoghe
Big Bill Blues
DaCapo
The first blues autobiography, originally published in 1955, this is not always reliable as history but packed with fascinating stories and rich in the flavour of a great man's life.

Paul Oliver
Blues Fell This Morning
Cambridge University Press
First published in 1960, approximately halfway between the birth of the blues on record and the present day, this remains the standard work on early blues and the social milieu in which it developed. Oliver uses the lyrics of recorded blues as keys to unlock the concerns of African-American life.

Charlie Gillett
The Sound Of The City
Souvenir Press
Now in its third edition since 1970, this is still the best history of rock 'n' roll and the 1940s–1950s blues and country music that sired it, with crisp accounts of the major musicians and record companies and clear-sighted analyses of stylistic change.

Peter Guralnick
Feel Like Going Home
Penguin
Affectionate, informed and superbly written essays on blues and rock 'n' roll figures including Muddy Waters, Howlin' Wolf and Johnny Shines, drawing on candid interviews. Blues "New Journalism" at its finest.

Arnold Shaw
Honkers And Shouters: The Golden Years Of Rhythm & Blues
Collier Books
An oral-history companion to Gillett's *The Sound Of The City*, full of interviews with pioneer record business figures, written by an insider. An indispensable guide to 1940s–1960s blues.

Larry Cohn (*ed.*)
Nothing But The Blues
Abbeville Press
Beautifully illustrated collection of essays by a team of experts, discussing every period of blues from the early days to the 1980s.

Stephen Calt
I'd Rather Be The Devil: Skip James And The Blues
DaCapo
This acerbic and intelligent book is not only the most revealing biography of a bluesman but airs many icono-clastic ideas about the blues itself.

Paul Trynka
Portrait Of The Blues
Hamlyn
A patchwork history of the blues told chiefly in the words of living musicians of all ages, enhanced by sensitive photographs by Val Wilmer.

Robert M.W. Dixon and Howard Rye
Blues & Gospel Records 1902–1943
OUP
Unrivalled for almost 30 years, now in its fourth edition, this discography contains virtually all the information an enthusiast will ever need about early blues recordings: what they were, when and where they were made, who played on them. Includes the African-American material in the Library of Congress's Archive of Folk Song.

Mike Leadbitter, Neil Slaven and others
Blues Records 1943–1970 Volumes 1 & 2
Record Information Services
Two fat volumes continue the documentation of the blues on record from the 78 and 45 rpm single into the LP era, listing all the known data on major and minor artists alike.

SUPPLIERS
As a source of these and other books on blues and popular music in general, the author recommends these mail-order suppliers:

A&R Booksearch, High Close, Winnick Cross, Lanreath, Looe, Cornwall PL13 2PF, England. (Publishes an annual catalogue.)

Red Lick Records, Porthmadog, Gwynedd LL49 9DJ, Wales. (Publishes bimonthly lists of records, books and magazines.)

BLUES MAGAZINES

Blues Access

1455 Chestnut Place, Boulder, CO 80304-3153, USA.
Tel: (303) 443 7245
email: Roosterman@aol.com
Subscription hotline: (800) 211 2961
Web site: http://www.he.net/~blues

Founded 1990. Quarterly. A pleasant-looking magazine, fond of interviews, with no perceptible axe to grind. The large team of reviewers includes Tim Schuller, Scott Dirks and Mary Katherine Aldin.

Blues & Rhythm

Editorial: Tony Burke, 82 Quenby Way, Bromham, Beds MK43 8QP, England.
Tel: 44 (0) 1234 826158
email: tony@bluestb.demon.co.uk
Subscriptions: Byron Foulger, 1 Cliffe Lane, Thornton, Bradford, Yorks BD13 3DX; tel: 44 (0) 1274 832147; email: byron@roker.demon.co.uk
Web site: http://www.bluesworld.com/

Founded 1984. Ten issues a year. Knowledgably covers a wide range of blues-related music, specializing in collector-oriented historical features. Record reviews are extensive and quick off the mark, and writers like Chris Smith, Neil Slaven, Keith Briggs and Ray Templeton are always worth reading.

Blues Revue

Editorial: Andrew M. Robble/Debra DeSalvo, 916 Douglas Drive – Suite #101, Endwell, NY 13760, USA.
Tel: (607) 786 3622
email: Ja916zz@aol.com
Subscriptions: Rt. 2, Box 118, West Union, WV 26456, USA; tel: (304) 782 1971; email: BluesRevue@aol.com

Founded 1991. Quarterly. A glossy, upmarket-looking title, primarily featuring contemporary blues. Older forms are treated in David Evans' 'Ramblin' column and occasional record reviews.

Juke Blues

P.O. Box 148, London W9 1DY, England.
Fax: 44 (0) 171 286 2993

Founded 1985. Three issues a year. This attractively presented magazine concentrates on post-war blues and some soul music. Dick Shurman contributes a news column from Chicago, while Chris Smith keeps a sharp eye on blues literature.

Living Blues

Center for the Study of Southern Culture, The University of Mississippi, University, MS 38677-9836, USA.
Tel: (601) 232 5742
email: lblues@barnard.cssc.olemiss.edu

Founded 1970. Bimonthly. It describes itself as "The Magazine of the African-American Blues Tradition" and reflects that emphasis in its features, though the reviews are a little more catholic. Jim DeKoster, Bill Dahl, David Whiteis and Peter R. Aschoff are experienced and trustworthy reviewers.

Real Blues

302-655 Herald St, Victoria, BC, Canada V8W 3L6.
Tel: (250) 384 2088

Founded 1996. (Formerly *Westcoast Blues Review*, 1993–1996.) Bimonthly. Packed coverage of the contemporary blues scene in the United States and Canada, with some attention to soul and gospel music but not much to historical blues.

78 Quarterly

626 Canfield Lane, Key West, FL 33040, USA.

Founded 1967. Occasional. A quirky house journal for the fraternity of 78 rpm record collectors. It contains no news or CD reviews but publishes revelatory articles on early blues, jazz and hillbilly artists and recording history by excellent researchers like Stephen Calt, Gayle Dean Wardlow, Doug Seroff and Lynn Abbott. Very occasional indeed: 9 issues in 30 years.

Soul Bag

C.L.A.R.B., 25 rue Trézel, 92300 Levallois-Perret, France.
Tel: 33 1 47 57 64 66

Founded 1971. Quarterly.
Despite the title there is plenty of blues material, both contemporary and historical, and occasional excellent artist discographies. Premier reviewers include André Hobus, Gérard Herzhaft, Robert Sacré and Jacques Demêtre.

THE BLUES MAGAZINE SCENE HAS NEVER BEEN HEALTHIER. SOME OF THE TITLES DESCRIBED ARE WIDELY AVAILABLE IN MAJOR RECORD-STORE CHAINS AND ON NEWSSTANDS. OTHERS ARE MORE SELECTIVELY DISTRIBUTED, AND READERS ARE RECOMMENDED TO TAKE OUT SUBSCRIPTIONS: IT NOT ONLY ENSURES SUPPLY BUT BENEFITS THE PRODUCERS, WHO ARE OFTEN DEDICATED AMATEURS.

BLUES FOR STARTERS

News & The Blues: Telling It Like It Is
Columbia

Twenty fascinating songs spanning two decades of US history, from the Southern floods of 1927 (Bessie Smith's 'Back Water Blues') and the Depression (Big Bill Broonzy's 'Unemployment Stomp') to World War II and the atomic bomb. Contributors include Charlie Patton, Blind Boy Fuller, Memphis Minnie and Lucille Bogan. No album puts the blues in its social context better.

The Prewar Blues Story
Best Of Blues

Double-CD set with 44 songs by as many artists, from Skip James and Son House by way of Big Joe Williams and Roosevelt Sykes to Big Maceo and T-Bone Walker. Many are heard with their best-known songs, making this an unrivalled collection of blues hits like 'How Long – How Long Blues', 'Bumble Bee', 'Milk Cow Blues', 'Key To The Highway' and 'Worried Life Blues'.

Slide Guitar Blues
Indigo

Steel or glass sliding on a guitar string yield some of the most characteristic sounds of the blues, and this 22-track CD investigates a medley of 1920s–1940s styles. Alongside classic recordings by Blind Willie McTell, Barbecue Bob, Kokomo Arnold, Robert Johnson and Muddy Waters are lesser-known but first-rate pieces like Hambone Willie Newbern's 'Roll And Tumble Blues'.

Country Blues Hard Hitters: 'How You Want It Done'
Pigmeat

No theme holds this 24-track collection together except the almost unwavering excellence of the performances, which include such masterpieces as Skip James's 'I'm So Glad', Blind Willie McTell's 'Statesboro Blues', Blind Blake's 'Diddie Wa Diddie' and Lottie Beaman's 'Rolling Log Blues'. A splendid, colourfully presented lucky dip into the blues of the 1920s and 1930s.

Blues Masters, Volume 1: Urban Blues
Rhino

As good a single collection as you will find of blues that jump and shout from the 1940s–1960s. Pee Wee Crayton's 'Blues After Hours', Lowell Fulson's 'Reconsider Baby' and songs by T-Bone Walker, Charles Brown and Jimmy Witherspoon represent Californian approaches while others of the 18 tracks stand up for New Orleans (Guitar Slim's 'The Things That I Used To Do'), Chicago, New York, etc.

Blues Masters, Volume 2: Postwar Chicago
Rhino

Muddy Waters, Howlin' Wolf, Little Walter, Sonny Boy Williamson II, Jimmy Reed, Otis Rush, Magic Sam, Buddy Guy, Junior Wells . . . with a cast list like that, and a programme of very well-known songs in their original recordings, this must sound like an almost faultless introduction to Chicago blues. And it is.

Mojo Working: The Best Of Ace Blues
Ace

Intended as an inexpensive sampler of a leading blues reissue label, this turns out to be a fine selection of mostly 1940s/50s blues from all over the place, with many famous recordings like Elmore James's 'Dust My Blues', John Lee Hooker's 'Boogie Chillen' and Slim Harpo's 'I'm A King Bee'. Also B.B. King, Howlin' Wolf, Lowell Fulson, Albert King and more.

Down Home Country Blues Classics
Arhoolie

Another mid-price sampler of a great blues label, this 15-track selection offers such heroes of the 1960s blues renaissance as Fred McDowell, Lightnin' Hopkins, Mance Lipscomb, Booker White and Big Joe Williams.

The Alligator Records 20th Anniversary Collection
Alligator

A charismatic blues label looks back over two decades in a 35-track double CD. The Alligator catalogue has held Albert Collins, Koko Taylor, Clifton Chenier, Clarence "Gatemouth" Brown, Walter Horton, Johnny Winter, Son Seals and Hound Dog Taylor, and all of them are here, with many more.

The Blues Album
Virgin

A remarkable 40-track double CD that juxtaposes Robert Johnson, John Lee Hooker, Muddy Waters, Albert King, Sonny Boy Williamson II and other masters with inheritors like Robert Cray, Stevie Ray Vaughan, Eric Clapton and Canned Heat, then widens the circle to embrace Fleetwood Mac, Dire Straits, Santana, Little Feat and The Commitments. It moves a long way from the blues, but that's all right: so does the blues, sometimes.

TEN COMPILATIONS FOR READERS WHO ARE CURIOUS ABOUT THE MUSIC DISCUSSED IN THIS BOOK AND WOULD LIKE TO SAMPLE IT IN ALL ITS DIVERSITY ON A MODEST BUDGET. NOT COMPREHENSIVE, BUT A SOUND FOUNDATION FOR A COLLECTION.

ACKNOWLEDGEMENTS

My friends and fellow bluesologues Chris Smith, Neil Slaven, Mike Rowe and Cilla Huggins generously supplied facts and debated theories. Ken Smith (Red Lick Records) and Mike Gavin (Ray's Blues & Roots) kept me up to date with new releases.

Many friends and contacts in the music business provided valuable assistance. Thanks in particular to Bruce Bastin (Interstate Music), Ed Chmelewski (Blind Pig), Larry Cohn (Sony US), Richard Cook (PolyGram), John Crosby, Tony Engle (Topic), Miles Evans (Topic/Direct Distribution), Paddy Forwood (BMG), Richard Ganter (MCA), Marc Lipkin (Alligator), Adam Sieff (Sony UK), Harriet Simms (Topic/Direct Distribution), Mal Smith (Delta Publicity), John Stedman (JSP), Chris Strachwitz (Arhoolie), Pat Tynan (Koch International) and Richard Wootton.

I am indebted to that ever reliable source of basic biographical data, Sheldon Harris's *Blues Who's Who*, and for information on some current artists to Robert Santelli's *Big Book Of The Blues*. I have also drawn gratefully on back issues of *Blues Access*, *Blues & Rhythm*, *The Blues Collection*, *Blues Revue*, *Blues Unlimited*, *Juke Blues*, *Living Blues* and *Mojo*.

PICTURE CREDITS

The publishers would like to thank the following sources for their kind permission to reproduce the pictures in this book:

Corbis-Bettmann/Amalie R Rothschild, UPI; **Frank Driggs Collection; London Features International**/Gie Knaeps, Steve Rapport; **Dave Peabody; Pictorial Press**/Escott, William Rutten, Showtime/S G Shoenfeld; **Sylvia Pitcher Photo Library**/Sylvia Pitcher, Ken Powell, Brian Smith, The Weston Collection; **Redferns**/Glenn A Baker Archive, James Barron, Rogan Coles, Brigitte Engl, Patrick Ford, William Gottlieb, Mick Hutson, Max Jones Files, Marc Marnie, Leon Morris, Michael Ochs Archive, Roberta Parkin, David Redfern, Simon Ritter, Ebet Roberts, Barbara Steinwehe, Chuck Stewart; **Tony Russell Collection; Nick Wright.**

Every effort has been made to acknowledge correctly and contact the source and/or copyright holder of each picture, and Carlton Books Limited apologises for any unintentional errors or omissions which will be corrected in future editions of this book.